Religious Revolutionaries

Religious Revolutionaries

THE REBELS WHO RESHAPED AMERICAN RELIGION

Robert C. Fuller

palgrave
macmillan

First published 2004 by PALGRAVE MACMILLAN™
175 Fifth Avenue, New York, N.Y. 10010 and
Houndmills, Basingstoke, Hampshire, England RG21 6XS.
Companies and representatives throughout the world.

PALGRAVE MACMILLAN is the global academic imprint of the Palgrave Macmillan division of St. Martin's Press, LLC and of Palgrave Macmillan Ltd. Macmillan®is a registered trademark in the United States, United Kingdom and other countries. Palgrave is a registered trademark in the European Union and other countries.

ISBN 1-4039-6361-4 hardback

Library of Congress Cataloging-in-Publication Data
Fuller, Robert C., 1952-
    Religious revolutionaries : the rebels who reshaped American religion / Robert C. Fuller.
      p. cm.
    Includes bibliographical references and index
    ISBN 1-4039-6361-4 (cloth)
      1. United States--Religion. 2. United States--Church history. 3. Religious leaders--United States
    --History. I. Title.

BL2525.F85 2004
200'.973--dc21   2003054928

A catalogue record for this book is available from the British Library.

Design by Planettheo.com

First edition: January 2004
10 9 8 7 6 5 4 3 2 1

Printed in the United States of America.

Contents

List of Graphs

Source of all graphs: Edwin Scott Gaustad and Philip L. Barlow, New Historical Atlas of Religion in America *(New York: Oxford University Press, 2001).*

List of Photographs

Preface

A GOOD FRIEND RECENTLY ASKED ME to recommend a readable history of religion in the United States. I began pondering which of the many fine textbooks and scholarly reference volumes I would suggest. I worried, however, that none was quite right for a general reader like my friend, who wanted an overview of American religious life written with the nonspecialist in mind. So instead I sat down at my computer and began retelling the story of religion in America in a way that might entice readers to consider some of the nation's most creative religious thinkers as possible stepping stones along their own spiritual journeys.

This book hopes to provide a readable, even entertaining history of religious life in America. It focuses on the persons who proved to be sources of change and creativity over the course of American religion. For this reason each chapter offers an initial overview of an era's mainstream religious practice, then highlights one or more persons who blazed new spiritual paths. The particular approach I have chosen makes no pretense of offering an exhaustive or even "objective" treatment of all the possible persons, organizations, and events that have shaped American religion. I have instead focused attention on ten of the most creative persons who were produced by—and who in turn produced changes in—the larger sweep of American religious history. Each of these persons was a religious revolutionary. These rebels opened up new ways of being religious—ways that continue to illuminate our spiritual lives. Their lives not only shaped the subsequent history of religion in America, but also provide interesting examples of what it might mean for any of us to live a creatively religious life.

I am not claiming that these "religious revolutionaries" are the most representative individuals of their historical eras. Indeed, most of them were dissatisfied with what they understood to be the consensus religiosity of their time. Their personal difficulties with existing religious organizations prompted them to travel new spiritual paths—paths that over time have led countless others to new and more meaningful religious lives. My criterion for identifying the nation's religious revolutionaries is thus not that they embodied what most Americans of their time believed. On the contrary, I selected them because they were iconoclasts. They were alert to spiritual tensions and problems that most church members simply overlooked. Facing these tensions and problems forced them to ask more of religion than did most of their contemporaries. By arriving at spiritual formulas that enabled them to assuage these tensions at a personal level, they simultaneously became agents of change and creativity in American religious history.

Some of the religious revolutionaries featured in this narrative are familiar names. Thomas Jefferson, for example, is one of the most beloved presidents in American history. Ralph Waldo Emerson is covered in most high school surveys of American literature. Anne Hutchinson, Joseph Smith, and William James are names we come across less often, but we have probably heard of them at one time or another. The remaining agents of religious change that I have chosen to highlight are known by relatively few. Paul Tillich, Mary Daly, and James Cone are recognized by those who have formally studied recent religious thought, but they are hardly household names. Meanwhile, Phineas P. Quimby and Andrew Jackson Davis are downright obscure. Yet all of these religious rebels were able to identify pressing spiritual issues of their age. And all were able to step outside existing paradigms and become true religious revolutionaries.

I am self-conscious about the fact that none of these religious innovators is either Catholic or Jewish (with the exception of Mary Daly, who began her career as a Roman Catholic). I am also acutely aware that only two are female. This is not meant to suggest that Jews and Catholics have lagged behind Protestants in terms of creativity, or that women are less likely than men to be agents of religious change. Many readers will wish that I had expanded my narrative to include a more diverse array of religious innovators (e.g., Ellen White, Mary Baker Eddy, Helena Blavatsky, Isaac Wise, Walter Rauschenbusch, Mordecai Kaplan, Thomas Merton, Starhawk, Alan Watts, Martin Luther King, or Charles Curran). My goal, however, was to identify just a few of the progenitors of revolutionary change in American religious life. I wanted to focus upon only those persons who were iconoclasts in the eyes of their contemporaries, who broke with existing tradition, and who opened up genuinely new ways of spiritual life and thought. And, rather than trying to be as inclusive as possible, I chose instead to settle on as few religious revolutionaries as possible while still chronicling the major episodes in which religious dissatisfaction has given rise to new and vital forms of spirituality. I am not arguing that these ten rebels should be regarded as the most revolutionary thinkers in the nation's religious history. My objective is more modest. I have simply tried to tell the story of change and creativity in American religious life as this has been reflected in the lives of a few innovative thinkers.

The history of religion in America is both rich and exciting. This story of the nation's religious revolutionaries helps bring this excitement to life. Their voices of change and creativity not only shaped the spiritual life of our nation, but invite us to reexamine our own spiritual lives as well.

𝒞

Colonial Beginnings

Forging Consensus
and Banishing Anne Hutchinson

HISTORY RARELY HAS TIDY BEGINNINGS. American religious history is no exception. North America had already been occupied for almost 20,000 years before the first European settlers arrived. The full story of religion in America thus begins with the religion of the continent's native inhabitants. We need to be careful, however, about assuming that there was any one "Native American religion" existing in North America prior to the age of colonization. There were over one thousand different ethnic groups occupying North America during this long time period. They lived in geographically separated regions. They created separate and distinct societies, using hundreds of different languages. Some were hunting and gathering societies, whereas others developed fairly advanced agricultural economies. Few statements apply to all of these cultures.[1] There was, therefore, no such thing as *the* Native American religious tradition awaiting Europeans when they first journeyed across the Atlantic.

Even if there had been a unified Native American religious tradition in place before the first Europeans arrived, it could not have remained intact for very long. William Bradford was typical of the European settlers who eagerly anticipated landing in the "vast and unpeopled countries of America." Bradford really didn't mean that Protestant settlers such as himself expected to find a vacant world awaiting them. By "unpeopled" he meant not yet populated by civilized Christians. Earlier explorers and Jesuit missionaries had already flooded Europe with accounts of "the nations of savages" that populated the Americas. Bradford was thus expressing the Pilgrims' belief that it was their mission to erect a New Jerusalem in a place "devoid of all civil inhabitants, where there are only savage and brutish men which range up and down, little otherwise than the wild beasts of the same."[2]

European settlers were determined to eradicate Native American religions from the outset. They usually listed their desire to convert pagan Indians to Christianity as one of the principal reasons they were venturing across the Atlantic. As early as the mid-1500s Spain began opening up settlements in what are now the states of Florida, Arizona, Texas, New Mexico, and California. With these settlements came Catholic missions and the arrival of priests dedicated to the task of Christianizing North America. The French also spread the Catholic faith as they set up trading outposts in what are now eastern Canada and the United States' northern Midwest. Eager to see that Protestant Christianity not be left behind, England clothed its own desires for land and wealth in the rhetoric of service to God. King Charles asserted in 1628 that the conversion of the natives was "the principal Ende of this plantacion," and the original charter granted to Massachusetts charged the governor and company to "wynn and incite the Natives . . . [to] the onlie true God and Saviour of Mankinde." These public professions of concern for the religious well-being of Native Americans shouldn't be taken too seriously, however. Within weeks of arriving on the shores of Plymouth, the Pilgrims were forced to raid Indian storage bins for corn and native crafts. Violent skirmishes broke out when the settlers realized that it would be necessary to forcibly remove Indians from the land they coveted for themselves. The quest for survival and dominance caused the colonists to abandon their lofty goal of converting Indians and brought home the realization that, in a barren wilderness, might makes right. For better or for worse, Christian theology made it easy for them to demonize their enemies and thereby justify their crusade not to convert—but to overpower—the savages who stood in the way of their mission to erect a Kingdom of God on earth.[3]

COLONIZING THE NEW WORLD

Europeans ventured across the Atlantic for a variety of reasons. Motives were probably mixed, but tended to fall into three main categories: (1) the quest for economic opportunity, (2) the desire to escape social disgrace or criminal punishment in the anonymity of a foreign frontier, and (3) the search for greater freedom of thought and lifestyle.[4] Of these three reasons for immigrating to the American colonies, only the last has anything to do with religion. Indeed, only about one in five persons throughout the colonial period would have considered her- or himself very religious. Most came for wholly nonreligious reasons. Europe had shifted from an economy based on inherited status to one based upon money and capital. Trade opportunities lured ambitious persons—particularly those with little economic opportunity in the Old World—to set out in search of a better life. In our rush to create an inspiring religious picture of America's beginnings, we often forget that the first English settlement in the United States was a commercial venture in Jamestown. And although Americans reverently hold on to images of the pious Pilgrims at Plymouth, their small settlement was soon eclipsed by the larger Massachusetts Bay Colony, which was largely mercantile in nature.

Many came to the colonies to escape disgrace or even punishment at home. Among the early colonists were more than a fair share of male drifters, troublemakers, heavy drinkers, thieves, and thugs. It is estimated, for example, that between 1718 and 1775 at least 50,000 criminals were forcibly transported to the colonies by order of English courts. Approximately 16,000 more were sent over by the courts in Ireland.[5] Drunken revelry, barroom brawling, gambling, and extramarital sex were more prevalent in early America than attending church.[6]

Of course, many of those who journeyed to the New World were in search of greater religious opportunity. We need to be careful, however, not to view this important motive for colonization out of perspective. Most Americans hold to an almost mythic view of their country's origins. School children, for example, are usually taught that this country began when the Pilgrims landed at Plymouth Rock ready to create a Bible-oriented society that would be pleasing to God. Illustrations of pious Pilgrims celebrating the first Thanksgiving or of the spires of Congregational churches looming over New England towns reinforce this myth of national origins. In history classes most of us have read excerpts from William Bradford's history *Of Plymouth Plantation* or John Winthrop's account of the settling of the Massachusetts Bay Colony. Both give the impression that the early colonists were a cohesive community of Bible-reading souls. Yet we must be cautious about taking these "official histories" at face value. There is no certain way to gauge the depth and seriousness of most colonists' religious beliefs, especially given the fact that church membership never reached higher than 20 percent throughout most of the colonial period. In his famous chronicle of life in the American colonies, the Frenchman Hector St. John de Crevecoeur observed that "religious indifference is imperceptibly disseminated from one end of the continent to another, which is at present one of the strongest characteristics of the American people."[7] And, too, we must remember that not all of the colonists' religiosity fit into the categories of orthodox Christianity. Most early Americans engaged in a wide array of magical and occult practices such as astrology, divination, fortune-telling, and folk medicine. Unchurched religious practices of this sort have a long history in America, too.[8] Colonial Americans were, in fact, more likely to turn to magical or occult techniques in their effort to avail themselves of superhuman power than they were to Christian rituals or prayer.[9]

We must thus be wary about overestimating the degree to which conservative, Bible-based Christianity shaped the everyday life of colonial Americans. But it remains a fact that when the colonists signed the Declaration of Independence in 1776, about 80 percent of the nonslave population was white, Anglo-Saxon, and Protestant. WASPS they were, and a particular kind of WASP at that. The Englishman Edmund Burke observed that "the people [of the colonies] are Protestants, and of that kind which is most adverse to all implicit subjugation of mind and opinion."[10] This was probably his way of saying that they had both a cross to bear and an axe to grind. They were Protestants who self-consciously opposed almost every other kind of Christianity they knew about. They were determined to see that, at least in the New World, Christians would finally get it right.

THE PURITAN WORLDVIEW

Those who settled the eastern seaboard were overwhelmingly white, Anglo-Saxon (British), and Protestant. It is estimated that at the time of the Revolutionary War as many as 83 percent of all colonists were of British ancestry. Very few were Catholics (1.8 percent). Fewer yet were Jews (no more than 0.2 percent). Nearly all British were Protestant, belonging to the established Anglican Church (or Church of England). Many English Protestants, however, believed that the religious reformation in their land had not gone far enough. They believed that the Church of England preserved too much of the ornate ritual and ecclesiastical structure of Catholicism. Nor in their eyes did the Church of England put sufficient emphasis on the plain Bible-centered faith that Protestantism claims can alone guide us to salvation. They thought that the Church of England was not sufficiently separated from the government of England, risking too great a corruption of faith from secular influences. A large group of these English Protestants found themselves with no option but to be dissenters and separatists. Their hope was to purify the Church of England. Known as Puritans, they separated from the established Church of England and clustered together in a number of fledgling denominations such as the Congregationalists, Presbyterians, and (although the relationship here is a bit more complex) Baptists. It was among these separatist and nonconformist groups that the most interest was generated in leaving England for America. Part of their motivation was to erect a bulwark against Catholic Spain and Catholic France. An even greater motivation was to at last correct the corruption found in the unpurified Church of England. They were taking up God's own errand. Theirs was a mission to plant a New Zion where at last God's true faith would prosper over and against all opposition. With such a serious mission it is easy to see why others viewed them as Protestants "of that kind which is most adverse to all implicit subjugation of mind and opinion."

Not only did the Congregatonalists, Presbyterians, and Baptists carry the Puritan cause to America's shores, but even those colonists who remained Anglicans (later to be Episcopalians) were largely committed to Puritan theology. Thus, by 1776, fully 70 percent of all church members shared a particular religious vision. In this sense Puritanism was the principal ideology or worldview of the American colonies at the time of independence. The lasting influence of the Puritan worldview on American religious life is readily apparent to anyone who surveys its basic tenets.

Puritan theology centered around three basic beliefs. First and foremost is Puritanism's belief in the sovereignty of God. While all Christian groups would surely share Puritanism's belief in God as the source of all creation, few place such emphasis upon viewing God as the ruler, law-giver, and magistrate to whom we owe unswerving obedience. The Congregationalists, Presbyterians, Baptists, and even Episcopalians who settled the American colonies were grounded in the theological tradition stemming from the Protestant reformer John Calvin. Calvin was convinced of the absolute gulf separating God from His lowly creation. The human mind is thus incapable of grasping the true nature or will of God. Fortunately for us, God has made His will known through the Bible. Puritans embraced the Bible as the literal word of God. They believed that the Bible provides a complete and absolute code upon which we must order our personal lives, organize our churches, and regulate society. The first major theological tenet of Puritanism thus commanded persons to obey God by following the letter of his Word as given to us in scripture.

The second theological tenet of Puritanism follows logically from the first. Because Calvinism attributes all sovereignty and glory to God, humans are by contrast in a condition marked by inherent sinfulness. Calvinist theology does not simply state that humans have certain flaws or shortcomings. Instead, it insists that the human condition is wholly depraved and in total rebellion against God. In Calvin's view, humans are so bereft of worth or merit that there is nothing they can do to be pleasing to God. God, and God alone, chooses who will be saved. He has, in fact, already preordained which souls will warrant Heaven and which will remain damned for all eternity. Certain Christians of the day had moderated the Calvinist insistence upon human depravity by embracing instead a position known as Arminianism. The Arminian outlook emphasized humanity's capacity to initiate some improvement and to exert efforts that will make us more pleasing to God (and thereby merit salvation). The Calvinist outlook held by so many of the early colonial churchmen was utterly opposed to this more optimistic interpretation of humanity's position before God. Their Puritan faith held that humans can do nothing to earn or merit their salvation. Even the best-acting persons stand before God as rebellious sinners, with no hope whatsoever of achieving salvation through their own efforts. As we shall see in the next chapter, American Protestantism gradually abandoned the strict Calvinist position on this matter when it committed itself to a strategy of winning converts at religious revival meetings. But in the early colonial period any wavering on this issue would come under ardent theological attack. Humans are born sinners, and their only source of hope is the gracious activity of a distant and inscrutable God.

A third distinguishing feature of Puritan theology was its emphasis upon conversion experiences. Conversions were viewed as specific signs that one has been elected to salvation. A conversion was understood to be a sudden episode during which God's spirit initiates the death of one's worldly preoccupations and signals one's rebirth as a regenerate saint. Puritan ministers knew that some persons might falsely interpret their emotions and sentiments as an authentic conversion experience. Human error in such matters was always possible, and thus no one could ever be wholly confident whether they were part of the elect few that God had chosen for eternal glory. But despite our inability ever to be certain of God's ways, conversion experiences were a prerequisite for full membership in a Puritan church that was to consist only of visible saints (i.e., those who had been "born again" in a conversion experience).

These beliefs in the sovereignty of God, the literal truth and authority of the Bible, the sinfulness of humans, and the need for a conversion or "born again" experience continue to be characteristic features of American Christianity. The Puritans got here first and were thus able to set the terms for what would count as "authentic spirituality" in America. For this reason they have cast a long shadow over the nation's religious history. They are, simultaneously, the original source of many of the beliefs and practices that our religious revolutionaries eventually had to struggle against before venturing forth along new spiritual paths.

PURITANISM AS A CULTURAL AGENDA

Puritanism was more than a theological creed. It was also a program for society. Puritans believed that uniformity in religion was the only proper foundation for a moral society. While they had come to America for their own religious freedom, they had no intentions of granting it to others. The

British government itself imposed no such system upon the colonists (except for a short time in Virginia). The free exercise of religion made good economic sense for European governments eager to find as many potential colonists as possible. It was the colonists themselves who envisioned a cohesive order in which civil and ecclesiastical law would blend seamlessly together. Most religious groups sought establishment (i.e., official recognition of their predominance by the civil government, which would collect taxes to support their churches and clergy). The Congregationalist denomination succeeded in procuring establishment throughout the colonies in New England, while Episcopalians enjoyed legal establishment in New York, Virginia, Maryland, North and South Carolina, and Georgia.

This quest to force religious conformity was rooted in the Puritans' sense of spiritual mission. Protestants had, from the outset, believed themselves to be championing the cause of true faith against seemingly insurmountable opposition. Nowhere was this zealous faith more clearly evidenced than in John Foxe's *Actes and Monuments*, popularly known as "The Book of Martyrs." The first edition of Foxe's book in 1554 was a small octavo volume recounting the martyrdoms of those who came before the Protestant Reformation. By the time it reached its final form in 1583, it had expanded to a work of almost 2,500 pages detailing the Roman Catholic Church's persecution of righteous English Protestants. Foxe explained that God had foreordained the eventual establishment of rule of righteousness on earth. The sweep of history was already bearing this out. First God acted to lay the foundations of His rule among the Jews in Jerusalem. Then God's providential power helped the Catholics to prevail in Rome before empowering the Protestants in western Europe. The progressive cause of salvation was moving from east to west. The tumultuous religious struggles of the sixteenth century were all the proof that English Protestants needed to know that the stage was being set for the final push to establish a Kingdom of God on earth. As historian Peter Gay has written, "Anglicans and Puritans alike loved the Book of Martyrs, memorized it, told their children stories from it. . . . And less than half a century after Foxe's death, Englishmen took his book, and his philosophy of history, across the Atlantic into the American wilderness."[11]

A tremendous sense of expectancy propelled the Puritans to settle the New World. To their way of thinking, European Protestants had proved unequal to the task to which God had summoned them. For this reason God chose to send a certain small remnant forth to form a new Zion. Here, in America, the world would at last witness a holy and uncorrupted commonwealth. John Winthrop, governor of the Massachusetts Bay Colony, promised his compatriots that theirs was to be "a city set on a hill." They were to demonstrate before "the eyes of the world" the glory that would usher forth when the entire population was bound together in a covenant with God. A Puritan minister by the name of Edward Johnson explained that when old England "began to decline in religion," Christ raised "an army out of our English nation, for freeing his people from their long servitude." Christ was creating "a new England to muster up the first of his forces in." New England was thus destined "to be the place where the Lord will create a new heaven and a new earth, new churches and a new commonwealth together."[12] William Penn voiced this same sense of expectancy when he declared the colonies to be God's "holy experiment," which He intended to be "an example . . . unto the nations" of how life might be remodeled according to Bible-centered faith. And, in a sermon delivered in 1670, Rev. Samuel Danforth provided his parishioners with "A Brief Recognition of New England's Errand into the Wilderness."[13] God had a special purpose for gathering his saints in the North American wilderness. They were engaged in an errand to show the world what it would be like if people organized themselves according to what Governor Winthrop described as "a due form of government both civil and ecclesiastical."[14]

The Puritans knew that a society entrusted with something as important as God's errand must be bound together by a common sense of purpose. There could be no divisions or conflicts of interest. From the outset, then, American Puritanism embraced an authoritarian and hierarchically organized conception of society. They were to be bound together in what Plymouth's William Bradford called a "civill body politick." The famous Mayflower Compact shaped this resolve into a political platform founded on obedience and submission to the word of God—which, of course, would be explained by the New England clergy:

> In ye name of God, Amen. We whose names are underwritten . . . having undertaken, for ye glorie of God, and advancemente of ye Christian faith . . . doe by these presents solemnly & mutualy in ye presence of God, and one of another, covenant and combine our selves togeather into a civill

body politick, for our better ordering & preservation, & furtherance of ye ends aforesaid . . . unto which we promise all due submission and obedience.[15]

John Winthrop further clarified what a society based upon "all due submission and obedience" required of its citizens. The colonists had long ago entered into a contract or covenant with God. God would bless them with His providential guidance provided that they keep up their end of the covenant through sustained moral and religious piety. The civil government they were forming extended this notion of covenant to require also that "we must be knit together in this worke as one man, we must entertaine each other in brotherly affection."[16] The kind of social solidarity that Winthrop and other Puritan leaders envisioned was one in which there would be no economic rivalry, no jostling for social position. Social gradations were to remain what God had originally appointed. People were not to seek any reward other than the reward of knowing that one was furthering God's errand. Although there would be hard work for everybody, prosperity would be bestowed not as a consequence of labor but as a sign of God's approval of the errand itself. For the first time in the history of humanity, there would be a society so dedicated to God's purposes that worldly success would not lead to sinful diversions or a lapse in piety. All would remain obedient to both the civil and ecclesiastical branches of the body politic.

To ensure the successful implementation of their social vision, the Puritans (particularly in New England) held tightly to their ideal of the congregational form of church polity. What this meant was that each local church was to be comprised only of men and women who could be certified to be "visible saints." As early as 1635, credible evidence that one had undergone a thorough religious conversion became a requirement for adult church membership. In practice this meant that one needed to provide a public narration of one's personal religious experience in order to become a full church member and hence be eligible for receiving the sacraments. This was a radical demand. For the first time in the history of Christianity, a state-established church was requiring that its members pass a test that entailed not only uniformity of belief, but also uniformity of inner experience. The Puritans were not so naïve as to think that every person who successfully narrated a conversion experience was really a saint. But their strict standards of church membership did assure them that, by and large, their churches were comprised only of visible saints.

Puritan churches, then, were comprised only of professing Christians.[17] The rest of the community was excluded. The local government still forced the rest of the community to attend church and listen attentively to the sermons intended for their moral edification. The government collected their mandatory taxes and used these taxes to provide the minister's salary and maintain the church building. But they could not be actual members. Of crucial importance was the fact that in most New England settlements, only church members had the right to vote. To this extent the Puritans envisioned an ideal "civill body politick" not so much as a democracy but a theocracy (rule by God and those with the authority to speak for God). Technically, Puritan communities were faithful to their tradition of "separatism." Their clergy were not allowed to hold public office. But the civil magistrates saw to it that the community's religious and moral standards were enforced. The civil government regulated almost all public behavior, including dress. They were even empowered to prosecute individuals for religious offenses, as was seen in the famous Salem witchcraft trials in 1692. And although the ministry was formally barred from holding public office, it still had great influence over public life. Ministers determined church membership (and thus determined who did and who didn't have the right to vote) and were able to use their pulpits to influence public opinion. Thus although Puritan society endeavored to maintain a technical line of demarcation between church and state, this was more to keep the state from meddling in church affairs than to curb influence from flowing in the opposite direction.

DISSENSION IN THE WILDERNESS

Puritan culture produced a certain toughness of temperament. It inculcated the self-discipline needed to execute difficult tasks or achieve distant goals. Puritan clergy worked diligently to direct this strenuous type of character toward the achievement of social stability. But the character traits fostered by Puritan culture were also capable of fueling the impulse to individual freedom. Puritans believed themselves obedient to a "truth" higher than that of any worldly authority or government. Authority rests in personal conscience, not civil institutions. The social order thus depends upon the clergy's continuous efforts to help persons see why serving God requires us to sacrifice our personal interests for the common good. Social harmony could be achieved only to the extent that individuals could be coaxed into acquiescing and submitting themselves to the social order thought to be ordained by God. This was not so difficult to achieve among the first generation of settlers. They were more likely to have freely chosen this model of life as adults. Furthermore, economic necessity drove first-generation colonists to a more communal, interdependent form of life. But this delicate balance between the impulse toward individual freedom and the demands of social authority was more difficult to maintain among subsequent generations. This was particularly the case when some members of the community experienced a degree of material prosperity and saw opportunities to seek even greater economic gain.

Puritan culture had difficulty getting a handle on the economic and social conflicts that soon emerged in the colonies. The only strategy available to colonial leaders was to view those pursuing material prosperity as enemies of God. Conservative Protestants were well aware that Satan and his colleague the Antichrist were determined to thwart their errand into the wilderness. It was thus only to be expected that these agents of deception would try to stir up trouble right within their midst. And this is apparently just what happened in Salem, Massachusetts.

In 1692 Salem Village had an adult population of 215 persons. The population was growing and economic opportunities were expanding. The emergence of preindustrial capitalism was pulling people toward an ethic of personal freedom and self-determination. Puritanism's "corporate" notion of society in which self-interest was to be subordinated to the public good didn't mesh well with the actual lives of Salem Village's more prosperous citizens. The problems that Salem Village faced were by no means unique in the late seventeenth century. All across New England the centers of social authority were shifting. Wholesalers and retailers were beginning to earn more than farmers, who had formerly been the colonies' economic corner-stone. Outlying areas were breaking away from their parent towns, creating new centers of economic prosperity that were less connected to older patterns of authority. Tensions such as these became especially acute in Salem Village. It was located just a few miles from the more prosperous and commercial Salem Town. Salem Town was more than a political and economic rival of the older, more agrarian-oriented Salem Village; it was also a symbol of the looming moral threat concerning the very nature of New England's errand. The tensions mounted during a series of disputes over who had the authority to call or dismiss the minister of Salem Village's church. In the midst of the debates over who would occupy the village's pulpit, the citizenry became increasingly aware that they had now divided into two very different camps. The division between the citizens of Salem Village pertained to their degree of economic prosperity and the degree of their acceptance of the new mercantile economy symbolized by nearby Salem Town.

The residents of Salem Village were separated by three main factors: church membership, wealth, and geographical proximity to the commercial enterprises in Salem Town. The witchcraft episode that ensued did not create these divisions, but it did expose their cultural significance. Paul Boyer and Stephen Nissenbaum, the authors of the single most perceptive study of the witchcraft episode, have observed that if we are

> to understand the intensity of these divisions, we must recognize the fact—self-evident to the men and women of Salem Village—that what was going on was not simply a personal quarrel, an economic dispute, or even a struggle for power, but a mortal conflict involving the very nature of the community itself. The fundamental issue was not who was to control the Village, but what its essential character was to be.[18]

These volatile social tensions ignited when a few young girls came together to play and to speculate about such things as boyfriends and the future. One of the girls devised a small crystal ball from the white of an egg and in its murky fluid thought she saw the outlines of a coffin. The girls became both frightened and excited. Some kind of hysterical episode ensued. Nobody knew then, much less now, what the girls actually experienced. Modern interpreters have argued that these witchcraft episodes were a symptom of sexual hostility, the consequence of generational conflict, the result of the intoxication caused by fungus-tainted rye bread, and an outbreak of racial hostility stemming from the experiences of captivity by the Indians.[19] The girls themselves never really said much. But the grown-ups already possessed a set of interpretive categories and were eager to apply them to the situation at hand. The parents were alarmed at their children's unruly behavior, which they described as "fits," "distempers," "odd postures," and "foolish, ridiculous speeches." Under intense questioning from their parents, the children shifted attention to a young slave girl by the name of Tituba who had apparently brought a great deal of occult lore with her from the Caribbean. A few weeks later, again under the adults' directive questioning, the children accused two other local women of tormenting them. These two, along with Tituba, were the first to be arrested for suspicion of witchcraft. It would not be long before another 140 people faced the same accusation.

Accusations and arrests multiplied in the following months. After the initial arrest of a few social misfits and general malcontents, the accusations began to target persons of increasingly higher social stature. A high percentage of those accused of witchcraft were persons of real social respectability; persons, that is, who were prospering from the very social forces responsible for the reduced status of Salem Village's old guard. The young girls who supplied most of the names at the beginning of the witchcraft epidemic had never even met most of those whom they accused. But the girls had heard their names mentioned around their homes and had picked up on their parents' resentment of these strangers' education, wealth, and growing social influence. What information the girls could not provide on their own was helpfully supplied by the adults who stepped in to make the accusations complete. Historical perspective allows us to see how members of the older cultural order, unable to relieve their frustrations in any normal political way, employed the only means at their disposal for ridding themselves of unwelcome persons: They accused them of being agents of the devil. The village authorities went after the more vulnerable of these social deviants not by making rational or empirical arguments, but by framing the dispute in the language of theology. The trials consequently revolved around private judgments of what ways of life constitute the way of God and what the way of Satan.

Published sermons and other church records leave little doubt about the role of religion in mythologizing the conflicts present in Salem Village. Salem's minister, Samuel Parris, had been preparing villagers to view their worldly enemies as nefarious agents of Satan long before the outbreak of accusations. As Parris put it, there existed "a lamentable harmony between wicked men and devils in their opposition of God's kingdom and interests."

In a sermon describing why King Saul had become "haunted with an evil and wicked spirit," Parris explained that Saul had gone for advice "to the Devil, to a witch."[20] Right after the young girls first broke into their fits and convulsions, Parris preached a sermon entitled "Christ Knows How Many Devils There Are." In this sermon Parris meticulously explained to the residents of Salem Village that satanic influences were present wherever Christ's moral order was being subverted. Two weeks later, accusations of witchcraft began.

Parris originally stated that wicked people were in league or association with the devil. During the protracted witchcraft proceedings, however, Parris' sermons collapsed even this fragile distinction between the human and supernatural realms by suggesting that the wicked persons in their midst actually were devils. He explained that persons with pronounced "villainy and impiety" had become devils in "quality and disposition." More to the point, he added that "there are such devils in the Church."[21] This subtle theological shift justified the sense of outrage felt by his parishioners at the way in which their "errand" was being betrayed by people in their own community. Devils were afoot in Massachusetts in the guise of prospering merchants and their families. Parris's theological dissertations on how human persons might actually embody the devil in "quality and disposition" adequately formulated the citizenry's desire to vent their jealous hatred and extract revenge from those who had strayed from the errand (and had prospered for doing so). Those who they accused as witches were suspected of being devil-like in quality and disposition. If found guilty they must be dealt with accordingly. And sure enough, many of them were.

After the trials were finally concluded, the governor of the colony asked the Rev. Cotton Mather to write a book that would explain and justify the court's actions. Mather's narrative of the witchcraft proceedings, *The Wonders of the Invisible World*, provides insight into the theological rationale that made these trials and the execution of the "guilty" appear to Puritans as an exercise in righteousness. "I have indeed," he wrote, "set myself to countermine the whole PLOT of the Devil, against New England, in every branch of it."[22]

For Mather, the witchcraft trials needed to be understood against the larger background of the Devil's plot to thwart the saints' errand into the wilderness. He explained that "the New-Englanders are a people of God settled in these, which were once the Devil's territories."[23] The early colonists had formed a "true utopia" and were a chosen generation whose godliness was without parallel. As could be expected, their inroads against vice and iniquity irritated the devil. For this reason the "Devil is now making one Attempt more upon us; an Attempt more Difficult, more Surprising, more snarled with unintelligible Circumstances than any we have hitherto Encountered."[24] As unintelligible and snarled as the evidence against the accused residents of Salem Village was, a person with keen theological vision could see right through all outer appearances and discern the shape of the devil's influence. The Devil was, after all, growing more cunning all the time. Now, just as New Englanders were poised to usher in a godly commonwealth, "an army of Devils is horribly broke in upon the place which is the Center . . . [even assuming] the shapes of innocent persons."[25] The fact that proper authority and government had been undermined was now understandable. The Devil's malevolence was the only acceptable answer to the bitter fact of the "animosity and misunderstanding among us."

The witchcraft episode was thus a major test of the Puritan community's moral resolve. The devil and all who resemble him in "quality and disposition" had to be exterminated. Although Puritan ministers like Cotton Mather were concerned that innocent persons might be mistakenly convicted of witchcraft, they insisted that protection of the errand nonetheless required steadfast loyalty and resolve. If dissenters had to be labeled witches or devils, then so be it. Clergymen such as Mather couldn't grasp the abstract social and economic transformations that would render Puritan ideals obsolete. But they could engage in name-calling. And so they did, venting their resentment against those whose nonconformity threatened to raise "animosity and misunderstanding among us."

ANNE HUTCHINSON AND THE
FIRST GLIMPSE OF REVOLUTIONARY THOUGHT

Those accused of witchcraft weren't the only citizens of New England who threatened the Puritan order. Roger Williams, for example, was welcomed as "a godly minister" when he first arrived in Massachusetts.[26] Unfortunately, Williams didn't find the churches in New England nearly so godly. The New England Puritans had never officially separated from the Church of England, for reasons of political expediency. Williams wasn't one to compromise on principles just to make life easier. He was adamant that all true Protestants formally sever any connection with the Catholic-like practices of the Anglican Church. He therefore refused to accept a call to serve the Boston Church. Ministers and civil leaders alike realized that Williams' position could alienate British authorities, whose goodwill was important to the colonies. As if Williams hadn't already done enough to rock the boat, he then began criticizing the colony's leadership for its practice of using the civil government to prosecute persons for not following religious precepts. Then, to make matters worse still, he denounced the colony's charter from the king as an unlawful expropriation of lands rightfully belonging to the Native Americans.

The problem with Williams' views was not that they were theologically unsound but that they failed to take into account the political and social realities of the age. Williams was embarrassing colonial leaders by pointing out that American Puritanism had still not separated church and state. Instead, the state still had the power to stamp out what it considered to be religious heresy by prosecuting persons for disrupting the civil order. The only difference was that whereas in England it was the Puritans who stood to be prosecuted for threatening the established order, in New England the system worked to suppress those who dared to challenge Puritan authority. What Williams soon discovered was that the nonconforming were no freer in New England than they had been in England itself. Williams' theological positions threatened to push the church toward a more democratic system and thereby roused the fears of civil and church leaders alike. Following a series of summonses before ministers and magistrates, the General Court found Williams guilty of disseminating "newe & dangerous opinions, against the authoritie of magistrates." The Court ordered him banished, forcing him into exile in Rhode Island. The Puritan order prevailed, the heretic was expelled.

Another test of the Puritan order began innocently enough in the home of a woman in her middle forties, Anne Hutchinson.[27] Hutchinson was born in England in 1591. Her father was something of a role model of religious rebellion, having been censured and even imprisoned for his contentious arguments with established religious authority. Anne married a cloth merchant, William Hutchinson, in 1612. Together they had sixteen children between 1613 and 1636 (three of whom died in childhood). It was while living in England that Anne became a devoted follower of the Puritan-leaning Anglican preacher, John Cotton. Cotton sensed that Anglicanism was endorsing what amounted to a "Covenant of Works." By this he meant that the Anglican clergy were suggesting that a morally responsible lifestyle was certain evidence of inward grace. This teaching was in part intended to help anxious persons gain certainty of their salvation. It was also intended to encourage moral behavior and thus promote social stability. Cotton, however, preached that we are not free to grow morally until we have first inwardly felt the "witness of the Spirit itself." Cotton went on to emphasize that the inwardly regenerated individual would surely strive to lead a morally responsible life. Cotton was thus only offering a slight shift of emphasis from "outer" moral works to "inner" spiritual receptivity, but his message clearly called into question the clergy's equation of holiness with socially responsible behavior.

It appears that Anne Hutchinson heard only half of Cotton's message. She took Cotton to be arguing that those who inwardly receive the gift of grace are already mystically united with God. She concluded that the elect were thus under no burden to produce any kind of outward works as evidence of their salvation. Her failure to add, as Cotton did, a strong exhortation to moral behavior gave her views the appearance of falling into the "antinomian heresy." That is, Anne's argument that Christians are freed from the moral law by a new dispensation of grace was so strong as to undermine the relevance of moral conduct in the Christian life. This slight modification of Cotton's views would make them dangerous commodities in a new community struggling to forge social cohesion.

John Cotton's teachings eventually got him into trouble with the Anglican authorities. By 1633 he was forced to flee to Boston in the Massachusetts Bay Colony. Anne Hutchinson promptly informed her family that a revelation from God directed her to follow Rev. Cotton and, in 1634, the Hutchinsons emigrated to Boston, where William became a successful merchant and Anne a nurse and midwife. Anne soon won the respect of her fellow New Englanders for her vigorous intellect and her kindly disposition. Her avid interest in religious issues prompted her to convene informal meetings of women at her house, during which she led discussions of the sermons of the previous Sunday. It is clear that Anne possessed a remarkable ability to debate the most obscure points of Puritan theology. The theological subtleties that most interested Anne were probably obscure even in her own day. Their importance, however, was never really theological but, rather, political. Hutchinson began to argue that the Rev. John Wilson, who shared the pulpit with John Cotton, put far too much emphasis upon the need for moral sanctification and far too little on the new terms of a covenant of grace. In her view only two of the ministers of the Bay Colony were "walking in a covenant of grace." The others all preached a "covenant of works." The juxtaposition of "covenant of grace" and "covenant of works" revived the Protestant Reformation's rejection of Catholicism's belief in the efficacy of ecclesiastical and moral works. To Protestant Reformers such as Calvin, sinning humans can do nothing to earn or warrant their own salvation. Even though every Puritan minister knew this, it was difficult for them to mold their parishioners' behavior unless they implied that conscientious living would earn a heavenly reward. Thus when Anne drew attention to this distinction she was questioning whether the clergy were justified in their efforts to mold citizens' behavior ("works").

Hutchinson was probably correct in her charge that colonial preachers had subtly shifted their emphasis from salvation by grace alone to the necessity of compliance with the community's moral standards. The clergy argued, of course, that they had never returned to the discredited covenant of works. They were not arguing that outer conformity to social mores earned salvation, but that such conformity was a convenient way of demonstrating that one had already received God's saving grace. On this basis they defended their practice of screening candidates for church membership by judging who had or had not experienced a true conversion experience. They also maintained that even the surest saint must submit to church discipline and be governed by the will of the congregation, not because this would earn salvation, but because a person must be adequately prepared for the gift of grace when it came.

Unfortunately, Anne saw right through the clergy's convoluted efforts to pretend they were teaching a covenant of grace when, in actual practice, their sermons assumed a covenant of works. Anne remained steadfast on the issue that godly behavior on earth was no evidence of salvation. In this she was true to Puritanism's Calvinist roots. But she was undermining the fragile basis on which New England clergy sought to control the nation's errand. For good or for bad, Hutchinson did not quite appreciate how the world had changed in ways that made the "covenant of grace" an insufficient basis for religion to serve as an agent of social control. Her opponents correctly saw her as a theological antinomian and thus a threat to social order. They accused her of advocating a religion that absolved its adherents from obedience to moral law. The case against her thus really wasn't heresy. It was sedition.

In the beginning, Anne had sufficient support to fend off her enemies. About one hundred citizens were sympathetic to her cause, including Governor Vane, Rev. John Cotton, and her brother-in-law, Rev. John Wheelwright. Unfortunately for Anne, Vane returned to England; Cotton acquiesced to his pastoral colleagues and softened his support; and Wheelwright did not even have enough clout to keep himself from being officially banished from the colony. Once cut off from effective allies, Hutchinson was brought to trial for holding meetings not "fitting" for her women, promoting divisive opinions, and "for traducing the ministers and their ministry." There was one troublesome point for the court, however. Even though the General Court knew in advance what her punishment should be, it didn't have the foggiest idea what crime she had committed. The transcript of her civil trial reveals how confused and frustrated the colonial authorities were as they cast around for a charge that would stick against their theologically adroit opponent. Even though Anne Hutchinson stood before the court a single woman in poor health and without legal counsel, all the male authorities knew that she was seeking to sabotage all that they held dear in life.

The opening sessions introduced a host of theological errors that Hutchinson was said to have made. It was clear, however, that she was better versed in scripture and intellectually quicker than her accusers. Asked, for example, what right she—a woman—had to hold meetings in her house, she promptly replied that in Titus it is counseled that the elder women should instruct the young. But the trial was never about theology. It was about who had the right to determine the standards of conduct to which the colonists must conform. And on this Hutchinson was not willing to back down. Given several opportunities to soften her stance in order to escape punishment, Anne kept right on firing away—seemingly hell-bent on undermining the authority of the male officials she saw standing before her. One after another, the assembled ministers offered testimony about the indignities they had suffered from the impudent Mrs. Hutchinson. Ex-governor Thomas Dudley sought to summarize the essence of her guilt:

About three years ago we were all in peace. Mrs. Hutchinson from that time she came hath made a disturbance . . . [she has] vented divers of her strange opinions . . . she now hath a potent party in the country. Now if all these things have endangered us as from the foundation, and if she particular hath disparaged all our ministers in the land . . . why, this is not to be suffered.[28]

Everyone already agreed on Hutchinson's guilt. Her "strange opinions" endangered the very foundations of Puritan society. It only remained to find the legal grounds for banishing her from the holy commonwealth before she could do more damage. Dudley again came to the rescue by uncovering the true source of this "potent party" of dissension. Much like those in Salem would do about fifty years later, he accused his adversary of diabolical influence by testifying that "I am fully persuaded that Mrs. Hutchinson is deluded by the devil." This had actually been suspected for some time. Just the year before, Anne's close friend and supporter, Mary Dyer, had given birth to a stillborn and premature baby, "so monstrous and misshapen" that Governor Winthrop was able to conclude unequivocally that the devil was working through these women. Then, a few months later, Anne herself gave birth to a deformed baby that further implicated her in the devil's diabolical plot against New England. As time would tell, a pattern was emerging: anyone whose talk or actions went against the grain of Puritan order risked being accused of collegiality with the devil.

Modern readers find it difficult to read the transcript of Anne Hutchinson's trial without viewing it as a blatant example of judicial prejudice. This is, however, to fail to realize that it was a social drama whose outcome was certain from the outset. At one point in the trial, Governor Winthrop became so exasperated at Hutchinson's theological arguments that he cut her off by simply proclaiming, "We do not mean to discourse with those of your sex." Then, at the end of many hours of legal posturing and without having produced any hard evidence that Anne had committed a crime, Winthrop announced the court's verdict: "Mrs. Hutchinson, the sentence of the court you hear is that you are banished from out our jurisdiction as being a woman not fit for our society, and are to be imprisoned till the court shall send you away." Still baffled as to why her theological arguments had not demonstrated the purity of her cause, Hutchinson responded, "I desire to know wherefore

Banished for Her Staunch Defense of Individual Conscience in Religious Matters
Credit: The Granger Collection, New York.

I am banished." Winthrop, without hesitating, scolded, "Say no more, the court knows wherefore and is satisfied."

Of course, the court did know why Hutchinson had to be banished even if it did not have any formal laws or statutes to cite. As sociologist Kai Erikson notes, "The settlers were experiencing a shift in ideological focus, a change in community boundaries, but they had no vocabulary to explain to themselves or anyone else what the nature of these changes were. The purpose of the trial was to invent that language, to find a name for the nameless offense which Mrs. Hutchinson had committed."[29]

In brief, Anne Hutchinson was guilty of being a religious revolutionary. It is true that she used the language of conservative theology. But she used it to vent "strange opinions," opinions that "disparaged all our ministers in the land . . . [and] endangered us as from the foundation." Anne Hutchinson refused to submit to a coercive social order. She refused to acquiesce to established male authority just because she was ordered to do so. In striking out for individual conscience and spiritual liberty she incurred the wrath of a repressive cultural regime. Ironically, Hutchinson was in many ways championing the very essence of Puritanism's original vision. She championed the decentralization of ecclesiastical authority and the primacy of each person's internal relationship with God. But Anne was out of step with the uses that colonial leaders needed to make of religion. She didn't share the clergy's interest in using theological standards to mold the citizenry in ways it saw fit. It was obvious to all the proper authorities that the only way anyone could doubt their vested authority was to have been invisibly influenced by Satan. Given such a crime, banishment was the most lenient sentence Anne Hutchinson could possibly have hoped for.

The civil authorities imprisoned Hutchinson in Boston until weather conditions permitted her and her children to depart from the Massachusetts Bay Colony. They traveled first to Naragansett Bay in what is now Rhode Island and then to what is now New York City. There, about a year later, she and all but one daughter were massacred by Indians. Although during her lifetime Anne Hutchinson failed to triumph over the male-dominated Puritan leadership, she has become a symbol of America's revolutionary religious spirit. Her brave commitment to the principle of individual conscience in spiritual matters looms large across the landscape of American religious history.

REVIVALISM AND THE FIRST GREAT AWAKENING

By 1700 a certain stability had begun to set into colonial religious life. The Congregationalists were clearly the leaders, closely followed by the Episcopalians (Anglicans).[30] Baptists and Presbyterians were third and fourth. Quakers were the fifth largest group, trailed by the Dutch Reformed, Roman Catholics, and Lutherans. The Congregationalists predominated in the New England colonies; Presbyterians were the most dominant in the middle colonies where Episcopalians, Quakers, German Reformed, and Dutch Reformed also had significant support; and Episcopalians, Baptists, and Presbyterians somewhat shared control of the southern colonies with a slight nod to the Episcopalians, who enjoyed establishment in five southern colonies.

Historical perspective reveals that religion is like any other human activity. It is driven by our needs, hopes, fears, and desires. Specific religious groups vary in how well they meet these needs, hopes, fears, and desires. For this reason the "religious marketplace" is a volatile one. Groups grow or decline depending upon their ability to target their message to the people's changing interests. Over any span of time there are always going to be winners and losers as measured by overall market share. Winning and losing, however, have little or nothing to do with the "truth" or "falsity" of the group's theology; instead changes in the religious marketplace usually reflect timing and marketing savvy—whether these derive from intentional proselytizing strategies or just plain luck.

Even as stability set into American religious life in the early 1700s, the stage was being set for the first round of market volatility. Three denominations—the Congregationalists, Episcopalians, and Presbyterians—were closely aligned with the colonial power structure. The ministers of these three denominations were the most likely to be educated. They were thus exposed to a wide array of ideas that expanded their religious and intellectual interests beyond the narrow confines of Bible-based faith. Their sermons were more likely to stress the rational rather than the emotional side of religion. And, because their denominations were the most likely to enjoy the economic stability of state establishment, they had the least incentive to take initiatives that might lead to a larger market share. The lay members of these denominations were also part of the social and economic establishment. They were often second- or third-generation colonists with obvious economic advantages over newly arriving immigrants. Commercial opportunities brought a degree of prosperity, and enticed them into pursuing worldly comforts or self-interest at the expense of older notions of community obligation. Worldly prosperity was a threat to the traditional piety of Puritan groups such as the Congregationalists. As the Puritan minister Cotton Mather so perceptively observed, "Religion brought forth prosperity, and the daughter destroyed the mother." Mather realized that "there is danger lest the enchantments of this world make them to forget their errand into the wilderness."[31] By 1720 the older Puritan code was no longer a viable cultural program. Life had changed. If religion was to remain vital, it would have to accommodate to these new social, economic, and psychological realities. Some segments of the religious world refused to change. Their market share was destined to decline. Others embraced the opportunity for new spiritual initiatives. Conditions were ripe for the advent of what was to become the

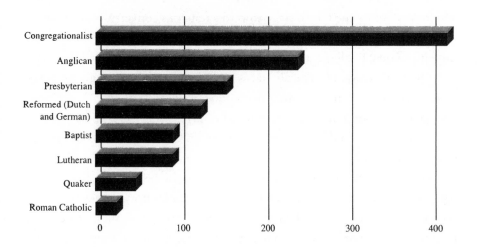

Number of Churches: 1740

single most distinctive institution in the history of American religion: revivalism.

A revival is an emotionally laden type of preaching aimed at producing conversions. Revivals heighten people's sense of sin, bring them to a crisis of conscience, and finally lead them to repentance and a heartfelt commitment to a new life in Christ. As such, revivals presuppose the basic model of religious conversion that Puritans had long held as the core of authentic spirituality. Some conversions appear to be spontaneous, others come after months or even years of personal struggle. But all tend to conform to a fairly distinct pattern of personal transformation. Allowing for individual variations, persons undergoing a religious conversion typically pass through five distinct stages. The first stage is the increasing sense that something is missing in our life. Typical human experiences such as a close call with death, an emotional hurt, guilt over lost opportunities, or even a general sense of meaningless can all lead to the conclusion that our life is somehow off the mark. The second stage begins with a growing awareness of the futility of relying on our own energies and efforts. If simple adjustments or quick fixes can turn our life back around, then a complete conversion wouldn't be necessary. But when we realize that all of our usual strategies for coping with life are of no real help, then a more complete change will inevitably be required. The third stage is that of despair, a bitter realization that we lack the resources to effect a cure. In theological terms, this is the "conviction of sin." From this sense of despair and futility comes the fourth stage toward a religious conversion—a sense of humility and powerlessness. The old self is humbled, giving up all conceit and pretense. Then, finally, comes the fifth stage, what might be called the "leap of faith." At this moment a person turns his or her life over to a higher power. This turn to a higher power brings tremendous relief and comfort. Wholeness and well-being are not achieved, but rather given from "above," as it were. Having died to our old self, a new self is born. In Christian terms, our life has been renewed in Christ.

Revivalist preachers are somewhat unique in the history of Christianity. They are often without formal credentials. Their authority comes not from formal training but from their personal power of persuasion. Successful revivalists possess an uncanny ability to arouse emotions, to bring persons to an emotional crisis. Their skill lies in the use of persuasion and pressure not only to elicit such a crisis, but to resolve it by bringing persons to a moment of decision. In this way they compress the long process leading to conversion into a compact time frame. In a couple of hours or less, revivalists bring persons to a conviction of sin and lead them to surrender their lives to Christ.

To many it seemed that religion had settled into a lifeless and routine formalism by the first few decades of the 1700s. As the Puritan preacher Jonathan Edwards observed, "an extraordinary dullness" seemed to pervade the churches. The colonies' preachers were capable enough at producing theologically sound sermons, but their weekly worship services were devoid of spontaneity or enthusiasm. Slowly but surely, things began to heat up. First a Dutch Reformed minister, Theodore Frelinghuysen, evoked strong emotional response by vigorously encouraging his parishioners to strengthen their religious resolve. Frelinghuysen was alarmed by the lax state of religion in the colonies. His preaching consequently forced listeners' attention to their own personal sin and demanded repentance, followed by conversion.

Whether Frelinghuysen was aware of it or not, he began a movement that lasted from 1720 until the early 1750s. This movement, often called the Great Awakening, was America's first mass religious revival.[32] Ministers and itinerant preachers picked up on the theme of "the necessity of the New Birth" and brought audiences to a conviction of their sinfulness, followed by highly emotional conversions whereby they committed their lives to Christ. Charismatic preaching drew large crowds of unprecedented size. The Great Awakening stretched into every colony, forging intercolonial alliances and shared experiences on the eve of the Revolutionary War.

Frelinghuysen's fame sparked others to intensify their preaching style. William Tennent and his son, Gilbert Tennent, took up the call to challenge sinners and lead them to the experience of rebirth lest they run headlong toward eternal damnation. So intense were Gilbert's sermons that his hearers sometimes "were compelled to cry out in the public assembly, both under the impression of terror and love."[33] As the Tennents (Gilbert's two brothers also joined the cause) continued to win converts, it became clear that revivalism was implicitly criticizing more established forms of ministry. Gilbert, in fact, delivered an inflammatory sermon on "The Danger of an Unconverted Ministry." Tennent argued against the spiritual authority of ministers who had not themselves undergone an intense episode of spiritual rebirth and thereby cast deep suspicion on the established ministry. Revivalism was thus destined to divide many Protestant denominations. New Light (pro-revivalism) and Old Light (anti-revivalism) contingents would forever after find themselves opposed to one another's understanding of what constitutes authentic Christian commitment.

The Great Awakening accelerated in the mid-1730s when Jonathan Edwards presided over a sudden revival of religious emotion in Northampton, Massachusetts. Edwards was a staid, emotionally disciplined rationalist. Having graduated from Yale at the age of seventeen, he was quite possibly the first real genius that the colonies had yet produced. Edwards was a sophisticated theologian and found himself particularly called upon to champion Calvinism over and against what he saw to be the colonies' proclivity for adopting Arminian views. At stake was the issue of whether humans are utterly characterized by sin and thus wholly dependent upon God's saving grace (Calvin) or possess sufficient moral strength to move toward God's grace through personal decision and sustained effort (Arminius). Toward this end Edwards delivered a number of sermons that vividly depicted what he knew to be the precariousness of the human condition. To this day American schoolchildren read excerpts from one such sermon, "Sinners in the Hands of an Angry God." In this sermon Edwards explained that at the moment of death every soul goes immediately to heaven or to hell. Following Calvin, Edwards taught that every human is deserving only of hell.

Our eternal fate is almost certain to be that of damnation unless we are one of the few whom God freely elects for salvation. We are thus not without hope. God's infinite love makes it possible for the gates of heaven to be yet open to some of us: "And now you have an extraordinary opportunity, a day wherein Christ has flung the door of mercy wide open and stands in the door calling and crying with a loud voice to poor sinners; . . . many, that were very likely in the same miserable condition that you are in, are now in a happy state, with their hearts filled with love to him that has loved them and washed them from their sins."[34]

Much to his own surprise, Edwards' sermons were met with intense and enthusiastic response. Edwards succeeded in converting over 300 people within six months. He recounted this amazing revival of faith in a tract titled *A Faithful Narrative of the Surprising Work of God*. By his account people were so fearful of "dropping into hell" that they committed every last energy "to get the kingdom of heaven." Not only did the local citizens increase their church attendance, they also formed into small groups to meet in private houses for Bible study and mutual encouragement. Of note is the fact that despite all the lip service Edwards had given in support of Calvinism, the upshot of his "hellfire and brimstone" preaching was to encourage an Arminian faith in humanity's ability to make a conscious choice to be saved.

The Great Awakening escalated to an even higher level of religious fervor when the British evangelist George Whitefield made the first of his seven trips across the Atlantic in 1738. By all accounts Whitefield may have been the single most impassioned, charismatic preacher in the history of American religion. Whitefield was young (in his early 20s when he first hit the lecture circuit), tall, and striking in appearance. He knew that his special mission was to be a catalyst for religious conversion and he had a natural gift for pushing the right emotional buttons necessary to elicit repentance. Whitefield had a certain flair for turning preaching into an impassioned performance. He would wave his arms, sing hymns, vary the cadence of his delivery, and weep in both pain and joy as he prayed for the deliverance of those in attendance. And when he preached, pandemonium broke out. Many cried out loud, others shouted. Still others fell to the ground, too smitten by the Holy Spirit to preserve self-control. All felt the intense relief of knowing that they had now joined the ranks of God's chosen. Whitefield's oratory and highly dramatic style were so powerful that David

Garrick, the most famous English actor of the time, claimed that Whitefield could move a crowd to frenzy merely by saying the word "Mesopotamia." Benjamin Franklin was no less impressed with Whitefield's powerful style. As we shall see in the next chapter, Franklin was something of a religious skeptic. But he knew a good commercial opportunity when he saw one. Once when Franklin heard Whitefield preach in Philadelphia he began pacing off the distance from the podium to the back of the crowd. He quickly calculated that as many as 25,000 persons were present, all avidly attending to Whitefield's every word. When Whitefield finished speaking Franklin approached him, contract in hand, to get the rights to publish Whitefield's sermons and sell them to a ready-made audience.

Whitefield was even more astute about marketing religion than was Franklin. He publicized his appearances well in advance of his arrival. He promoted his forthcoming lectures in newspapers and leaflets, making religion one of the first industries in America to seize upon the value of advertising. He also sold sermons and books, preserving the market share he first won with personal appearances. During one lecture circuit in the fall of 1740, Whitefield traveled over 800 miles to preach to 130 audiences in a 73-day period. The crowds were often enormous. One sermon alone was estimated to have drawn 30,000 people; this in a day in which the entire city of Boston had a population of only 20,000. Whitefield carried the Great Awakening up and down the Atlantic seaboard, delivering the same revivalist message to those in the northern, middle, and southern colonies.

By the early 1750s the Great Awakening began to subside. But its legacy was to live on in American religious life, up to and including the present day. First and foremost, the Great Awakening established revivalism as a unique and distinctive feature of American religion. From that time forward groups that could effectively utilize revivalist techniques to gain new converts would prosper in the American religious marketplace. Those that couldn't would languish (unless, in the case of Catholicism, immigration and large families could offset a lack of evangelizing zeal). Already the Baptists, previously lagging far behind the Congregationalists and Episcopalians, were gaining membership as they ventured out with their revivalist-friendly message. Second, the Great Awakening deepened the evangelical outlook of American religious thought. The term "evangelical" refers to a religious outlook emphasizing that the only way to salvation is through a conscious, personal commitment to Jesus as one's Lord and Savior. The evangelical outlook places conversion at the core of religion. This is in opposition to those forms of Christianity that emphasize participation in church rituals, ecclesiastical authority, formal theology, or morality as central to Christian commitment. While the Puritans who first settled the colonies surely embraced an evangelical piety, the Great Awakening deepened this strain of Protestant belief and interjected it deeply into popular religiosity. Third, the Great Awakening created a sense of national consciousness that would prepare the colonists for the impending push toward independence from England. The Great Awakening popularized a rhetoric of liberty, a conviction that true authority rested in personal conscience rather than in established authority. The Great Awakening involved citizens of every colony in a common event (even those who opposed the basic themes of emotional, revivalist religion). It further gave the colonists a sense of special destiny, a confidence that they were somehow preparing the world for a more complete establishment of a kingdom of God on earth.

JONATHAN EDWARDS: TENSIONS BETWEEN CONSENSUS AND CREATIVITY IN PURITAN THOUGHT

The colonial period was marked by the struggle to construct viable institutions. So much effort was expended in the effort of building consensus that few cultural revolutionaries emerged. Anne Hutchinson surely never sought such a role. In some ways she wasn't a revolutionary at all. She never doubted the veracity of orthodox Christian teachings. Theologically, her faith was fairly conservative. But she voiced beliefs that exposed vulnerabilities in the Puritan cultural code. Hutchinson, much like the colonial Quakers who were viewed with equal suspicion, claimed that she received direct revelation from God. The Holy Spirit dwelt in her heart. For this reason she didn't need the guidance of male church officials to interpret the Bible or to apply it to the tasks of everyday life. Anne Hutchinson's reliance on the inner light of Christ undercut Puritanism's concern with equating spiritual piety with capitulation to cultural authority. By doing this she championed spiritual freedom over and against social conformity. She was surely a religious revolutionary, but it was never her intention to encourage others to seek out new spiritual paths.

Anne Hutchinson was by no means the most brilliant or even the most original religious thinker during the colonial era. This distinction undoubtedly belongs to Jonathan Edwards. Edwards was something of a theological prodigy. He entered Yale at thirteen, graduated at seventeen. After a few years as a tutor he began an assistantship under the direction of his grandfather, Solomon Stoddard, who was pastor of the Congregationalist church at Northampton, Massachusetts. When Rev. Stoddard died two years later, Jonathan Edwards assumed the pulpit at the age of twenty-six. We have already seen how approximately five years into his ministry Edwards presided over a great outburst of spiritual revival among his parishioners. The spiritual enthusiasm that Edwards witnessed caused him to ponder many of American Puritanism's most puzzling questions: How to sustain and renew the personal virtue that a virtuous nation would require? How to cultivate the moral persons who alone could people a moral nation? How to distinguish between those who possess true Christian faith and those who profess it without really having it? How to determine whether a conversion experience originated in God's saving spirit, or whether it was the result of self-deception or even the guile of Satan?[35]

"True religion," Edwards proposed, "consists in holy affections."[36] By "holy affections" Edwards meant something qualitatively different than any other operation of the human mind or personality. In strict Calvinist terms Edwards explained that the holy affections aren't something natural to us or achieved through effort. They are imparted to us directly from God. A sermon delivered in 1734 explained that the holy affections originate in "A Divine and Supernatural Light, Immediately Imparted to the Soul by the Spirit of God, Shown to be Both a Scriptural, and Rational Doctrine." True religion was thus very much an inner affair. It comes, however, not from our own will or our own emotions but rather from a supernatural spiritual agency. Edwards was thus not reducing religion to mere moralism or even willed belief. He insisted that religion was something far more exhilarating. It included an intensely mystical encounter with a more-than-human reality and it utterly transformed one's inner being.

A difficult problem in Edwards' time was that many of those who claimed to have undergone a personal religious conversion must have surely been mistaken. But how was one to know who was a true, visible saint and who was either mistaken or simply pretending? Edwards conceded that we probably never know such things for certain. But he was pastor of a Puritan church that wished to have only "visible saints" as full members. It was therefore important for him to determine how we might evaluate a person's spiritual credentials. Edwards explained that the religious affections grow out of inner sensations that are distinct, lively, and vigorous. These sensations should be expected to grow or intensify over time. But Edwards was never equating true religion with emotionalism, like many modern revivalists do. He insisted that inward realities must necessarily express themselves in, and can therefore be tested by, outward behaviors. True saints will, for example, display a quickened sense of the gospel's truth. They will love God for the sake of God's loveliness rather than for personal benefit, continue in humility, and yearn for increased spirituality. The crucial test of sainthood, however, is moral in nature. True religious affections must, in Edwards' view, result in a wholly new stance toward the world. A saint is thus characterized by disinterested virtue. By this Edwards meant that the saving work of God's spirit displaces our natural tendency to act out of self-interest. A true saint acts only out of a duty to serve and obey God. In a roundabout way, therefore, the final test of true religion for Edwards was the degree to which a regenerated saint conforms to the community's moral code.

Much in Edwards' thought was both original and inspiring. His writings reveal a religious passion. The main themes of his work amplify Puritanism's historic hunger for spiritual intensity. As historian Perry Miller explains, Puritanism always contained "an indestructible element which was mystical, and a feeling for the universe which was almost pantheistic."[37] Edwards picked up on this strain of Puritan piety. He wanted to show that God's saving presence is palpably present within the saint's inner constitution. He argued that God—or more properly, the supernatural light that emanates from God—is present to the properly receptive individual.

> The great and last end of God's works . . . is fitly compared to an effulgence or emanation of light from a luminary. . . . It is by this that all nature is quickened and receives life, comfort and joy. . . . In the creature's knowing, esteeming, loving rejoicing in, and praising God, the glory of god is both exhibited and acknowledged; His fullness is received, and returned. *Here is both emanation and remanation. The refulgence shines upon and into the creature*, and is reflected back to the luminary.[38]

These references to the "effulgence" or "emanation" of divine light reveal how far Edwards had unwittingly strayed from traditional Calvinism's emphasis upon the distance or remoteness of God. Edwards' eagerness to explain how a saint's natural constitution had in some fundamental way been altered by God's "emanations" led him to hint at God's radical immanence within the natural order. He even went so far as to suggest that the holy affections render us capable of perceiving "images or shadows of divine things" all about us in nature. This notion had intriguing implications. It suggested that God is all about us, but awaiting us to expand our perception and behold His beauty. It simultaneously suggested that the barrier separating us and God is not sin or disobedience, but limited spiritual vision. But neither Edwards nor his Puritan contemporaries were prepared to follow this idea of God's "effulgence" to such daring conclusions. As Perry Miller reminds us, Puritanism was more than a passion for inward communication with God. It "was also a social code demanding obedience to external law, a code to which good people voluntarily conformed and to which bad people should be made to conform. It aimed at propriety and decency, the virtues of middle-class respectability, self-control, thrift, and dignity, at a discipline of the emotions."[39]

Edwards could never quite break free from his impulse to use spirituality as a means of social control. Even at the height of spiritual fervor in his own church, he couldn't step back and appreciate "inner illumination" for its own sake. Instead, he could only harp on moral duty. His goal was to purge the church of all who strayed from the Puritan cultural code. He resolved to measure every parishioner's saintliness by his or her conformity to Christ's law. New applicants for church membership were judged by an even stricter standard. For four years not a single applicant was able to pass Edwards' strict tests of moral obedience. Not surprisingly, the members of his Northampton church began to find Edwards exceedingly contentious, cold, and lacking in compassion. The congregation finally had no choice but to remove him from their church. Edwards was expelled and forced to relocate to the remote village of Stockbridge, where he was relegated to relative obscurity.

Edwards, while creatively attentive to the dynamics of spiritual transformation, fell short of being a religious revolutionary. His final goal remained that of fortifying Puritanism's theological and social boundaries, not expanding them.

ON THE EVE OF REVOLUTION

By the 1770s white, Anglo-Saxon Protestants—Puritan Protestants—had established their dominance in the American colonies. It is true that only about 20 percent actually belonged to a church. But many more attended, at least occasionally. And because most colonies enforced the establishment of one particular denomination (mostly Congregationalist churches in the northern colonies, Episcopal churches in the southern colonies), the vast bulk of the population found themselves paying taxes in support of the propagation of religion. The rough order of religious denominations in terms of membership was as follows: (1) Congregationalists, (2) Presbyterians, (3) Baptists, (4) Episcopalians, (5) Quakers, (6) Dutch and German Reformed, (7) Lutherans, and (8) Methodists. Catholics came in ninth. Jews hardly registered, with perhaps only five small congregations on the entire continent.

But things were poised for change. The Revolutionary War would soon bring independence from England. Independence was looming on the religious front, too. A wave of free thinking would soon embolden many to break from inherited religious patterns.

ళ

Religion and the Early Republic

The Era of Thomas Jefferson

WHEN THE DECLARATION OF INDEPENDENCE WAS SIGNED in 1776 nearly 20 percent of the American population were slaves of African descent. Another 8 percent of the population consisted of Native Americans. The remaining 72 percent were of European ancestry—the vast majority of whom (over 83 percent) were English. But, as we have seen, these were Englishmen "of that kind which is most adverse to all implicit subjugation of mind and opinion." This resistance to subjugation made revolutionaries of them. They were engaged in a war for independence, and religion was to play a significant role.[1]

Religion helped forge colonial unity even before the first shot was fired. Since a majority of English settlers had some connection with Puritanism, they consequently saw themselves as united against the Catholic-like Angli-

NUMBER OF CHURCHES: 1780

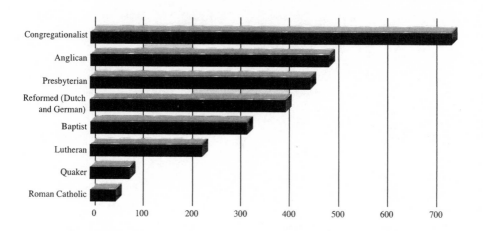

can Church. The federation of church and state in England was one of the reasons that had led to the colonization of the New World in the first place. Puritan leaders had long viewed human history as a dramatic battle between the forces of good (followers of Christ) and evil (followers of the Antichrist). As the Revolution approached, colonial ministers preached an increasing number of sermons that identified both King George III and the Anglican Church as agents of the Antichrist. The image of England as the Antichrist justified violent rebellion. Ministers described the revolutionary cause as a sacred quest against "the prince of darkness," "all the powers of Hell," "the serpent," or "the antichristian beast." Such apocalyptic rhetoric refocused the colonists' belief that they were engaged in God's special errand into the wilderness.[2] The Great Awakening had also aroused hope concerning America's spiritual destiny. Revivalists whipped crowds into a frenzy with the message that "the dust of Babylon" could be shaken off in the twinkling of an eye. A new life was possible for those who stepped forward to accept their divinely appointed destiny as free and morally pure agents of righteousness.

Not every American religious group embraced armed rebellion. Episcopalians were intimately connected with both the government and the established religion of England. Episcopal clergy, particularly in the north, were thus prone to see the war as an unjustified revolt against established authority. Yet Episcopal laymen from southern colonies were among the most ardent supporters of independence. A few of the smaller denominations were pacifists. Quakers, Mennonites, Dunkers, and Moravians kept to the sidelines out of long-standing principle. Lutheran, Dutch and German Reformed, Roman Catholic, and Jewish congregations were by and large aligned with the colonial cause. The most zealous advocacy of independence came from the Baptists, Presbyterians, and Congregationalists, who saw their own cause closely linked with the establishment of a new government wholly emancipated from the established order of British culture.

When the Revolution finally ended, the Congregationalists, Presbyterians, and Baptists were the three largest religious organizations in the new nation. Their clergy were euphoric and quickly turned their attention to planning the next stage in the establishment of a Kingdom of God on earth. They knew they were in a privileged position to direct the nation's future. Evangelical revivalism was destined to extend pure Christian faith to the whole American populace and then throughout the world. The prospects for inaugurating the Kingdom of God on earth had not seemed so auspicious since the Pilgrims first set foot on Plymouth Rock. As the former chaplain to the Continental Congress, George Duffield, boldly proclaimed during a sermon in 1784, "Vice and immorality shall yet here become banished . . . and the wilderness blossom as the rose."[3]

The nation's Protestant citizens eagerly anticipated the establishment of a complete Christian commonwealth. Little did they realize that some of the very leaders who had helped secure independence from foreign rule would now insist upon independence from religious rule as well.

EARLY CULTURE WARS

In 1780 the essential nature of the new American nation was still undecided. Two opposing parties contended for cultural supremacy. To see how these two opposing philosophies have vied for control of American culture we need only look at the two sides of a coin. One side of an American coin reads "In God We Trust." Western culture, we are reminded, is deeply rooted in the Judeo-Christian heritage. In the case of the United States, it was the Calvinist formulation of this heritage that most forcefully informed those who gathered in the 1780s to write our Constitution and Bill of Rights. Calvinism teaches that since Adam's fall human nature has been utterly corrupted and that human reason is not to be trusted because it ultimately serves humanity's basest passions. Rather than rely on human powers, we should instead humble ourselves before the Almighty Lord and obey His will as it has been revealed to us in the Holy Bible. The proper goal of life is to wage an unceasing war against our tendencies for self-expression. Through incessant self-scrutiny we must abase ourselves and thereby become worthy of Christ's redeeming love. Faith is thus to be valued above any form of human reason. Faith, here, is understood to mean accepting Jesus as one's Lord and Savior. It also requires us to abandon reason and instead place trust in the literal truth of the Bible as well as the church authorities, who can help us interpret and apply the Bible to our everyday lives.

On the other side of an American coin, however, is the Latin phrase "E Pluribus Unum." This use of classical Latin reminds us that Western culture is also grounded in the rationalist and humanist heritage of the Greco-Roman world. We can become "one out of many" not only by obeying God's laws but also by using the rational powers celebrated by Greek and Roman philosophers. The philosophers of the classical era were unhindered by notions of sin or the need for self-abnegation. They believed that the basic impediment to human happiness was insufficient knowledge about how the natural universe operates. We can improve our lives by using our innate capacities for rational inquiry to extend our knowledge about the world. Classical thought was therefore humanist, emphasizing human abilities, human rights, and human potentials. For this reason classical humanism opposed any kind of nonrational faith that threatened to suppress humanity's creative powers.

The two strands of Western thought have each enjoyed periods of relative predominance. For example, we commonly think of the Middle Ages as an era dominated by Christian faith. The rationalist outlook gained ascendancy during the Renaissance and again during the Enlightenment or Age of Reason. The Enlightenment captured the imaginations of European intellectuals during the period that directly preceded the American Revolution. A major impetus for this widespread faith in reason was the career of Sir Isaac Newton (1642-1747). Prior to Newton, men and women were completely at the mercy of the natural universe. They had no real way of understanding, much less controlling, the universe they inhabited. Newton's scientific and mathematical accomplishments made the universe seem more intelligible. More important, Newton's discoveries established a new, scientific method for progressively understanding the laws of nature. His contemporaries believed that they were at last freed from fear, ignorance, and superstition. The universe could now be understood as a vast machine—lawful, harmonious, and comprehensible by the human mind. Alexander Pope captured Newton's influence on the spirit of the age when he wrote: "Nature and Nature's Laws lay hid in night. / God said 'Let Newton be!' and all was light."[4]

Newton demonstrated that the movement of the planets in distant space can be explained with the same mathematical formulas that explain nearby objects. His work thus made the universe seem intelligible and thoroughly rational. Newton's influence is hard to overestimate. Those who encountered his work could not help but observe the precision with which reason and science could describe the workings of the universe. Religion and faith paled by comparison.

The British philosopher John Locke (1632-1704) further contributed to the buoyant spirit of the Age of Reason. Locke's philosophical writings overthrew Calvin's distrust of human reason. Locke argued that the mind begins as a blank slate (in direct contrast to Calvin's insistence upon humanity's innate depravity). Our knowledge of the world comes through sensory impressions, which are gradually grouped into ideas or concepts. In his treatise titled *The Art of Thinking*, Locke explained how the mind is capable of testing and, if necessary, correcting its judgments about the nature of the world. Although Locke himself remained a Christian, his writings effectively undermined belief in divine revelation. Since ideas come only from sensory experience, and revelation is extrasensory, no "truth claim" based on alleged revelation meets Locke's criteria of true human knowledge. "Reason," Locke wrote, "must be our last Judge and Guide in every Thing."[5]

The writings of Newton and Locke inspired an unprecedented faith in the powers of human reason. As a cultural and intellectual movement, the Enlightenment was defined by five basic commitments.[6] First, the Enlightenment championed experience and reason as the twin foundations of human knowledge. Observation and inductive reasoning—not faith in unproven dogmas—were thought to be the only road to reliable knowledge. Second, the Enlightenment directed persons to the study of nature and the "here and now"—as opposed to speculating about heaven or eternity. Third, those with confidence in humanity's rational powers were deeply suspicious of authority—political or religious. They urged all to use their own minds, think for themselves, and resist pressure to conform for the sake of conformity. Fourth, the Age of Reason spread commitment to the ideals of individual freedom and political equality. Fifth, the Enlightenment inspired confidence in the inevitability of progress. The Enlightenment outlook became synonymous with belief in human perfectibility and in humanity's capacity to use newly gained understandings of the natural universe to shape a better future.

Most Enlightenment thinkers began to reexamine religion in light of the era's confidence in reason. Some, especially the French *philosophes* like Voltaire and Diderot, followed reason to an atheistic conclusion and held all religion in contempt. Others, however, were drawn to a religious philosophy known as deism. Deism had roots both in the Enlightenment and in liberal ("latitu-dinarian") sentiments among many eighteenth-century Englishmen who stressed the rational side of Christian faith. Briefly stated, deism held that God exists, that the true worship of God consists of moral actions, and that there is an afterlife in which virtue will be rewarded and vice punished. Beyond these three principles, deism had nothing more to say. There was, therefore, nothing distinctively Christian about deism. Its rational outlook cast suspi-cion on such topics as the special nature of Christ, the existence of miracles, or the reliability of scripture. Deism was devoid of mystery or ritual, and offered little in the way of emotional comfort to those seeking guidance from a Higher Power. But deism did make it possible for educated persons to affirm a "rational faith." And, for many in the Age of Reason, this was the only alternative to rejecting religion altogether.

Many colonial leaders embraced deism as the only religious outlook consistent with the progressive temperament of their era. Thomas Paine, for example, was less famous among his contemporaries for his patriotic treatise *Common Sense* than his deistic manifesto *The Age of Reason*. Several other respected thinkers of the era—Ethan Allen, Joseph Priestley, and Elihu Palmer—also popularized a religious outlook that openly challenged conven-tional Christian faith. Deistic influence spread so widely among the educated ranks of American society that the Protestant minister Lyman Beecher, who entered Yale in 1793, later recalled that the "college was in a most ungodly state. The college church was almost extinct. Most of the students were skeptical. . . . That was the day of the infidelity of the Tom Paine school. Boys that dressed flax in the barn, as I used to, read Tom Paine and believed him. . . . Most of the class before me were infidels, and called each other Voltaire [and other French atheists]."[7] Infidelity, atheism, and the wild ideas of French libertines were seemingly rampant among the nation's educated citizenry. A 1789 alumnus of Dartmouth College recorded that his fellow students were "very unruly, lawless, and without the fear of God" and lamented that ten years later, "but a single member of the class of 1799 was publicly known as a professing Christian."[8]

Culture wars had broken out in the new republic. Christianity and Enlightenment rationality were contending for the right to define the essential nature of the American people. The friction between the two contending parties became readily apparent in the public debate over the role that religion would have in the official constitution of the United States. Many of the nation's churched citizens argued for the establishment of churched religion. The argument for establishment rested upon two basic assumptions: that the existence and well-being of any society depends upon a body of commonly shared religious beliefs, and that the only guarantee that these necessary beliefs will be sufficiently inculcated is to put the power of the state behind the institution responsible for their dissemination.[9] Enlightenment thinkers tended to find both assumptions offensive. They were suspicious of all religion and wanted to make sure that it wouldn't have any role in the new nation. Passing a constitution would prove difficult as long as no middle ground could be found between the two opposing sides.

Resolving this ideological war required a particular kind of American revolutionary: someone who could respect the first assumption concerning the relationship between religion and social order (that the well-being of society depends upon commonly shared beliefs) without embracing the second (that the only guarantee of culturally shared beliefs is to put the power of the government behind a particular religious group). Fortunately for the United States, two such revolutionaries were ready at hand. Benjamin Franklin and Thomas Jefferson appreciated belief in the necessity of commonly shared basic religious ideas. Both, however, rejected the necessity of establishment (coercion) in favor of complete religious freedom (persuasion) as the best means of ensuring productive religious thought over the long haul of American history. Franklin's thoughts about religion are surprisingly sophisticated even by today's intellectual standards. But it is finally Jefferson who emerged as the early republic's most foresighted religious revolutionary. His deistic outlook enabled him to sustain faith in "the essentials" of religion while yet spearheading the movement to guarantee complete religious freedom in the United States. Jefferson became the architect of what he called the "wall of separation" between church and state, giving rise to a system that to this day fosters a great diversity of religious belief without sacrificing the stability of the social order.

PROPHET OF AMERICAN VIRTUE: BENJAMIN FRANKLIN

Benjamin Franklin (1706-1790) was born into a pious Puritan household. His father, Josiah, was a candlemaker and skilled mechanic. His mother, Abiah Folger Franklin, was, in her son's eyes, "a discreet and virtuous Woman." Benjamin was the eighth of ten children and grew up in the family home located across the street from Boston's Old South Church, where his parents were fully covenanted members. Josiah Franklin subscribed wholeheartedly to the Calvinist scheme. He regularly attended the church's worship services and embraced its teachings concerning the serious purpose of life. By word and example Josiah taught his children the importance of living a frugal, self-disciplined life. Benjamin later described his father as an honest man, a doer of good works, and in every way a paragon of moral rectitude.

By his early teens, however, Benjamin came to resent his parents' stern piety. Weekly attendance at Old South Church's somber services became an unpleasant duty. He particularly reacted against Calvinism's emphasis on guilt and fear. The Puritan outlook struck him as repressive and thus inherently incapable of helping persons find happiness, spontaneity, or purpose in their lives. Benjamin had by this time become an avid reader. He had learned the physics of Isaac Newton and the social philosophy of John Locke. He had also devoured the writings of several deists, confirming his intuitive rejection of doctrinal Christianity and his movement toward a more rational and practical religious philosophy.

Franklin absorbed the intellectual currents of the day. He particularly devoted himself to the study of science. The worldview that science opened up contrasted sharply with the seemingly backward stance of Calvinism. The emphasis on reason, observation, and continuous revision of ideas was more in keeping with Benjamin's practical bent of mind. He soon followed reason to a point of view almost completely opposite that of his parent's traditional Puritanism. For a short time he adopted a purely materialistic philosophy of life. Seeing life as a machine-like system, Franklin temporarily denied free will and came to conceive of God in a way that was so intellectually abstract as to make God irrelevant to everyday life. In this way Benjamin succeeded in freeing himself from the constrictions of Calvinist theology. But the starkly rationalist philosophy he championed in place of Calvinism was no better at filling life with happiness, spontaneity, and sound moral purpose.

Over the course of his life Franklin slowly fashioned his own deistic philosophy. At a purely intellectual level he was never able to affirm any concept of God other than Deism's notion of God as the First Cause that set the universe into motion. Like all deists, Franklin rejected belief in divine revelation. Humans can therefore know nothing about God directly. The only ideas that we can really have about God come by inference; logic tells us that there must be a First Cause or Grand Architect who established the system of physical laws that govern our universe. Franklin wasn't strident about his deistic views. He was committed to toleration, embracing a "live and let live" approach to life in a society with so many contending religious sects. His confidence that knowledge develops progressively over time made him self-conscious of the fact that his own views were limited and must undoubtedly contain elements that would later need to be corrected or revised. We might also note that Franklin appreciated how important conventional religion was to society even if most of its doctrines were untrue ("if men are so wicked as we now see them *with* religion what would they be if *without* it?").[10]

Benjamin Franklin's most succinct explanation of what he understood to be the essentials of religion appear in an especially lucid passage of his *Autobiography*:

> I had been religiously educated as a Presbyterian; and tho' some of the dogmas of that persuasion, such as *the eternal decrees of God, election, reprobation, etc.*, appeared to me unintelligible, others doubtful, and I early absented myself from the public assemblies of the sect, Sunday being my studying day, I never was without some religious principles. I never doubted, for instance, the existence of the Deity; that he made the world, and govern'd it by his Providence; that the most acceptable service of God was the doing

of good to men; that our souls are immortal; and that all crime will be punished, and virtue rewarded, either here or hereafter. These I estimated to be *the essentials of every religion*; and being to be found in all the religions we had in our country, I respected them all, tho' with different degrees of respect, as I found them more or less mix'd with other articles, which, without any tendency to inspire, promote, or confirm morality, serv'd principally to divide us, and make us unfriendly to one another.[11]

Franklin's delineation of "the essentials of religion" largely mirror the deistic philosophy of his day. But in certain important respects Franklin went beyond deism and championed a highly innovative spiritual outlook. Prefiguring the philosopher William James, who lived almost a hundred years later, Franklin seems to have made a distinction between what might be called "pure reason" and "practical or moral reason." While "pure reason" will forever remain skeptical about religious issues, humans nonetheless find themselves adopting spiritual perspectives when engaged in the actual practice of life. Intellectually, Benjamin Franklin never strayed far from the Enlightenment-inspired view that humans know nothing certain about God except the rational inference of the existence of a First Cause. Yet he also realized that people do—and should— believe in ways that sustain them spiritually and ethically. All of us need "useful fictions"—beliefs that help us envision the universe in ways that comfort us, provide daily life with a sense of purpose, and encourage virtue.[12] The various doctrines espoused by the nation's churches fall into this category of useful fictions. Franklin didn't believe that religious doctrines were true in any literal sense. But he appreciated how they helped make the universe more actable. For example, he personally believed in divine providence (i.e., the belief that God actively guides human history toward some ultimate destiny) despite the lack of any conclusive evidence. Most Enlightenment thinkers rejected the idea of divine providence since it presupposes belief that a Supreme Being occasionally intervenes in the otherwise lawful affairs of our world. Some Enlightenment thinkers adopted a watered-down view of providence that while repudiating belief in miraculous intervention nonetheless accredited the Supreme Architect with having designed the laws of nature in such a way as to make progress likely if not inevitable. Franklin, however, went one step further. In a talk delivered to friends who met as a club to discuss science and philosophy, he argued that God "sometimes interferes by his particular Providence and sets aside the Effects which would otherwise have been produced."[13] Reason alone didn't drive Franklin to assert belief in "particular" Providence. It was that he couldn't live with the alternative points of view. He surely didn't want to affirm that God controls every last event on earth, leaving no room for the role of free will or energetic human action. Nor could he settle for a universe in which God was so aloof as to be wholly uninterested in our personal or collective fates. Franklin was thus left with no option other than to affirm the rather anti-intellectual belief that God can and does sometimes exert guiding influence into the affairs of this world. In similar fashion Franklin came to affirm the existence of an afterlife. True, he had no sound intellectual reason to believe in life after death. Yet his will to look forward and marshal his energies for new tasks prompted him to affirm a "hope for the Future, built on Experience of the Past."[14]

The fact that religious beliefs often serve as useful fictions did not mean that they were all equally valuable. Franklin acknowledged that some religious beliefs serve humans better than others. Much like Jonathan Edwards before him, Franklin believed that the ultimate test of spirituality was the degree to which it gives rise to virtuous living. Edwards investigated the nature of true virtue with the intention of showing that it must ultimately lead to disinterested service (i.e., obedience to the cultural order). Franklin, on the other hand, tried to discover which specific virtues produced practical consequences for the individual who emulated them. In his *Autobiography* he enumerated thirteen such virtues: temperance, silence, order, resolution, frugality, industry, sincerity, justice, moderation, cleanliness, tranquility, chastity, and humility.

It was not that Franklin was exceptionally expert in his practice of any of these virtues. He seemed particularly in short supply of temperance, chastity, and humility. And unlike a Jonathan Edwards, Franklin deemed neither self-abnegation nor a pious surrendering of one's rational powers to be the proper goal of life. He instead equated authentic spirituality with the art of practical living (i.e., finding happiness, spontaneity, and purpose in our everyday lives). This requires intelligence, humor, tolerance, and a commitment to individual freedom. And all of these, in Franklin's view, were indispensable to spiritual living. Franklin knew that he lived in an age that viewed these traits as the antithesis of religious piety. In his opinion the religious groups of his era misunderstood spirituality and turned it into the enemy of happiness rather than the agent of its procurement. The result was that "every sect believing itself possessed of *all truth,* and that every tenet differing from theirs was *error,* conceived that when the power was in their hands, persecution was a duty required of them by that God whom they supposed to be offended with heresy."[15] Over and against Calvinism's grim and humorless stance toward the world, Franklin dared to poke fun at himself and his attempts at theological understanding.[16] He not only preached religious tolerance, he practiced it both by donating funds to many denominational causes and by befriending those of different faiths. Franklin was, in fact, a close personal friend of the revivalist preacher George Whitefield despite the fact that the two men could hardly have been more theologically opposed. Whitefield's entire ministry was predicated upon theological doctrines (e.g., original sin, the divinity of Jesus, salvation through Christ's vicarious sacrifice, the literal truth of scripture) that Franklin repudiated. Yet Franklin found Whitefield an honest man and a relentless advocate of the kinds of social reform that Franklin himself identified with the virtuous living that alone would enable the new republic to flourish.[17] Thus Franklin the printer, scientist, inventor, and statesman was also a progenitor of a spiritual outlook that substituted the practice of civil virtue for Puritanism's call to civil and ecclesiastical obedience.

POLITICAL AND RELIGIOUS REVOLUTIONARY: THOMAS JEFFERSON

Thomas Jefferson (1743-1826) was admired for his intellectual brilliance and political leadership even in his own day. He authored the Declaration of Independence. He served with John Adams and Benjamin Franklin as America's ambassadors to European governments, from whom America desperately needed financial support during the Revolutionary War. He then became the nation's second vice president before being elected to two terms as the nation's third president. In retirement Jefferson spearheaded the development of the University of Virginia, serving as its principal architect. Throughout all of this he was an inventor, scholar, farmer, and man of letters. For all these reasons Jefferson is widely regarded by contemporary Americans as one of the most revered presidents of all time, probably ranking behind only George Washington and Abraham Lincoln.

What most Americans probably don't remember about Jefferson was that he was also a philosopher, with especially distinct opinions about religion. This was something not lost on his contemporaries. For while he was widely admired as a political revolutionary, he was simultaneously reviled for his daring religious views. Newspapers, political pamphlets, and Sunday sermons alike smeared his reputation by labeling him a "French infidel and atheist." Clergy warned that, if elected president, Jefferson would overthrow all churches and have every Bible in the country destroyed. Others, however, lauded his courageous defense of "rational religion." Jefferson's Enlightenment-inspired views illuminated a path toward achieving spiritual peace in a nation full of contending—and contentious—religious sects.

Jefferson was something of an aristocrat by birth. His mother, Jane Randolph, came from one of the most famous families in Virginia. His father, Peter Jefferson, was a successful planter and surveyor. The Jeffersons saw to it that Thomas received the finest possible education. In his youth he was trained in the classics, giving him a thorough background in rationalist and humanist moral philosophy. He later graduated from the College of William and Mary before taking up the study of law. Through all of this Thomas Jefferson picked up the excitement being generated in both Europe and in the colonies by proponents of Enlightenment thought. He absorbed the intellectual "spirit of the age," especially its aversion to intolerance and its unbridled confidence in the perfectibility of human nature.

The writings of Isaac Newton and John Locke had a powerful effect upon Jefferson, leading him to value free intellectual inquiry as humanity's surest guide to a better future. He concluded that "reason and free inquiry . . . [are] the only effectual agents against error."[18] This commitment to rational inquiry provided him with an intellectual compass with which he could take his bearings on any new topic that presented itself. This included religion. Jefferson couldn't see why either religion or ethics should be exempt from rational analysis. He was convinced that there was no end to the progress that could be made in religion and ethics once they were investigated with the same scientific methods then being used in other fields of human endeavor. His bold approach to religious thought was bound to bring him into conflict with the era's clergy. Threatened, they resorted to calling him an atheist and infidel. To this Jefferson had a cool-headed response:

My opinion is that there would never have been an infidel, if there had never been a priest. The artificial structures they have built on the purest of all moral systems, for the purpose of deriving from it pence and power, revolts those who think for themselves, and who read in that system only what is really there. These therefore they brand with such nicknames as their enmity chooses gratuitously to impute.[19]

Jefferson could withstand the misguided accusations against him because he had his own kind of faith and his own kind of courage. He had faith that reason was the greatest gift that God had imparted into creation. Loyalty to reason, then, was humanity's most important religious obligation: "for the use of reason everyone is responsible to God who planted it in his breast, as a light for his guidance."[20] Throughout his life Jefferson had the courage to follow the God-given gift of reason wherever it might lead, trusting that humans have nothing to fear from truth. For the rest of his life he would believe that "Almighty God had created the mind free" and he must therefore vow "never to bow to the shrine of intolerance."[21]

It is true that Thomas Jefferson spent a great deal of time in France and that many of his French acquaintances fashioned themselves atheists. But he never even came close to embracing an atheistic outlook. He was philosophically a deist, believing that the great canvas of nature is sufficient evidence for the existence of "a first cause, possessing intelligence and power; power in the production, and intelligence in the design and constant preservation of the system."[22] Writing to John Adams, he expressed amazement that anyone could deny the existence of "an ulterior cause, a Creator of the world, a Being whom we see not and know not." Jefferson revealed the depth of his religious sentiments when he explained to Adams that

I hold, on the contrary, that when we take a view of the universe; . . . the movements of the heavenly bodies, so exactly held in their courses by the balance of centrifugal and centripetal forces; the structure of our earth itself . . . perfectly organized; it is impossible, I say, for the human mind not to believe, that there is in all this, design, cause and effect, up to an ultimate cause, a Fabricator of all things from matter and motion.[23]

Jefferson's scientific studies, far from leading him away from belief in an "ultimate cause," made him even more inclined toward a religious outlook on life. Newton, Locke, and others inspired in him an enthusiasm for the design

Architect of Religious Freedom and the Separation of Church and State
Credit: The Library of Congress.

and order in nature. The more he learned about the lawful order of nature, the stronger grew his belief in God, the Creator of it all. His scientific bent caused him to adopt a deistic outlook. Deism enabled Jefferson both as philosopher and as politician to steer a "middle course" between the extremes of rationalistic atheism and dogmatic religion.

Jefferson and other deists believed in God as necessary to explain the First Cause of the universe. Jefferson argued that the intelligent design evident in creation is itself compelling reason to believe in God. True, he rejected most traditional conceptions of God. He could not, for example, believe in God as a Father sitting on a Heavenly Throne. His belief in the lawful operations of the universe made it impossible for him to believe in a God who occasionally suspends the laws of nature to perform a miracle.

Instead, Jefferson preferred to think of God in such deistic categories as "Creator," "Giver of Life," "Infinite Power," "Fabricator," or "Intelligent and Powerful Agent." Jefferson often went further and affirmed belief in God's continuing presence in our world. His belief in human perfectibility, for instance, was ultimately grounded in his belief that God had implanted in human nature an impulse toward progress and self-development. He even argued that God is engaged in the "constant preservation" of the operations of the universe. Jefferson thus had faith that living beings have God as "their Preserver and Regulator and their regenerator into new and other forms. We see, too, evident proofs of the necessity of a superintending power to maintain the universe in its course and order."[24] Jefferson never pushed this confidence in God's providential powers to advocating specifically religious actions (i.e., intercessory prayer, ritual, worship, hoping for miracles). He was too much of an Enlightenment rationalist for that. Yet in his public addresses he often used religious language that he knew would comfort and reassure his listeners. He could thus invoke faith in "that overruling Providence which governs the destinies of men and nations" and pray that God "will enlighten the minds" of America's leaders and "guide their councils."[25] Jefferson, the public leader, felt comfortable using a religious discourse that invoked symbols belonging to the nation's churched population, yet doing so in a way that avoided sectarian differences.

Jefferson devoted a great deal of his life to the study of the Bible. Few of his contemporaries could claim that they had studied it more systematically. Indeed, Jefferson was a pioneer of what in the late nineteenth and early twentieth centuries would evolve into the scholarly exegesis of the Bible. He devised an intricate theoretical framework that allowed him to see the Bible as a humanly constructed text (as opposed to a text delivered once and for all through divine revelation). He reasoned that nothing truly grounded in divine reality could be irrational, for this would be contrary to the very order and design God imparted to the universe. He then proceeded to identify those passages that were blatant nonsense from the standpoint of a scientifically educated, Enlightenment thinker. It was thus possible for him to find "so much ignorance, absurdity, untruth, charlatanism and imposture" existing alongside lofty ethical principles.[26] He described his method of textual criticism in a letter to his nephew:

Fix reason firmly in her seat. . . . Read the bible then, as you would read Livy or Tacitus. The facts which are within the ordinary course of nature you will believe on the authority of the writer, as you do those of the same kind in Livy or Tacitus. . . . But those facts in the bible which contradict the laws of nature, must be examined with more care. . . . Here you must recur to the pretension of the writer to inspiration from god. . . . Examine upon what evidence his pretensions are founded, and whether that evidence is so strong as that its falsehood would be more improbable than a change of the laws of nature in the case he relates. . . . Your own reason is the only oracle given you by heaven.[27]

Jefferson's exegetical method was designed to discriminate between the sound principles contained in scripture and the "vulgar ignorance and superstition" that ancient writers imposed upon the text. The application of this method became most controversial when it came to New Testament attestations of the divinity of Jesus. Many deists dismissed Jesus altogether, viewing him as deluded or mad in his claim to be the divine son of God. Jefferson, however, remained a serious student of Jesus all of his adult life. He was convinced that Jesus had been a sublime moral teacher. He saw in Jesus' teaching the three main principles of a rational religion: (1) That there is one God, and that He is all perfect; (2) That there is a future state of rewards and punishments; and (3) That to love God with all they heart and thy neighbor as thyself, is the sum of all religion. The problem, in Jefferson's view, was that Jesus' original ethical teachings were later transmitted by "unlettered and ignorant men." He singled out Paul in particular as a "corruptor of the doctrine of Jesus." Jefferson's point was that although Christianity originated in the lofty ethical and religious principles taught by Jesus, over time it degenerated into irrational and superstitious beliefs. Jefferson's rationalism caused him to reject such traditional Christian beliefs as the virgin birth, miracle stories, the resurrection, and atoning sacrifice. As he wrote to John Adams about the virgin birth, "The day will come when the mystical generation of Jesus, by the Supreme Being as his father, in the womb of a virgin, will be classed with the fable of the generation of Minerva in the brain of Jupiter."[28]

If being a Christian means believing in the divinity of Jesus and the doctrine of the triune nature of God, then Jefferson was surely no Christian.

He referred to the Christian belief in the Trinity sarcastically as "an unintelligible proposition of Platonic mysticism that three are one, and one is three; and yet one is not three, and the three are not one." In a letter declining to be the godfather of a friend's child, Jefferson confessed that "I had never sense enough to comprehend the Trinity and it has always appeared to me that comprehension must precede assent."[29] But Jefferson was not willing to concede that this is the only definition of being Christian.

> To the corruptions of Christianity, I am indeed opposed; but not to the genuine precepts of Jesus himself. I am a Christian, in the only sense in which he wished any one to be; sincerely attached to his doctrines, in preference to all others'; ascribing to himself every human excellence, and believing he never claimed any other. . . . I am a *real Christian*, that is to say, a disciple of the doctrines of Jesus, very different from the Platonists, who call *me* infidel, and *themselves* Christians and preachers of the gospel, while they . . . [espouse] heathen mysteries beyond the comprehension of man, of which Jesus, were he to return on earth, would not recognize one feature.[30]

Of interest is the fact that Jefferson spent many of his evenings in the White House sitting before the fire studying the teachings of Jesus. Using a pair of scissors he carefully cut out all of Jesus' basic moral lessons, leaving behind all references to his supposed divinity, miracles, etc. He labeled the first version of his own, edited New Testament a "Syllabus of an Estimate of the Merit of the Doctrines of Jesus, Compared with Those of Others." A second version was more simply titled "The Life and Morals of Jesus of Nazareth." This second version, commonly known as the "Jefferson Bible," still resides in the Smithsonian Museum in Washington, D.C. His concern was to strip away "the mysticisms, fancies and falsehoods by which the religion-builders have distorted and deformed the doctrines of Jesus and get back to the pure and simple doctrines he inculcated."[31] He believed himself to be rescuing the essential foundations of Christianity, "the most sublime and benevolent code of morals which has ever been offered to man." Jefferson cut these moral teachings verse by verse out of the New Testament so that they might be "as easily distinguishable as diamonds in a dunghill."[32]

For Jefferson, as for deists generally, the final test of religion was not whether it leads to doctrinal conformity but whether it leads to virtuous living.

He wrote, "I have ever judged of the religion of others by their lives. . . . For it is in our lives not from our words, that our religion must be read."[33] In another context he explained that "I must ever believe that religion substantially good which produces honest life."[34] For Jefferson, a religion capable of producing "honest life" must be built upon the firm foundation of reason and free inquiry. As he put it, "comprehension must precede assent" in matters of religion as in any other area of life.

Thomas Jefferson repeatedly found himself in positions where he was entrusted with the responsibility of speaking for the entire nation: As one of Virginia's delegates to the Continental Congress; as principal author of the Declaration of Independence; as ambassador to France; and as president of the United States of America. Yet he believed that his most important task as a national leader was leading the debate over the role that religion would play in the new American system. When the Revolution ended, attention turned to the writing of a constitution. Most governments with which the framers of the Constitution were familiar had an established religion. Jefferson, the political revolutionary, now found himself called upon to be a religious revolutionary as well. He felt it necessary to speak out against religious establishment. Jefferson's *Notes on Virginia*, written at the height of his home state's constitutional debate, argued that establishing any religion was tantamount to "religious slavery." Americans, who had risked their lives for establishing civil freedom, should not now opt for a system that denies them complete religious freedom. Americans must never submit their conscience to any worldly institution:

> We are answerable for them to our God. The legitimate powers of government extend to such acts only as are injurious to others. But it does me no injury for my neighbour to say there are twenty gods, or no God. It neither picks my pocket nor breaks my leg. . . . Reason and free inquiry are the only effectual agents against error. Give a loose to them, they will support the true religion by brining every false one to their tribunal, to the test of their investigation.[35]

Jefferson's most eloquent statement on religious liberty appears in his "Act for Establishing Religious Freedom" submitted to the Virginia state legislature. The "Almighty God hath created the mind free," Jefferson argued. It was thus imperative that the State of Virginia ensure "that no man shall be compelled to frequent or support any religious worship, place or ministry whatsoever, nor shall be enforced, restrained, molested, or burthened in his body or goods, nor shall otherwise suffer on account of his religious opinions or belief; but that all men shall be free to profess, and by argument to maintain, their opinions in matters of religion."[36] Many of Jefferson's friends among the Virginian gentry did not share his aversion to government regulation of religion. They were especially concerned that, without government support, the churches might prove unable to overcome religious indifference or sufficiently inculcate public morality. It was not that Jefferson was insensitive to the importance of public morality. But the battle for religious freedom was still in doubt at the time. Jefferson consequently threw his influence behind the complete separation of church and state in order to ensure freedom of individual conscience. He actually believed that disestablishment would make the churches strong by forcing pastors to make their case convincingly in the free market of opinion. Even if the reverse should prove to be the case, he still believed that disestablishment was necessary because the danger of religious oppression and tyranny outweighed the danger of public conformity to a fixed moral system.[37] Jefferson's arguments eventually won the day. After a few years of debate, and with the considerable help of James Madison, the Virginia legislature eventually passed Jefferson's Act for Establishing Religious Freedom.

What Jefferson accomplished at the state level was not immediately achieved at the federal level. The Constitution of the United States was passed without a Bill of Rights safeguarding freedom of religion. This disturbed Jefferson and he worked diligently to see that the very first amendment to the Constitution clearly defended the cause of religious freedom. When he later became president he repeatedly reminded the nation's leaders that government has no proper jurisdiction over religious beliefs. He even went so far as to refuse to declare Thanksgiving a national holiday because he believed that it was too closely associated with a particular religious outlook. His persistent defense of religious freedom drew attacks from both clergy and citizens who felt their particular denomination's cause betrayed. Accusations of being an infidel and atheist plagued him for the rest of his life. Yet Thomas Jefferson, the third president of the United States, considered his tireless efforts on behalf of religious freedom to be one of the crowning achievements of his life. He died on July 4, 1826, while the country was celebrating the fiftieth anniversary of the signing of the Declaration of Independence. He left directions that his gravestone should bear "the following inscription, and not a word more:

Here was Buried
Thomas Jefferson
Author of the Declaration
Of American Independence,
Of the Statue of Virginia
For Religious Freedom,
And Father of the University of Virginia

by these testimonials that I have lived I wish most to be remembered." Thomas Jefferson didn't want to be remembered as an administrator. He saw himself as a visionary, a revolutionary. As a political revolutionary he fought against tyranny of government to secure individual liberty. As a religious revolutionary he fought against intolerance and sectarianism to secure freedom of religious belief. And this, he hoped, was one of the three most important contributions he made to American life. Thomas Jefferson is, to this day, the most self-consciously theological president in American history. And, even more important, together with James Madison he dedicated himself more steadfastly to the cause of religious liberty than any other president in history. Jefferson's whole life was dedicated to the cause of helping all of us see that reason and free inquiry are indispensable to the attainment of spiritual integrity—for individuals and for American society as a whole. His personal spiritual philosophy enabled Americans to construct a political system that makes it possible for us to assume the risks of granting religious freedom in a diverse and democratic society.

DRAWING A LINE OF SEPARATION

Those who drafted the Constitution of the United States were reluctant to give the federal government the power to interfere in matters that seemed to belong more properly to the individual states. One of these matters was religion. Thus the only reference to religion in the Constitution itself was

Article VI, stipulating that "no religious test shall ever be required as a qualification to any office or public trust under the United States." This provision, however, applied only to federal offices. Several states banned Catholics or Jews from holding other public offices for years to come. The belief that orderly government could be ensured only through the coercive power of religion thus still had pockets of support.

As the constitutional process advanced, it became increasingly clear that Americans would at last guarantee complete freedom of religion. Several states had already moved toward a policy of religious liberty. Rhode Island, Pennsylvania, New Jersey, and Delaware had adopted policies of religious freedom even before the war. New York, Maryland, Georgia, and the two Carolinas dropped their establishment of the Episcopal Church shortly after the war started. This left only Massachusetts, Connecticut, New Hampshire, and Virginia where the debate still raged. It was in Virginia where the arguments were the fiercest. And, as we have seen, Thomas Jefferson clearly and decisively carried the day with his "Act for Establishing Religious Freedom in Virginia." Jefferson's argument resounded throughout the states. He had articulated what were henceforth to be considered inalienable American rights: individuals are to be left free to make up their own mind about religion; they are to have liberty to express their opinions freely; they may seek to persuade others to their view; and they may not be forced to contribute to the support of any ecclesiastical institution.[38]

Those influenced by Enlightenment rationality were in favor of a constitution that clearly spelled out the terms of religious freedom (particularly citizens' freedom from religion). Pressure for religious freedom was mounting within the churches, too (particularly for churches' freedom from government interference). Most denominations probably wanted government establishment, hoping to extend their religious and moral vision to the whole populace. But they obviously feared the possibility that this establishment might be granted to a competing denomination. They realized that the only way to ensure their own freedom was to grant such freedom to all others. So the churches, too, were largely in support of complete religious liberty. The upshot was that the Constitution wasn't going to be ratified until it contained amendments that specifically defined the rights and freedoms that the Revolution had been fought to secure. Jefferson's "Act for Establishing Religious Liberty in Virginia" provided a ready-made argument that led to the formulation of the very first amendment to the Constitution of the United States: "Congress shall make no law respecting an establishment of religion, or prohibiting the free exercise thereof."

The First Amendment thus grants every citizen the right to believe and profess whatever religious doctrine he or she chooses. It ensures that the government may not compel affirmation of religious belief, punish the expression of religious doctrines it may believe to be false, impose special disabilities on the basis of religious views, or lend its power to one side or the other in a religious controversy. It also grants the freedom to perform— or abstain from performing—such religious actions as congregating for the purpose of worship, wearing distinctive clothing, proselytizing, and abstaining from certain foods. In Jefferson's words, the Constitution had erected "a wall of separation between church and state."[39] Jefferson's friend and colleague, James Madison, referred instead to "the line of separation between the rights of religion and civil authority." Madison's metaphor of a line is probably more apt than Jefferson's wall. Nothing solid was ever erected once and for all. The line has had to be redrawn virtually every time the courts have had to ponder the specific dilemmas that arise when freedom of religion is granted in a diverse and democratic society: Can government funds be used to pay for lunches at parochial schools? May a Jehovah's Witness refuse to allow his or her child to have a blood transfusion because this might be in violation of God's commandment in Leviticus 17:10? Can prayers be offered at high school graduation ceremonies? Can Native Americans have special permission to use peyote for certain traditional rituals? Such issues make it difficult to decide just where the line of separation must be drawn if we are to both protect public welfare and grant religious liberty. Surely the government cannot permit people to break any law of their own choosing just because they say it interferes with their religious beliefs. Yet religious freedom has from the outset been an essential element of American liberty. Both sides of America's early culture wars fought long and valiantly to ensure that complete religious liberty can be curtailed only under the most compelling of circumstances.

Whatever else we make of the line of separation that Jefferson and others drew between church and state, this line has had two major consequences. First, it has ensured that diversity would prevail in American religious life. The First Amendment's prohibition against the establishment of any religious organization leveled the playing field and made religious pluralism a permanent fact of American life. Second, the First Amendment's line of separation also ensured that the American spiritual marketplace would be a volatile one. A consumer-driven marketplace inevitably fluctuates with changing whims, fads, and fashions. The subsequent history of religion in the United States was destined to be characterized by dynamic, market-driven change.

Dynamic change was already beginning. Deism was dying out as a distinct movement by the first decade of the 1800s. Its basic ideas would live on, of course, but repackaged in any number of new, nineteenth-century "isms." The population was moving westward, into the furthest regions of New York, Kentucky, Tennessee, and the Ohio River valley. A brand new "awakening" of revivalist activity was soon to erupt in these frontiers. There were soon to be winners and losers in the competition for church clientele. The era of Jefferson was giving way to a new century whose revolutionaries would include Joseph Smith, Ralph Waldo Emerson, Phineas P. Quimby, and Andrew Jackson Davis.

❧

THREE

Sectarian Heyday

Joseph Smith and the Golden Era
of Religious Innovation

GROWTH AND EXPANSION CHARACTERIZED THE UNITED STATES at the dawn of the nineteenth century. Kentucky joined the union in 1792 with a population of 73,000. By 1810 Kentucky had grown almost sixfold to a population of over 400,000. Tennessee achieved statehood in 1796 with 77,000 inhabitants. By 1810 it contained more than 260,000. The westward flow of population continued as Ohio became a state in 1803, Louisiana in 1812, Indiana in 1816, Alabama in 1817, Illinois in 1818, and Missouri in 1821. The nation's growth went well beyond westward expansion. It also included unprecedented rates of urban growth. When Kentucky became a state the entire country had only six cities with a population of at least eight thousand (Philadelphia, New York, Boston, Charleston, Baltimore, and Salem). Yet within a few years Cincinnati and New Orleans grew to become important commercial centers. Pittsburgh, Rochester, Buffalo, Detroit, Cleveland, Chicago, Louisville, and St. Louis soon followed.

America's geographical, economic, and political boundaries were being redrawn. The boundaries of the nation's religious institutions would likewise undergo radical change.

THE SECOND GREAT AWAKENING

Scholars caution us about using tidy labels to explain the past. Some historians, for example, argue that the concept of a religious awakening is an oversimplification. Evidence suggests that there has been a steady stream of revival meetings in American history. It therefore makes little sense to designate certain eras as undergoing a distinct "awakening." But history is both a science and an art. It requires narrative structures that alert us to subtle changes in a people's life and thought. The concept of a Second Great Awakening is just such a narrative device. Even had the period between 1800 and 1830 not experienced unprecedented outbursts of revival activity, it nonetheless witnessed changes that forever restructured the nation's religious marketplace. Congregationalists, Episcopalians, and Presbyterians were the big losers, surrendering the market dominance they had enjoyed throughout the colonial era. Baptists and Methodists, meanwhile, were the big winners. By mid-century they were clearly established as the nation's two largest denominations. Several other upstart groups were also successful at garnering significant market shares in the new religious climate. Two of the religious organizations indigenous to American religious history—the Seventh-Day Adventists and the Church of Jesus Christ of Latter-day Saints—emerged during this heyday of sectarian innovation. The concept of a Second Great Awakening is thus an eminently useful one. It draws attention to the dynamic change and creativity that in the span of a single generation produced a host of permanent changes in American religious life.

The Second Great Awakening is ordinarily associated with the revivals occurring in the nation's western frontiers. Yet it also intensified religious life along the eastern seaboard. In 1802 Yale president Timothy Dwight was distraught over the student body's "freethinking" religious views. He felt compelled to respond to their Enlightenment-inspired beliefs in a series of chapel sermons. Dwight warned that Americans would follow the path of

French infidels toward cultural anarchy unless they returned to God-fearing piety. Much to his surprise, Yale students responded to his pleas. A full third of the study body claimed to have undergone a religious conversion in response to his impassioned arguments. Most proceeded to join the student "Moral Society." Dwight concluded that revival meetings such as he had conducted were an effective means of turning infidelity into a passionate embrace of biblical faith. He was thus one of the first prominent New England clergy to break with American Protestantism's earlier understanding of conversions. During the First Great Awakening, Puritan clergy such as Jonathan Edwards believed that conversions were stunning acts of God. It was thought that humans are separated from God by a chasm that cannot be bridged from the human side. Conversions are produced by God, not humans. All that individuals can do, therefore, is repent as sincerely as possible and then wait in hope that God would send them assurance of their election. In the older theological pattern, conversions were thought to signal—not create—the salvation that emanates from God alone. But Dwight was beginning to alter this understanding and to emphasize humanity's own role in procuring salvation. The urge to conduct revivals, win souls, and rekindle commitment to moral conduct lured Protestant clergy into affirming humanity's own power to reconcile themselves with God.

Other Yale theologians emerged as champions of a new strategy for winning souls. Nathaniel Taylor, for example, conducted a series of revivals based on his premise that "sin is in the sinning." Taylor argued that it is our own acts that make us sinners. The implication was that we have the power to quit sinning and make ourselves again worthy of God's grace. The further implication was that revival meetings could hasten this process and thereby serve as instruments for procuring conversions. Following Dwight's and Taylor's lead, preachers began orchestrating revival meetings to bring pressure to bear upon potential converts. Their words were carefully chosen to induce those in the audience to make the decision to become born again.

The Second Great Awakening flourished in the "camp meetings" held in Kentucky, Tennessee, and western New York. In 1800 James McGready presided over three Presbyterian parishes in southwestern Kentucky. He and four other ministers conducted a four-day camp meeting at Gasper River. By the meeting's end the search for individual salvation broke out into mass contagion. One of McGready's associates lost all inhibition and began "shouting and exhorting with all possible energy." Soon the floor was "covered by the slain." Their screams for mercy pierced the heavens. McGready later recorded that even the most persistent sinners among the crowd were "pricked to the heart" and cried out for salvation.[1] Revival meetings, it seemed, could be used to push people's emotional buttons to the point where they willingly surrendered. While critics might argue that they were surrendering to group contagion or the persuasive power of the preacher himself, the era's revivalists were certain that they had come upon the means of fostering surrender to the Holy Spirit.

Barton Warren Stone, one of McGready's converts, was so impressed by what he witnessed at Gasper River that he announced a great revival meeting to be held at Cane Ridge in the summer of 1801. Several Methodist and Baptist ministers joined Stone to preach to the crowd, estimated at somewhere between ten and twenty-five thousand. Services were conducted around the clock for an entire week. The impassioned preachers called upon those gathered to repent of their sins and to respond to the redemptive grace of God. Emotions soared. So did bodily agitations. Many fell to the ground, convulsed with physical spasms, "barked," danced wildly, or fell into trance-like states. These unusual phenomena were understood to be tangible evidence of the life-altering power of the Holy Spirit.

When it was over, Cane Ridge was widely acclaimed as the greatest outpouring of the Holy Spirit since Pentecost.[2] Neither supporters nor critics were entirely sure what role emotional enthusiasm had played in this massive soul-winning phenomenon. Barton Stone himself reported that, "Many things transpired there, which were so much like miracles, that if they were not, they had the same effects as miracles on infidels and unbelievers; for many of them by these were convinced that Jesus was the Christ, and bowed in submission to him."[3] Many factors combined to help the events at Cane Ridge seem "so much like miracles." Most of those who gathered for the week-long revival were used to living in relative isolation. Some of the exhilaration they felt came from the sociality itself. By day they circulated through crowds of frontier families. They made friends, shared news, and offered camaraderie in an exciting makeshift community. By night they gathered around campfires for music, storytelling, and even romantic liaisons. Much of the behavior at these frontier camp meetings was downright raucous, leading critics to charge that "more souls were begot than saved." Whatever the mixture of factors,

Cane Ridge became a symbol of the success of frontier camp meetings in winning new converts—especially for Baptist and Methodist denominations.

The individual who most clearly symbolized the theological spirit of the Second Great Awakening was Charles Grandison Finney. Finney was born in Connecticut, but his family moved to western New York State when he was a young child. He became a lawyer by the age of twenty-two and showed no initial inclination for the ministry. One day it occurred to him, however, that salvation was a very simple matter. All that salvation requires is for one to make a personal decision to accept Christ. Finney thus understood salvation as a legal or contractual agreement between two parties. If one sincerely accepts Christ's offer of salvation, he or she in turn will be accepted by God. That very night Finney affirmed his own decision to accept Christ and instantaneously received a mighty baptism of the Holy Spirit. "The Holy Spirit descended upon me in a manner that seemed to go through me body and soul."[4] Finney refused suggestions to study theology at Princeton and instead pursued a largely self-taught program of study before his ordination in 1824. His revival preaching met with almost immediate success. Finney was a commanding presence. Six feet two and with piercing eyes, he spoke in a firm and confident tone. His cool, straightforward manner was especially effective with the business and professional classes. Historian Whitney Cross has commented that "the exceptional feature was the phenomenal dignity of his awakening. No agonizing souls fell in the aisles, no raptured ones shouted hallelujahs. Rather, despite his doses of hell-fire, the great evangelist, 'in an unclerical suit of gray,' acted 'like a lawyer arguing . . . before a court and jury,' talking precisely, logically, but with wit, verve, and informality. Lawyers, real-estate magnates, millers, manufacturers, and commercial tycoons led the parade of the regenerated."[5]

What distinguished Finney was his forthrightness in presenting a new understanding of the conversion experience. In his *Lectures on Revivals*, Finney proposed that a conversion "is not a miracle or dependent on a miracle in any sense . . . it consists entirely in the right exercise of the powers of nature."[6] By implication, religious experience can be humanly engineered. He believed that he had hit upon a series of "new measures" that turned the conversion process into a lawful science. "New measures," he wrote, "are necessary from time to time to awaken attention and to bring the gospel to bear upon the public mind."[7] The new measures Finney described were not entirely original. Most, in fact, had already proved effective in procuring salvations at frontier camp meetings. What Finney really did was to systematize the revivalists' craft and adapt it to use in urban settings. First, he extended the time span of religious services—conducting them over several hours and often over a period of several days.[8] He used direct and forceful language, drawn more from his experience in the courtroom than from attending traditional worship services. Finney was direct and forthright. In his prayers he often singled out persons by name to direct public attention to their unrepentant ways. He even utilized the "anxious bench," where sinners were ushered down to sit in full view of the entire congregation and the forceful gaze of the revivalist preacher. These measures were all intended to "break down" even the most hardened members of the audience. The combination of Bible preaching and peer pressure was designed to bring sinners to a state of emotional distress and utter despair over their spiritual futures. Shame and embarrassment were important weapons in Finney's revivalist arsenal. The new measures were aimed at wearing down self-conceit. After hours or even days in this emotional furnace, persons would predictably break, crying out as they publicly proclaimed their decision to accept Christ. Many wept, convulsed, or fell into trances. All such reactions provided empirical confirmation of revivalism's power to move individuals to the point of a conscious, willed conversion.

THE REORDERING OF DENOMINATIONAL LIFE

The Second Great Awakening had profound consequences for the reordering of religion in the United States. First and foremost it permanently altered the balance of power among Protestant denominations. When the Awakening began, the Congregationalists, Episcopalians, and Presbyterians dominated the national religious scene. By the time the Awakening receded, Baptists and Methodists had established themselves as the two largest Protestant denominations in the United States. The reasons were clear.[9] Congregationalists, Presbyterians, and Episcopalians relied upon ministers who were well educated and who had been trained in denominational seminaries. Most were of middle- or upper-middle-class standing. Upon ordination they could expect to preach at a parish in a settled community and to receive a respectable salary.

PROPORTIONAL DENOMINATIONAL STRENGTH AMONG JUDEO-CHRISTIANS IN THE UNITED STATES: 1830

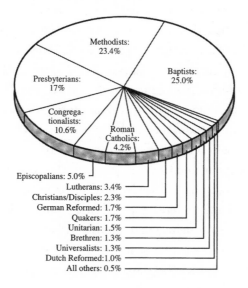

Methodists: 23.4%

Baptists: 25.0%

Presbyterians: 17%

Congregationalists: 10.6%

Roman Catholics: 4.2%

Episcopalians: 5.0%
Lutherans: 3.4%
Christians/Disciples: 2.3%
German Reformed: 1.7%
Quakers: 1.7%
Unitarian: 1.5%
Brethren: 1.3%
Universalists: 1.3%
Dutch Reformed: 1.0%
All others: 0.5%

Very few were inclined to forsake these professional comforts to relocate into the western frontiers, where living conditions were harsher and where their salaries would be a fraction of what they were accustomed to.

Baptists and Methodists, on the other hand, relied upon clergy who were "of the people." They characteristically had little education, received little or no pay, and spoke in plain but forceful language. Methodist clergy on the frontier were often assigned multiple parishes. They were expected to be "circuit riders," traveling from parish to parish so that they might serve the ministerial needs of sparsely populated frontier regions. Baptists, meanwhile, more typically relied upon the "farmer preacher." What set Baptist preachers apart from their congregations was not formal seminary training, but an innate talent for preaching from the heart. Anyone who felt "the call" might be chosen to occupy the local pulpit. Baptists and Methodists were thus likely to have a neighbor, friend, or relative as their local minister. Scholars have noted that even though "this may have meant that the clergy held the same prejudices as did their flocks—and thus hampered the prophetic role of religion—it fostered a close relationship between the minister and the people in the pews. The minister shared the wants, needs, and desires of the people, and he made every effort possible to share the same religion, too."[10]

Baptists and Methodists ran a far more efficient form of ministry than did the more established denominations. Baptists often paid their ministers nothing at all. Baptist ministers typically earned their living just like other members of the congregation six days a week and then voluntarily preached on the Sabbath. Methodist circuit riders didn't fare much better when it came to pay. Only by assuming duties at several churches or supplementing their income in other ways could they make ends meet. In this way both Baptists and Methodists could keep their overhead low and thereby afford to expand into the sparsely populated frontiers. None of this would have mattered, of course, if their message hadn't also been keenly attuned to the emotional and spiritual needs of the American populace. Ministers for the established denominations typically delivered sermons that were literate and intellectual. They often tried to connect biblical theology with contemporary events or new cultural trends. The Methodists and Baptists stuck to matters of salvation. Theirs was a revivalist-hewn theology that focused squarely on sin, hell, and the path to salvation. It is true that Baptists had historical roots in Calvinism, but both the style and substance of their message shifted to conform to the Second Great Awakening's emphasis upon personal decision and individual responsibility to God. Methodism had from the outset embraced a more Arminian faith in humanity's role in achieving salvation. Hence both of these upstart denominations appealed to people's desire for renewal. They promised that we can make a fresh new start. By letting go of our former, sinful ways, we can avail ourselves of Christ's redeeming spirit. And thus both the Baptists and the Methodists were promulgating a message that was perfectly in keeping with the needs of the nation's rapidly growing population.

Nineteenth-century Methodists and Baptists helped establish evangelical religion as the dominant form of American Protestantism. Evangelical faith focuses squarely on the belief that we are naturally in a condition of sin. It follows that the only means of procuring salvation is through a personal decision to accept Christ as one's personal Lord and Savior. Evangelical faith is thus distinct from other forms of Christianity that emphasize church membership, participation in the sacraments, or theological investigation as central to Christian faith. Evangelical Protestantism insists that the sole means of escaping damnation and procuring eternal life is to have a personal conversion experience (whether highly emotional or a simple moment of mental lucidity) in which we consciously accept the salvation made possible through Jesus Christ. Evangelical religion therefore emphasizes plain Bible reading and Bible preaching. Its worship services are fairly simple, avoiding the more ornate uses of music or ritual found in other forms of Christianity.

Evangelical Protestantism directs its message to individuals. Its goal is to save the world by saving individual persons one at a time. This is not, however, to suggest that evangelical Protestantism is solely individualistic. One of the other major results of the Second Great Awakening was a permanent coupling of evangelical faith with a resolve to work toward the moral renovation of society. Revivalist ministers counted selfishness as one of humanity's most egregious tendencies. Conversion, therefore, was understood as entailing a revitalized concern for the welfare of others. A genuine conversion is thought to result in a shifting of our energies to concern for the well-being of society. Conversion is therefore not the end of the Christian life but rather its beginning.

Revivals increased church membership. They generated a wave of enthusiasm that naturally aroused hopes that the world might soon be populated almost wholly by regenerated saints. Toward this end the churches began organizing a variety of missionary societies aimed at promulgating the gospel. At first the societies focused on explicitly evangelical goals: distributing Bibles, forming Sunday Schools, and sponsoring foreign missions. With time the goals became more ambitious, such as education societies formed to establish grammar schools, colleges, and seminaries. A good many of the liberal arts colleges functioning in the United States today were initially founded by Protestant denominations about the time of the Second Great Awakening.[11] Even more ambitious, however, was the formation of societies promoting a wide variety of humanitarian causes. Temperance societies promoted restraint from the consumption of alcohol. Abolition societies endeavored to harness the forces of evangelical religion to the effort to rid the nation of slavery (an effort that eventually led to bitter disputes between northern and southern Baptists and eventually led to the formation of the Southern Baptist Convention in 1845). Others helped establish hospitals, provide relief for the poor, and promote international peace. While some of these societies were backed by particular denominations, others were interdenominational. All were voluntary in nature. That is, they were comprised of persons whose regenerated hearts committed them to concerted action on behalf of the moral reform of society. "Voluntaryism," as it came to be known, became one of the Second Great Awakening's most important legacies to American religious life.

SECTARIAN PROLIFERATION

Finney's "new measures" were but one expression of the period's experimental approach to religion. Evangelical enthusiasm gave rise to innovation and adaptation. And in some cases it gave rise to the formation of wholly new religious movements. Up to the Second Great Awakening the main Protestant organizations in the United States had all originated in Europe and had been carried to the New World by immigrants. It is customary to refer to these Protestant organizations as denominations. Unlike the forms of the Christian church in Europe, American denominations are not principally territorial. And, due to Jefferson's wall of separation, none has official connection with a civil power. Instead, American denominations are voluntary associations of individuals united to further common beliefs. They are called, or denominated, by a given name (the name in some way descriptive of their historical origins or the defined doctrines and objectives they collectively seek to advance). Importantly, denominations implicitly recognize that they are but one of several branches of the larger church of Christ. They may have pride and confidence in their particular expression of Christian faith, but they do not regard themselves as alone the true or exclusive church. From a sociological point of view, denominations—even the smaller ones—fit comfortably into the larger culture. They are fully accepted as part of mainstream society and thus blend fairly seamlessly with the broader "American way of life."

What is significant about the Second Great Awakening is that it instigated the first outburst of sectarian development in American religious history. Several wholly original religious groups or sects emerged in a fairly brief span of years. The term "sect" is really sociological rather than theological in nature. It comes from the Latin *sequi* (to follow). The term thus alerts us to the social and historical dynamics prompting people to follow a novel religious path or teaching. Sects emerge out of a more stable or culturally dominant religious heritage—in this case the heritage of American Protestantism. They usually place a great deal of emphasis upon one or two elements of this inherited faith that they believe are being neglected or even forgotten (e.g., healing, the imminent end of the world, speaking in tongues). They also usually emerge under the direction of a charismatic leader. This leader's personality and particular way of drawing attention to a particular cluster of tenets are often what give the emerging sect its distinctive ethos.

The groups that historians label as sects differ from denominations in that they are more likely to regard themselves as alone possessing the true faith or at least the true interpretation of a shared faith. They see themselves as the one true church. The fact that a sect's members consciously secede from the culture's more established religious groups to join this "true church" often indicates preexisting disenchantment with the status quo. As historian Sydney Ahlstrom notes, sects are initially comprised of "people who are spiritually, socially, economically, educationally, or in other ways 'disinherited.' If not disinherited in this sense, the sect's following is at least in search of values, fulfillment, or fellowship that a dominant, socially acceptable church by its nature cannot ordinarily satisfy."[12]

It is easy to see how nineteenth-century revivalism fostered conditions that were ripe for the emergence of new religious sects.[13] First, revivalists demanded immediate confrontation with God. This emphasis upon personal encounters with God often gave rise to ecstatic experiences and mystical visions that were readily interpreted as new revelations. Second, revivalists stressed the possibility of becoming free of sin. They encouraged born-again Christians to commit themselves to a lifestyle aimed at achieving holiness and moral perfection. Finally, revivalists aroused expectation of a golden age to come, especially as inaugurated by the return of Christ as was thought to be prophesied in the biblical books of Daniel and Revelation. It is thus not surprising that American sectarian religious movements are often characterized by an emphasis upon such themes as (1) experientialism—a desire for intense religious experiences that may afford personal revelation of God's plan for humanity; (2) perfectionism—the quest for complete holiness and moral purity; and (3) millennialism—strong belief in the imminent Second Coming of Christ and the establishment of a thousand-year reign of righteousness preceding final judgment.

Baptists, Methodists, and the newly organized Disciples of Christ were three groups that embodied these revivalism-born enthusiasms. Yet all three are more aptly considered denominations, since they never saw themselves as pulling away from the cultural mainstream. More closely conforming to the sectarian pattern, however, were any number of newly emerging religious bodies: the Shakers, the Oneida community, the Rappites, and Millerites. The Shakers, formally known as the United Society of Believers in Christ's Second Coming, first took root on American soil when Ann Lee Stanley immigrated with eight followers in 1774.[14] "Mother Ann" Lee had joined a small group of Shaking Quakers back in England. This band of Quakers got their nickname from their tendency to tremble uncontrollably and to sing or shout when seized by the Holy Spirit. From them Mother Ann Lee acquired a fervent belief in the imminence of Christ's Second Coming and a consequent resolve to prepare herself for final judgment by disassociating herself from all sin and iniquity. Just before embarking to the New World, Ann received a revelation that, since Adam and Eve, engaging in sexual intercourse has been humanity's primal sin. Giving way to lust signals our willful disobedience of God's commands. Thus, in addition to calling upon her followers to live in expectation of the "final days," Mother Ann Lee also summoned them to live a celibate life. Her message won few converts at first but, after a series of revivals in western Massachusetts and Connecticut, she slowly gained adherents who were eager to make their lives pleasing to Christ.

Mother Ann Lee was herself a conduit of God's revelation. She entered into mystical states and offered inspired teachings. Enthusiasm escalated when her followers learned that Mother Ann was herself the Second Coming of Christ, appearing before them as the female element of God and about to usher in the new millennium. After her death in 1784, Joseph Meacham rose to leadership of the group and began organizing the sect into small communal societies. Shaker communities were fairly prosperous, relying both on farming and various commercial activities. By the time it reached the zenith of its popularity between 1830 and 1850, there were nineteen Shaker communities with a combined membership of about six thousand people. Its own success at inducing members to be celibate, however, ultimately led to the gradual dwindling of the group.

The Shakers were not the only religious group that saw communal living as a partial key to a life of ongoing moral perfection. John Humphrey Noyes came from an upper-middle-class family in Vermont.[15] After graduating from Dartmouth he enrolled first at Andover Seminary and then at Yale Divinity

School. He believed, however, that the established denominations were in error in asserting that conversion truly released one from sin. So fervent was he in his conviction that we must wholly separate ourselves from sin that he was refused ordination. He set out on his own as an unlicensed itinerant preacher, seeking those who yearned to pull away from the world's sinful ways and dedicate themselves wholly to God. In 1848 he finally succeeded in gathering a community of about 200 together at Oneida, in western New York. The Oneida Community was fairly progressive in spirit, becoming less interested in final judgment than in creating a mutually supportive community. The community was economically viable, relying first upon farming and logging and later upon light industry that produced silver-plated flatware. One of Noyes' teachings, however, symbolized the degree to which the Oneida Community resided both physically and theologically at the periphery of mainstream American culture. Noyes believed that the possessive nature of romantic relationships prevented us from true Christian love. For this reason he institutionalized a system of "complex marriage" in which each adult was a spouse to every other adult. Procreation was made a matter of overt communal decision. In all other sexual transactions, males were taught to withhold ejaculation. The Oneida Community's practice of "complex marriage" drew persistent scorn from surrounding communities, leading finally to the dismantling of the entire commune. By this time, however, the silver-plating business had become so successful that it was transformed into a joint-stock company with shares distributed to the community's members. Oneida silver is to this day a reminder of the heyday of sectarian formation in the wake of the Second Great Awakening.

Many other communitarian groups emerged in the early nineteenth century.[16] One of the better known was the pietistic community founded in Harmony, Pennsylvania, by George Rapp. Rapp's group stemmed from the German Anabaptist tradition. Their concern for religious purity had prompted them to separate fully from the established church in their German homeland. Like the Shakers, the Rappites expected the imminent return of Christ and were therefore anxious to separate themselves from any connection with worldliness or sin. Their goal was to form an entire community that would be pleasing to Christ upon His return. They established their Pennsylvania colony in 1804 and, in 1815, relocated in New Harmony, Indiana, before finally settling in Economy, Ohio, in 1825. The Rappites were actually but one of several German pietistic communities to appear in the first half of the nineteenth century (e.g., the Amana Society in Iowa and the Bethel community in Missouri). Meanwhile, other communal societies spread sectarian philosophies that veered even further from mainstream Protestantism. Brook Farm and Fruitlands were established by Transcendentalists to create non-Christian spiritual communities. Still other communal societies of the era were more philosophical and moral than religious in nature. Robert Owen, for example, established an early socialist community in the New Harmony settlement abandoned by the Rappites. While none of these societies attracted large numbers, we should not underestimate their overall contribution to the sectarian sentiments of the day. They all received a fair amount of publicity. And all were reminders that not everyone could in good conscience embrace the same set of religious doctrines. The very existence of these sectarian bodies kept alive the notion that we should hedge our bets and keep an eye on newly emerging spiritual insights.

Another fascinating example of sect formation in the early nineteenth century is the case of the Millerites.[17] Religion is never so exciting to Christians as when they believe that their Lord will appear before them at any moment. Expectation of the Second Coming intensifies spiritual desire. Believers hold nothing back, trying to do everything in their power to make their lives pleasing to God in expectation of imminent judgment. Beliefs concerning the "final days" are generally referred to as apocalyptic or millennial.[18] Millennialism has been a part of Jewish and Christian thought for over two thousand years. Interest in the biblical passages that seem to predict the final fate of sinners (and the rewards bestowed upon the righteous) seems to come and go over the centuries. Most socially stable organizations deflect attention away from end-times speculation and focus instead upon the prophetic task of world-building. When a small group seizes upon millennial belief as the key to a full understanding of God's will, it necessarily finds itself at the periphery of mainstream religious life. Nowhere is this more clearly seen than in the case of the Millerites.

William Miller was a farmer from upstate New York who claimed to have been a staunch Deist in his early twenties. A revivalist preacher brought Miller to a crisis of faith. His conversion to evangelical Protestantism set him upon a disciplined course of daily Bible reading. For reasons that are unclear, Miller became obsessed with the apocalyptic Books of Daniel and Revelation. He devoted countless hours trying to decipher the otherwise cryptic passages in Daniel and Revelation that he hoped would shed light on the precise moment at which Christ would return to pass judgment on the human race. Miller gradually developed a convoluted scheme that seemed to disclose the precise date of the Second Coming.[19] He arrived at the shocking conclusion that the Bible clearly and unequivocally identified 1843 as the year that biblical prophecy would finally be fulfilled. Miller checked his figures again and again. It was 1818 when he came to this startling discovery. The apocalypse was only 25 years away!

Miller described himself as a "worm," a "poor feeble creature" who was too weak to be a spokesman for God. He nonetheless accepted an invitation to speak on Bible prophecy at a Baptist revival in 1831. His lecture was received enthusiastically, and suddenly this shy farmer was transformed into a commanding revivalist preacher. The next year he published a pamphlet aptly titled "Evidences from Scripture and History of the Second Coming of Christ About the Year A. D. 1843." A year later he was granted a license to preach as a Baptist minister, and his apocalyptic message began to attract the attention of ministers and laity alike.

In 1839, a Boston minister by the name of Joshua Himes met William Miller. Himes was an active reformist in the abolition and temperance movements. He was enthralled by Miller's calculations and his ability to see how contemporary events were rapidly fulfilling the biblical prophecies connected with the end times. Himes joined Miller and brought to the movement a marketing savvy that placed the millennial cause at the center of national attention. Himes bought a circus tent that could seat four thousand people, reportedly the largest tent in North America. Soon Himes launched a newspaper, the *Signs of the Times*, and then a number of periodicals with titles such as *Advent Witness*, *Voice of Warning*, and *Midnight Cry*.

It is estimated that fifty thousand Americans became committed Miller-ites. Thousands more were fascinated by Miller's predictions and were consequently filled with religious excitement.[20] It is easy to understand why Miller attracted so many followers. Many had already become "born again" at earlier revivals. Over time their spirituality had understandably grown more sedate. When Miller came along they were ready for someone to light new fires of enthusiasm. Many had joined one of the voluntary societies spawned by the Second Great Awakening, but had become discouraged by the slow progress they were making toward renovating the entire world. It was only natural that they would be enchanted by a message promising an immediate and total resolution of the world's imperfections. This was particularly the case given that the financial panic of 1837 had set off a widespread depression and thus dashed the worldly hopes of many farmers and businessmen. Miller's message was perfectly tailored to such spiritual and economic disappointments. He told how, in the twinkling of an eye, every last problem in the world would be solved. The disintegrating kingdoms of earth would instantly give way to the glorious Kingdom of God.

As 1843 approached, millennial fever soared. Some Millerites even gave away all their possessions and gathered on hilltops to await Christ's descent from the clouds. When the predicted date came and passed, Miller made new calculations and reset the date to October 1844. But still there was no cataclysmic destruction and no appearance of Christ. Hopes were dashed. Enthusiasm was crushed. The "Great Disappointment" of 1844 dealt a serious blow to the adventist cause (named for the expected return or advent of Christ). Some became bitter and wary of all forms of enthusiastic religion. Others, like Miller himself, did not readily concede error but instead maintained that their basic prophetic scheme was still valid; they had erred only in relying upon inaccurate dates supplied by shoddy biblical scholars.

The most innovate response to Miller's failure was by Ellen Gould White. White's numerous visions afforded her the certain knowledge that October 1844 had indeed been a signal moment in the end-times scenario. God revealed to her that the "cleansing of the sanctuary" had indeed occurred on this date. Miller had erred in thinking that this was the date that Christ would return to earth. Instead, it was the date that Christ ascended to a heavenly sanctuary, where He is even now making His final preparation for His return. White's visions had the effect of keeping Miller's general framework intact while simply lengthening the timetable a bit. In a further revelation, she learned that Christ will not return until more Christians live up to His moral demands, which include keeping the true, biblical Sabbath on Saturday.

Ellen White was a charismatic prophetess.[21] Her revelatory visions ultimately gave rise to the formation of the Seventh-Day Adventists. The Seventh-Day Adventists have subsequently grown to over 500,000 members in the United States and continue to be one of the fastest-growing religious groups in the country. Even with this phenomenal success, however, their story does not quite rival the saga of America's largest home-grown religious group: the Church of Jesus Christ of Latter-day Saints.

JOSEPH SMITH: SEER, TRANSLATOR, AND PROPHET

Joseph Smith (1805-1844) was not only a creator of nineteenth-century sectarian spirituality. He was also its creature. His family hailed from Vermont, but in 1816 moved to western New York State in hopes of making a better economic go of it.[22] They finally settled near Palmyra, a town about twenty miles east of Rochester. The region turned out to be the epicenter of frontier revivalism. Revival after revival swept through the area, leaving many of its residents vacillating between religious enthusiasm and total bewilderment. In time the region became known as the "burned-over district," using an analogy equating the fires of the forest to those of the spirit. The best-known historian of this phenomenal episode in American religious life, Whitney Cross, has noted that the burning-over process did more than destroy older religious forms. It also fertilized luxuriant new growth.

Smith's early life is difficult to reconstruct. The first public record of his life comes when he was twenty-one. The record of a trial in Bainbridge, New York, indicates that a local farmer charged that "one Joseph Smith . . . was a disorderly person and an imposter."[23] The details are sketchy but it seems that at the time Smith claimed to possess "peep stones" (natural crystals thought to have divining powers) that could lead him to buried treasure. Affidavits later published in E. D. Howe's 1834 *Mormonism Unvailed* (sic) cite other local residents who also alleged that Joseph was a conniver. The court concurred and found Joseph guilty of the charges. All records of his early life thus indicate that he had a reputation for heightened fascination with magic and divination. It also seems that he was taken with local legends concerning the ancient history of North America, the origins of American Indians, and reports concerning the discovery of "brass plates" that had purportedly been buried in the region. Joseph believed that his "peep stones" might enable him to uncover lost treasures or, better still, ancient texts detailing the region's lost history. He lived in a world where there was no real line between magic and religion as avenues to the supernatural. He was young and curious. And he seemed to have deeply desired the power for supernatural sight.

In 1830, just four years after this trial, Smith's fortunes changed forever. This was the year that the Book of Mormon was published and offered for sale. It is also the year that Smith organized a small church that proclaimed itself to be "the only true and living church upon the face of the whole earth." Joseph and the handful of local residents who joined him in this church considered themselves to be a gathering of saints (because Christ's followers were known as saints, Smith's group understood themselves to be saints of the latter days). In time this church was to be known as the Church of Jesus Christ of Latter-day Saints. It is far and away the largest religious body ever to have emerged wholly on American soil. And its principal teachings are far and away the most original of any group to have emerged in the nineteenth century's sectarian heyday.

Smith related how on September 22, 1823, he had been visited by an angel named Moroni. He later identified Moroni as the angel mentioned in the Book of Revelation who flew "in the midst of heaven having the everlasting gospel to preach unto them that dwell on the earth." Moroni was thus the bearer of God's restoration of truth on earth in preparation for the final fulfillment of biblical prophecy. Moroni told Joseph of a glorious book etched on golden plates buried in the Hill Cumorah near Palmyra. Joseph went to the Hill Cumorah the very next day hoping to retrieve the buried tablets. But Moroni indicated that the time was not yet ripe and told him to return on the night of the next fall solstice. For three straight years Joseph faithfully came to the Hill Cumorah on the appointed day but was still denied access to the tablets. Finally, on the evening of September 22, 1827, the Angel Moroni allowed him to uncover the buried text.

Joseph found himself in possession of very strange golden plates. The text inscribed upon them wasn't in English, but in what he described as "reformed Egyptian" hieroglyphics.[24] Moroni had also entrusted him with two "ancient seer" stones known as the "Urim and Thummim." These stones mystically empowered Joseph to translate the tablets. A local farmer, Martin Harris, served as Joseph's scribe during the early translation work. Harris' wife actually threw away the first 116 pages of the translation after she had become angry with her husband. While praying on the matter, Joseph received a revelation from God directing him to forget about the missing piece of revelation and to begin translating a different section of the tablets instead. From this moment on God was to use Joseph as a revelator through which he would send instructions—both big and small—for the restoration of a true church into which saints might be gathered.

With the help of Oliver Cowdrey, a Palmyra schoolteacher, Joseph finished the translation work. The finished product was to become known as the Book of Mormon (named after the resident of ancient America who was both the author of the book and the father of Moroni). The Book of Mormon reads in a manner somewhat similar to the first five books of the Bible. It tells the story of a small group of Hebrews who escaped the Babylonian invasion of Jerusalem about 600 B.C.E. by constructing a boat and journeying to North America. These people settled in what is now the northeastern United States, constructing quite advanced cities and temples. The most amazing part of the story comes when, following His resurrection and ascension in Jerusalem, Christ appeared before these people and organized His church among them. With time, however, the people eventually divided into two separate tribes: the Nephites and the Lamanites. The Nephites were a God-fearing people. The Lamanites (said to be the ancestors of American Indians), however, were sinful. As conflict between the groups escalated, war finally broke out, with the final battle occurring at the Hill Cumorah. The last of the peaceful Nephites were a soldier-statesman by the name of Mormon and his son, Moroni. They buried tablets containing records of their people and of Christ's ministry among them in the side of this hill to keep them from being lost forever. And there these tablets remained until Moroni led Smith to uncover them more than two thousand years later.

It is easy to understand the spiritual excitement felt by the six elders and approximately fifty others who joined together to form the Church of Jesus Christ of Latter-day Saints in 1830. Like others of the era, they were full of millennial enthusiasm and lived in expectation of their Lord's return amid the tribulations that would destroy unbelievers. One of Smith's recent revelations had, in fact, called for the "gathering of the Saints" in order "to prepare their hearts and be prepared in all things against the day when tribulation and desolation are sent forth upon the wicked." They were aware that other groups such as the Baptists and Disciples of Christ were trying to return to the pristine teachings of "primitive Christianity." But they alone had the full gospel of Christ, a gospel including His teachings in North America. Indeed, in time they would not only have the Book of Mormon, but also other works (including the Doctrine and Covenants, and a Pearl of Great Price) stemming from Smith's prolific outpouring of revelations.

Latter-day Saints were but one of many groups in the burned-over district that emphasized inner experience and close relationship to God. Nor were they the only group claiming that some of their members entered into ecstatic states and were thus empowered to offer private interpretations of biblical writings. Yet the Latter-day Saints had within their midst an inspired prophet chosen especially by God. A few years later God sent a revelation through Smith explaining that He had sent "his servant Joseph to be a presiding elder over [the] church" and that Joseph had been sent to them "to be a translator, a revelator, a seer, and a prophet." Indeed, the Saints possessed a new scripture miraculously translated from plates of gold, a new prophet called by God Himself, and a new church restoring the ancient order of things under the direction of ongoing divine revelation.

The revelation of the Book of Mormon would alone have set Joseph Smith apart as a religious genius. True, outsiders have doubted the authenticity of the text from the outset.[25] Yet the Book of Mormon was only the beginning of Joseph's exceptional religious career. Until his tragic death in 1844, Joseph continued to occupy center stage in the greatest saga in American religious history. Over six feet tall and possessing athletic mannerisms, Joseph was a commanding physical presence. He was also full of personal charm, kindness, and endearing determination. More important, he had an uncanny ability to redirect the spiritual restlessness of his era into new and exciting directions. His continuing stream of revelations seemed to correspond perfectly with his followers' spiritual questions and aspirations. Smith responded to their spiritual doldrums by giving them a vivid sense of their role in building the Kingdom of God here on earth. He was himself a living symbol of the nearness we might have with God. And he promised his followers a heaven that would be an eternal continuation of all earthly pleasures—including wealth, achievement, sex, and endless personal progression.

Early Mormons (the nickname that soon attached to the fledgling group of Latter-day Saints) wrestled with the issue of their relationship to other Christian groups. It was within this context that Joseph announced an earlier revelation that in capsule form forged the Latter-day Saints' unique sense of identity and mission. In 1838, a full eight years after the initial publication of the Book of Mormon, Smith for the first time spoke publicly about a vision that had occurred to him as early as 1820. This episode during his teenage years has henceforth come to be known as the First Vision, coming as it did three years before the Second Vision, in which Moroni disclosed to him the existence of buried golden plates. At the time Joseph, who was only fourteen years old, was perplexed by the religious controversies that divided the residents of the burned-over district. His religious uncertainty led him to prolonged contemplation and prayer. After all, which of the many revivalist preachers was he to believe? In his autobiography he captured the dilemma of his early career: "In the midst of this war of words and tumult of opinions, I often said to myself, what is to be done? Who of all these parties be right? Or are they all wrong together?" Troubled, Joseph went strolling in the woods, where he saw a pillar of light descending from above. Within this light he saw "two Personages, whose brightness and glory defy all description, standing above me in the air." The two personages were none other than God and Jesus Christ. They instructed him to hold himself from all the contending denominations since not a single existing church continued to follow the full gospel. They promised him that he would play a crucial role in the restoration of the true church. This, of course, is precisely what happened three years later when he was visited by the Angel Moroni.

It is unclear whether Joseph Smith's family or close associates had ever heard of this vision prior to his announcement some eighteen years after it purportedly took place.[26] This account of Smith's early vision succinctly captures the Mormons' growing confidence that they were the one true church and that Joseph was specially called by God to serve as His appointed prophet.[27] It also provides succinct imagery upon which Mormons could ground several of their developing beliefs. It offered firm support, for example, that God is a physical being. It also showed Mormons that the conventional notion of the Trinity is wholly mistaken; Jesus and God are separate individuals. And, again, it provided ample justification for Mormons' sense of being a chosen people led by a chosen prophet.

The publication of the Book of Mormon in 1830 signaled the next phase of Joseph Smith's prophetic career. He had already received a vision in which John the Baptist appeared to him and Oliver Cowdrey, ordaining them in the ancient biblical Aaronic priesthood. This priesthood was open to all worthy males, giving them the power to administer "outward ordinances" such as baptism. Further revelations flowed. At a later date Smith was instructed to revise a higher order of priesthood, the Melchizedek priesthood, who alone would confer the church's other spiritual blessings. By June of 1830 he could claim twenty-seven followers. A few of his followers headed west to serve as missionaries to the Indians. As they passed through Kirtland, Ohio, they met a Campbellite minister by the name of Sidney Rigdon. Rigdon and his entire congregation were so moved by the story of God's ongoing revelation to latter-day saints that they all converted to the fledgling church. A few months later Smith moved his New York followers to Kirtland to begin the "gathering" of saints in anticipation of Christ's return.

For a time the Saints prospered in Kirtland. They sent a missionary party out to establish a new settlement in Missouri. Their temple in Kirtland was dedicated in 1836. But persecution began to escalate. Many outsiders were offended by the Mormons' seemingly outlandish claims. Others were threatened by the political power that their Mormon neighbors could collectively wield on election days. And still others were incensed that the Mormons often preached to black citizens, stirring up considerable racial tension in antebellum America. In 1832 Joseph Smith was tarred and feathered by a mob in Hiram, Ohio, while Sidney Rigdon was beaten severely. Even worse violence erupted in Missouri. Mobs attacked Mormon settlements and destroyed the office of their newly organized newspaper. Economic conditions were harsh in Ohio in 1837, leading to the collapse of the Mormons' bank. The Ohio group migrated to Missouri, but tensions continued to mount throughout the summer of 1838. Local citizens refused Mormons the right to vote in the election that August, leading to more violent skirmishes. That fall a Missouri-Mormon war broke out. The Mormons organized into militias, with the most violent group calling themselves the Danite Band. Separate battles at Crooked River and Haun's Mill killed at least two dozen Mormons, and the Missouri governor issued an order that they were to be expelled or exterminated. Joseph Smith was arrested and imprisoned for almost six months before being released to lead the Mormons to a new settlement in Illinois that they named Nauvoo.

It was in Nauvoo that Joseph Smith reached the full height of his prophetic powers. The State of Illinois granted Nauvoo a charter that gave the Mormons considerable autonomy in regulating their own affairs. And Joseph was up to the task. God sent a revelation to remind His gathered flock that He had sent him "his servant Joseph to be a presiding elder over [the] church." He had been given to them "to be a translator, a revelator, a seer, and a prophet." In many ways this seems like an excess of titles. But each title responded to needs of the developing community of Saints.[28] Smith served the gathered community as deliverer (Moses), military commander (Joshua), prophet (Isaiah), king (Solomon), and founder of a new church (Peter). Joseph was a high priest whose words and actions harnessed spiritual energies to perform the "ordinances of the Lord" as well as a king whose leadership would institute a political kingdom of God.

The fact that the Gentile world opposed them on every front did not detract from Joseph Smith's mission. On the contrary. Smith often exaggerated the persecution they faced as a way of helping his followers maintain exaggerated notions of their religious and cultural separateness. Historian R. Laurence Moore goes so far as to argue that without opposition, Smith's religious career might well have gone nowhere.[29] Persecution gave their struggle value and reinforced their identity as Saints called by God to separate themselves from a wayward world. In conscious and unconscious ways, they built a viable identity by stressing the degree to which they diverged from mainstream culture.

It is in this context of constructing a new and separate identity that the Prophet announced several startling revelations during the Nauvoo years. Smith had never dwelt upon original sin as did so many in the burned-over district. The people he ministered to were optimistic, hard-working, and held high hopes for their own worldly futures. Smith's revelations responded to these hopes and gave them new theological expression. Spiritual progress, he explained, is progressive and extends well beyond this lifetime. We all may in time evolve into gods. Indeed, God himself was once a man. This concept of eternal progression toward divine status had immediate religious appeal to the future-oriented community of Saints. Self-effort, stick-to-itiveness, and moral obedience pave the way to higher degrees of glory.

This doctrine of eternal progression raised a number of theological questions that resulted in continuing revelations. The Saints learned that there are many gods, all of whom evolved to this status through ongoing moral perfection. They learned that while salvation is available to all, there are three distinct degrees of glory: terrestrial, telestial, and celestial. Part of the path to godhood consists of developing the special creative powers made possible by marriage. Joseph's revelation on "celestial marriage" disclosed that temple ordinances can seal a marriage for eternity, permitting married couples

Prophet and Founder of America's Largest Native-Born Religion
Credit: The Library of Congress

to continue to evolve toward godhood in their future state. This doctrine of celestial marriage in turn connects with the single most distinctive Mormon tenet—that of pluralistic marriage. There is some evidence that the practice of plural marriage may have begun in secret as early as the Kirtland years. But in Nauvoo, Smith announced that God was reinstating the ancient biblical custom of males having more than one wife. Surely no doctrine has done more to symbolize "Mormon separateness" than this reinstatement of plural marriage (polygamy). Many Saints were themselves scandalized by Smith's announcement. Yet Joseph had once again succeeded in bringing clarity to the Mormon's distinctive spiritual style. To this day Mormons consider the activities of the world, everyday life, to be the chief concern of religion. Sexuality and marriage are thus both worldly and spiritual. It appears that Joseph was well aware of his own strong sexual impulses.[30] His revelations about plural marriage thus assured him that if he had these tendencies, they must finally be in accordance with God's will. It is, furthermore, a Mormon's duty to provide fleshly tabernacles for waiting spirits who need to come to earth to further their spiritual growth. Plural marriage enables one to fulfill this duty more completely. Smith was also sensitive to the role that sexual disorder and family disorganization played in tearing frontier communities apart. Plural marriage actually desexualized the family structure and bound men and women together in loyalty to the long-term purposes of the gathered community of saints. The revelation of plural marriage pointed to a new form of kinship ties that would strengthen social bonds.[31]

The Latter-day Saints flourished in Nauvoo. By 1844 the Mormon population in Nauvoo was in excess of 10,000—making Nauvoo the second-largest city in Illinois, next only to Chicago. As the community grew, so did the parameters of Joseph Smith's leadership. By this time he commanded a militia of 2,000 soldiers. Now known as King of the Kingdom of God, Joseph announced his candidacy for president of the United States in the upcoming 1844 election. He formed an internal organization known as the Council of Fifty to help execute his plans for the expansion of their worldly kingdom. The exact nature and activities of this secretive council are still not entirely known. It is probably safe to assume, however, that it was charged with helping Smith move into a more aggressive phase of extending Mormon influence over the region. Non-Mormon residents understandably feared the escalating political power wielded by the Saints. Further fear and outrage mounted as Mormon apostates circulated wild rumors about the polygamy and corruption allegedly connected with the highest levels of Mormon leadership. One ex-Mormon published a scathing article in the *Nauvoo Expositor* criticizing the Saints' polygamy and Smith's political ambitions. Smith promptly condemned the *Expositor* as a corrupting influence and ordered his militia to destroy its presses. On the evening of June 10, 1844, the Mormon troops broke into the newspaper office and destroyed it. In so doing, Smith seemed to substantiate the allegations concerning his increasingly despotic rule. Governor Ford came personally to the nearby village of Carthage in order to investigate. He wrote to Smith, promising him a safe escort if he surrendered pending a formal hearing. Smith agreed, but with an uncanny prescience about what was to unfold is said to have uttered "I am going like a lamb to the slaughter. . . . I shall die innocent, and it shall yet be said of me—he was murdered in cold blood."[32]

On the afternoon of June 27, 1844, Joseph Smith, his brother Hyrum, and two other Mormon leaders were huddled in the upstairs cell of the Carthage jailhouse. They saw a mob of about 150 armed men approaching. It seems that the militia assigned to protect the prisoners were in collusion with the attackers. Hyrum was killed by the first round of bullets fired from below. Joseph actually had a revolver that one of his friends had smuggled into the jail for him. He fired at the attackers, wounding three. The attackers stuck their guns into the partially opened doorway and fired repeatedly. Joseph attempted to jump from the second-story window, but was shot from behind before he could escape. Not yet forty, Joseph Smith died a martyr for the church he had founded some fourteen years earlier. His innovations proved too unsettling for most of his contemporaries. He died amid public outrage and ridicule.

Shortly after Smith's death, Brigham Young led the majority of Saints to Salt Lake City, where they would begin again. Other Mormon groups, notably the Reorganized Church of Jesus Christ of Latter-day Saints, who followed Joseph's son back to Missouri, also picked up the pieces of Joseph's dynamic faith and moved forward. Today the Latter-day Saints number more than 4 million, making it by far the largest native-born religious group in American history. The Saints' eventual prosperity is itself sufficient tribute to their founder's creative vision. Joseph Smith succeeded in binding his followers into a cohesive community in which every member works diligently to build the Kingdom of God upon earth. Their progress—individual and communal—is itself understood to be a sacred enterprise and will continue even into their heavenly futures. Joseph Smith helped his contemporaries come to believe that revelation is not something restricted to ancient biblical times. It continues even now to those who are close enough to God to receive it. The world is full of unexpected possibilities. Smith's message assured the Saints that continuing progress—both material and spiritual—is our divine inheritance. He helped his followers envision how they, too, shall eventually be as gods. And this vision lives on today in one of the nation's fastest-growing religious groups.

ULTRAISM UNLEASHED

The story of Joseph Smith draws attention to the wave of religious innovation unleashed by the Second Great Awakening. Contemporaries referred to this outburst of religious fervor as "ultraism." Ultraism, in the words of historian Whitney Cross, consisted of a "combination of activities, personalities, and attitudes creating a condition of society which could foster experimental doctrines."[33] Charles Finney's "new measures" were a prime example of this experimental approach to religion-making. "New measures," Finney declared, "are necessary from time to time to awaken attention and to bring the gospel to bear upon the public mind."[34] Implicit in Finney's remark is his assumption that the final test of religious beliefs is whether they produce results. Most of the new measures developed by Finney, Smith, and others of the era were intended to produce conversions. Mormons, Shakers, Adventists, and communitarians all hoped to seize upon innovative techniques that might induce the Holy Spirit to descend and symbolize the start of the New Life.[35]

Ultraism, however, knew no bounds. Once unleashed, it incited experimental fervor among the spiritually unorthodox as well. Many of the era's most innovative sectarian thinkers were inspired to pursue new measures that would take them far afield of biblical religion. The spiritual marketplace encouraged their efforts. Popular demand, whetted by the excitement of experiential religion, invited ever-more-novel approaches to establishing contact with the progressive power of the Holy Spirit. A number of religious revolutionaries responded with new and exciting spiritual philosophies that had little or no contact whatsoever with the nation's established churches. Ralph Waldo Emerson, Phineas P. Quimby, and Andrew Jackson Davis emerged in the mid-nineteenth century as progenitors of new spiritual traditions.

℘

FOUR

American Metaphysical Religion

The Countervailing Voices
of Emerson, Quimby, and Davis

BY THE TIME OF THE SECOND GREAT AWAKENING there were two basic forms of religiosity present in America's churches: the liturgical and the evangelical. The liturgical model of religiosity emphasizes personal renewal through participation in formal ritual and worship. Roman Catholics, Episcopalians, and Lutherans (the latter two groups began immigrating into the United States in larger numbers toward the end of the nineteenth century) are the clearest Christian examples of this liturgical orientation to religion. Presbyterians, Congregationalists, and Methodists are far less liturgical, but retain certain elements of this model. Baptists—along with most other conservative Protestants—have instead emphasized the evangelical model of religion. Evangelical Protestantism believes that personal renewal comes through the deeply emotional experience of conversion. It stresses fervent belief as the hallmark of salvation.

There was, however, already a third basic model of spirituality emerging in American life: the metaphysical model. The term "metaphysical" refers to a loosely organized range of beliefs concerning the existence of a more-than-physical reality surrounding everyday existence. As such, metaphysical religion thrives in cultural territory that exists somewhere between conventional religion and conventional science. Some forms of metaphysical religion are more overtly mystical than conventional churches. Metaphysical spirituality thus appeals to persons desiring a felt-sense of connection with something "more." Other forms of metaphysical religion are less concerned with inner experience than they are with establishing "objective" evidence for the existence of nonmaterial realities that are normally dismissed, ignored, or even denied by existing scientific theories. The common aim of all metaphysical religion is to understand the larger spiritual forces affecting human life in ways that bypass the categories of biblical religion or materialistic science. Metaphysical religion promotes what is often called harmonial piety. In contrast to either liturgical or evangelical models of piety, harmonial spirituality has no formal connection with the Bible or conventional theology. Instead, it comprises a wide range of beliefs and practices predicated on the conviction that spiritual composure, physical health, and even economic well-being flow automatically from a person's inner rapport with a metaphysical reality.[1]

American metaphysical religion has its roots in the magical and occult practices that the early colonists brought with them from Europe. This is particularly true of those whose curiosities prompted them to dabble in various forms of Western occultism such as Rosicrucianism, alchemy, and philosophies in the Hermetic tradition.[2] But the main emergence of metaphysical spirituality as a principal form of American spirituality began with the Transcendentalists and their principal spokesperson—Ralph Waldo Emerson.

THE BOSTON BRAHMIN

Many educated persons in nineteenth-century New England found themselves in a spiritual predicament. They often didn't know where to place their ultimate loyalty: religion or science. The religion being preached from the pulpit often came across as cold and irrelevant. Science seemed to be passing religion by. It was steadily uncovering the lawful principles by which the universe operates, giving people hope that they would soon hold the key to a better future in their own hands. Yet science had in many ways elbowed God out of daily human experience. Western science operated on the basis of the philosophy of John Locke, which proclaims that all knowledge derives from direct sense experience. The implication was that we have no direct knowledge about God or the soul. Doctrines about such spiritual matters therefore have less cognitive merit than scientific knowledge. It was possible, of course, to believe that the Bible contains God's revelation to the world. Yet, as we saw in the case of both Franklin and Jefferson, many educated Americans had long since ceased believing that the Christian Bible was essentially different than other ancient myths. They viewed the Bible as a fascinating collection of ancient superstitions and moral teachings that must be carefully scrutinized according to modern intellectual criteria. Their lack of faith in the Bible put the era's progressive thinkers in a precarious spiritual position. They had little to turn to except the intellectually solid, but emotionally cool, philosophy of deism. The God proclaimed by deism was even more removed from the affairs of everyday life than the God of classic Protestantism. To be sure deism was less pessimistic than Protestantism about the human condition. Protestantism insisted that humans are fallen, existing as "poor worms" in their state of sinfulness and depravity. Yet even though deism proclaimed faith in human abilities, it still suggested that humans find themselves alone in a wholly material universe.

Ralph Waldo Emerson (1803-1882) rebelled against both the scientific materialism and the biblical religion of his day. It is not that he rejected scientific rationality. He only insisted that the human spirit was far more expansive than could be explained in the narrow scientific categories of his day. He also believed that humans were far more than "poor worms." He had faith in humanity's capacity for free and creative action in the world. Emerson was thus unwilling to settle for the conventional philosophies of his day. He was spiritually restless, yearning for a mode of personal spirituality capable of unleashing humanity's highest intellectual and emotional powers.

Emerson's upbringing was fairly traditional. He was the son of the minister of Boston's First Church. Although his father died when Ralph was young, his family provided him with an environment that nurtured middle-

Transcendentalist Philosopher Who Celebrated Our
Inner-Connection with Universal Spirit
Credit: The Library of Congress.

class sensibilities. Emerson went to college at Harvard, receiving a classical
education consistent with New England's conception of a respectable gentle-
man. He then enrolled in Harvard Divinity School to be trained as a Unitarian
minister. In 1829 he was ordained as the junior minister at Boston's Second
Church. He resigned just three years later because he was uncomfortable with
public prayer and with administering the Lord's Supper to his congregation.
The next year he launched a career as a public lecturer and soon earned a
reputation for propounding a novel spiritual philosophy.

In 1836 Emerson published a slim volume titled *Nature*. This book ignited a
fire in his contemporaries' religious imaginations. It held out an exciting vision
of God's presence in our world. Indeed, Emerson confessed that when alone in
nature he opened up to an immediate sense of divine presence. The sacredness
he encountered in nature contrasted sharply with the coldness of ordinary
church services. Nature, he maintained, contains God's in-streaming spiritual
presence. Divine spirit surrounds us, awaiting our recognition. We need only

put aside our worldly rationality and open our inner spiritual faculties. A mystical encounter with God is thus an imminent possibility of human experience. Emerson found that the quiet of nature helped him to enter into states of spiritual receptivity. He wrote that when alone in nature, "All mean egotism vanishes. I become a transparent eyeball; I am nothing; I see all; the currents of the Universal Being circulate through me; I am part and parcel of God."[3]

Emerson had in one quick stroke cut a new spiritual path that avoided the limitations of both the science and biblical religion of his day. His vision of God's presence in the natural world did not ask persons to denounce scientific rationality; only to expand upon it. It didn't require belief in the Bible. Nor did it portray humans as wretched sinners in desperate need of forgiveness. It asked instead that we temporarily set aside the egocentric rationality of everyday life. We must first learn to become nothing in order to become open to the transparent presence of "Universal Being." Emerson was staking out a new, unchurched spirituality that offered his audiences the possibility of achieving a mystical connection with God without requiring them to dwell upon their personal sinfulness or to surrender their freedom of thought.

The same year that Emerson published *Nature,* a group comprised mostly of rebellious Unitarian preachers gathered in the home of George Ripley. The group called themselves "The Transcendental Club." The club included some of the period's greatest thinkers: Ralph Waldo Emerson, Theodore Parker, James Freeman Clarke, Frederic Hedge, William Henry Channing, and Orestes Brownson. Shortly thereafter they were joined by Henry David Thoreau, Bronson Alcott, Margaret Fuller, and Elizabeth Peabody. What they held in common was a rejection of the cold intellectualism that they thought dominated the "official" religious and moral views of their day. They had been influenced by the British Romantic writers and wished to infuse a certain mysticism into their liberal religious outlook. In truth, the Transcendentalists didn't even attempt to forge consensus among themselves. They were far too independently minded to expect conformity. The group could, however, agree upon three basic principles: (1) the immanence of God; (2) inward experience as the primary conduit of spiritual truth; and (3) a rejection of all external authority. They were called Transcendentalists, Ripley explained, because they believed "in an order of truths which transcends the sphere of the external senses." And since "the truth of religion does not depend on tradition, nor historical facts, but has an unerring witness in the soul," they relied upon each individual's inner experience of God rather than the Bible or traditional theological creeds.[4]

Though almost all of the Transcendentalists were prolific writers, Emerson was without question the group's leading spokesperson. In 1838, just two years after the publication of *Nature*, Emerson was asked to deliver the commencement address at Harvard Divinity School. This speech was destined to have important historical consequences. It announced to the theological world that Americans now possessed a striking new spiritual philosophy that had no formal connection to churched religion. Emerson crafted a poetic exposition of metaphysical spirituality that, with the exception of William James' *Varieties of Religious Experience*, has never since been equaled. The address begins by proclaiming that the world is the product "of one will, of one mind; and that one mind is everywhere active, in each ray of the star, in each wavelet of the pool; . . . All things proceed out of the same spirit, and all things conspire with it. . . . The perception of this law of laws awakens in the mind a sentiment which we call the religious sentiment, and which makes our highest happiness."[5] But Emerson was not content simply to draw attention to the immanence of God. He took this opportunity to point out what he judged to be the spiritual failings of the religious faith received "second hand" in the nation's churches. A primary faith, he argued, is a faith that wells up within one's own thought and experience. Put bluntly,

> In this point of view we become sensible of the first defect of historical Christianity. Historical Christianity has fallen into the error that corrupts all attempts to communicate religion. . . . (it rests upon) an exaggeration of the personal, the positive, the ritual. It has dwelt, it dwells, with noxious exaggeration about the person of Jesus. The soul knows no persons. It invites every man to expand to the full circle of the universe.[6]

Emerson's point was that in proclaiming Jesus' divinity, Christianity had lost sight of every human being's inner-connection with the currents of Universal Being. Christianity attributes divine nature to Jesus, but denies it to the rest of us. In so doing it loses any real sense of the spiritual inspiration of which we are all capable. Similarly, the church speaks of miracles in the distant past, but has become blind to the higher spiritual power available to all of us in the here and now. The churches have in this sense become the enemy of authentic spirituality; they divert our attention from the miraculous and divine possibilities of everyday human experience.

Emerson found in Hinduism a vocabulary befitting the modern spiritual situation. In the mystical texts known as the Upanishads, Hindus described God as the infinite, impersonal spirit known as Brahman. By conceiving God as an impersonal spirit, the Hindus had done away with the very imagery of God as a sin-hating Judge, King, or Father that Emerson found to be an obstacle to religious belief. Emerson translated the concept of Brahman into English as the Over-Soul. The metaphor of Over-Soul provides a succinct image of how each individual soul is connected with the all-embracing spirit of God. The notion of Brahman or the Over-Soul was also connected with the Hindu belief that God is ultimately ineffable and beyond literal designation. Hinduism teaches that the only real knowledge of God is not doctrinal knowledge, but the knowledge that comes through direct experience. Hindu mystical thought asserts that the mind is multi-layered. When we pierce beneath the layer of the outer, physical senses we eventually uncover the pure soul—the Atman. The individual soul, or Atman, is in continuous rapport with Brahman. At depth, then, each of us is in continuous harmony with God. This imagery of the intimate connection between the individual mind and the Over-Soul suggested that we have the capacity to receive "an influx of the Divine mind into our mind. It is an ebb of the individual rivulet before the flowing surges of the sea of life."[7]

This new vision of the self's inner-connection with God rendered biblical notions of sin and vicarious atonement obsolete. In the Transcendentalist view, what separates us from God is not disobedience but rather limited self-awareness. If we learn to explore the deeper levels of the mind we will simultaneously become "conscious of a universal soul within or behind our individual life, wherein, as a firmament, the natures of Justice, Truth, Love, Freedom, arise and shine."[8] This perception is nothing less than an ecstatic religious event. It is marked by "that shudder of awe and delight with which the individual soul always mingles with the Universal Soul"[9]

Inner-connection with the Over-Soul frees us from being at the mercy of outer conditions. It shows us that our true self is anchored in a transcendent reality. We have continuous access to a limitless supply of wisdom, spontaneity, and guidance. Emerson explained that "we lie in the lap of immense intelligence, which makes us receivers of its truth and organs of its activity."[10]

The byproduct of such spiritual awareness is the capacity for Self-Reliance. Spiritual insight helps us understand that the true "self" is neither the physically nor the socially defined self. It is, rather, the self that has first "become nothing" and thus receptive to the "exertions of a power which exists not in time, or space, but an instantaneous, in-streaming causing power."[11]

Emerson and his fellow Transcendentalists were among the Boston area's social and intellectual elite. They were well-educated and relatively affluent. Their interest in literary and cultural topics identified them as core members of what was then known as "the Boston Brahmin" (the word for "high caste" in India). The Transcendentalist vision had this elite aura about it. It attracted those who possessed the time and resources to explore the subtleties of spiritual philosophy. The Transcendentalists, it seemed, had somehow grown beyond the all-too-human need for a personal God who might hear and answer our petitionary prayers. Their willingness to dabble in Eastern mysticism and to picture God in impersonal terms made their religious system irrelevant to the vast majority of their contemporaries. But in historical hindsight, they were especially prescient. They were ahead of their time in appreciating the growing conflict between science and religion. Their distinction between ordinary rationality and the "higher" faculty of intuition enabled them to sustain a spiritual (as opposed to wholly secular) outlook while nonetheless repudiating the need to equate religion with belief in the literal truth of the Bible. The Transcendentalists' interest in Eastern mysticism was also ahead of their time, displaying a concern for tolerance, eclecticism, and multiculturalism long before these became fashionable in the area of religious belief. Many persons would also find the Transcendentalists ahead of their time in placing the individual, rather than institutional religion, at the center of their spiritual vision. Of course many of the trends discernible in Transcendentalism would eventually prove troublesome. For example, the very individualism that might be seen as one of Transcendentalism's major strengths can also be viewed as mirroring the excessive individualism that has helped corrode our nation's communal bonds. And, too, Transcendentalism's harmonial piety tends to divert attention away from the tough social, economic, and political decisions that we must make as a culture if we are to ensure "harmony" on a long-term basis. Yet, as historian Sydney Ahlstrom contends, these and other such criticisms of Emerson and other Transcendentalists "do not tell us why Emerson is, with William James, peculiarly

America's own philosopher. They fail to recognize that Emerson is in fact the theologian of something we may almost term 'the American religion.'"[12]

This "American religion" is based on neither the liturgical nor the evangelical model of personal spirituality. It is metaphysical through and through. Emerson and his Transcendentalist colleagues loom so large across the American religious landscape because they succeeded in creating a vocabulary of spiritual self-understanding predicated almost wholly on just three metaphysical doctrines: (1) the immanence of God; (2) the fundamental correspondence between the various levels of the universe; and (3) the possibility of "influx" from higher to lower metaphysical levels. Emerson's concept of God as the Over-Soul succinctly captured his faith in an ever-present, but impersonal, spiritual power. His spiritual philosophy offered a viable alternative to Christian theologies of the fall, original sin, and humanity's innate depravity. In Emerson's pantheistic view, God is always and everywhere present to the properly attuned mind. Instead of proclaiming that humans are separated from God by sin as most Christian churches did, Emerson maintained that the only barrier between God and human beings is limited spiritual understanding. The route to a more vibrant spiritual life thus requires greater self-awareness rather than the repentance called for in traditional Christianity.

Emerson's notions of correspondence and influx derived at least in part from the Swedish mystic Emanuel Swedenborg. Swedenborg (1688-1771) was a preeminent European scientist when he claims to have been visited by angelic beings. Swedenborg's angelic guides taught him that the universe consists of seven interpenetrating dimensions (the physical, spiritual, angelic, etc.). The doctrine of correspondence explained that each of the seven principal dimensions is intimately connected with every other dimension. God's divine spirit, as the source of all, works through every dimension. Although the divine nature is progressively obscured by the growing unresponsiveness of each successively "lower" realm, it is never obliterated. The doctrine of correspondence thus envisioned causal interaction between the material and spiritual dimensions of life while simultaneously explaining how each individual possesses a core of divinity. This metaphysical doctrine also explained that the universe is lawful throughout. The laws that govern our physical order are but reflections of the spiritual laws that govern every other level of existence. For this reason the study of the lawful operation of any one part of the universe simultaneously sheds light on the operations of the universe at other, higher levels. Even the loftiest of spiritual principles is, at least potentially, within the grasp of human understanding.

This vision of metaphysical correspondence led directly to Swedenborg's doctrine of influx. Swedenborg taught that causal power continuously emanates from God and gradually filters into each successively "lower" dimension of existence. All true progress proceeds according to influences received from above. The physical body achieves inner harmony by becoming attuned to the influx of energies coming from the soul, the soul through contact with superior angelic beings, and so on up the spiritual hierarchy. Through diligent study and by cultivating mystical states of awareness, anyone might obtain the requisite gnosis to make contact with higher spiritual planes.

Part of Emerson's spiritual achievement was his ability to translate Swedenborg's doctrines of correspondence and influx into a vocabulary more befitting the American public. Emerson, for example, never embraced Swedenborg's belief in angelic spirits. Whereas Swedenborg credited angels with mediating his metaphysical revelations, Emerson proclaimed that each individual could receive God's inflowing spirit without any mediation whatsoever. Emerson emphasized the message "that God must be found within," not that we should be seeking communion with angels. He did, however, embrace Swedenborg's conception of a multi-level universe. He, too, believed in the close, lawful connection between the material and spiritual worlds. And the Boston Brahmin, like the Swedish seer, taught that every human being has the capacity to become receptive to the inflow of spiritual energy. In short, the concepts of correspondence and influx became central to Emerson's metaphysical vision.

Belief in the principle of correspondence freed Emerson and other Transcendentalists from dependence upon scriptural terminology. The study of any facet of human experience (the microcosm) can potentially shed light on the larger universe (macrocosm). This was particularly true of the deepest recesses of the human mind. The concept of influx implied that the mind is constructed in such a way as to be intimately connected with higher, metaphysical realities. Self-reliant persons inhabit a higher sphere of thought, they are an "exponent of a vaster mind and will. The opaque self becomes transparent with the light of the First Cause."[13] Emerson never provided a concise description of our psychological capacity to become transparent to the in-streaming power of God. In certain contexts he emphasized the role of inner receptivity. He maintained, for example, that it is through mental *abandonment to the nature of things"* that we avail ourselves of a new energy.[14] Yet, in other contexts, Emerson identified a certain deliberately held spiritual outlook as the key to achieving correspondence with higher spiritual levels: "As fast as you *conform your life to the pure idea in your mind*, that will unfold its great proportions. A correspondent revolution in things will attend the influx of the spirit."[15]

It is thus clear that Emerson struck off in directions quite unlike those pursued by Anne Hutchinson, Thomas Jefferson, or Joseph Smith. He surely shared Jefferson's progressivist temperament and distrust of institutional religion. Yet his yearning for mystical connection with the wider spiritual universe caused him to find Enlightenment rationality too constraining. Like Anne Hutchinson and Joseph Smith, Emerson appealed to the authority of "inner experience" as well as to the authority of "higher revelation." But, unlike Hutchinson or Smith, Emerson believed that no one scripture itself contains ultimate truth. To Emerson, true revelation had to do with the self becoming open to the in-streaming energies that flow from the Over-Soul; it had nothing at all to do with ancient books or fixed dogmas. Emerson proclaimed that the human spirit must be free of all preset or "final" truths in order to interpret spiritual experience in fresh and ever-changing ways. The search for spiritual truth is unending, leading to deeper encounters with one's inner self and with nature, not with churches or inherited theologies.

While Emerson was certain that spiritual truths "arise to us out of the recesses of consciousness," he was unsure about the exact relationship between specific mental states and the divinity immanent in nature.[16] This is why his fellow Transcendentalist, George Ripley, announced that "the time has come when a revision of theology is demanded. Let the study of theology commence with the study of human consciousness."[17] True to Ripley's vision, the very next step in the evolution of American metaphysical religion came when a clockmaker from Belfast, Maine, set himself to the task of studying "the recesses of consciousness."

THE BELFAST MESMERIST

In 1838 Charles Poyen stopped in Belfast, Maine, on his proselytizing tour through New England. There a young and inquisitive Phineas P. Quimby (1802-1866) sat spellbound while Poyen demonstrated the astonishing powers unleashed through the science of animal magnetism. The science of which Poyen spoke stemmed directly from the Viennese physician Franz Anton Mesmer's "discovery" of an ultrafine fluid that he termed animal magnetism.[18] Mesmer postulated that animal magnetism constituted the etheric medium that links the physical universe together. He further explained that animal magnetism was evenly distributed throughout the healthy human body. If for any reason an individual's supply of animal magnetism was thrown out of equilibrium, one or more parts of the body would be deprived of sufficient amounts of this vital force and would eventually begin to falter. "There is," Mesmer reasoned, "only one illness and one healing." Medical science, therefore, should consist only of those procedures designed to supercharge a patient's nervous system with this mysterious life-giving energy.

Originally Mesmer passed magnets up and down his patients' spinal columns in an effort to induce an inflow of animal magnetism. Over time, however, he and his followers shifted their attention to putting patients into a sleep-like trance. It was thought that this trance enabled patients to become more receptive to the inflow of vital magnetic energy. Patients were "mesmerized." That is, they were put into a special state of consciousness in which they became oblivious to the outer world. While in this trance-like state they were aware of nothing except the voice and commands of the healer (mesmerist). Yet, when they returned to their normal waking state they felt refreshed and claimed either partial or complete cures. More astonishing was the fact that about 10 percent of all mesmerized persons spontaneously demonstrated extraordinary mental powers. Mesmerized subjects suddenly became capable of extrasensory perception such as telepathy or clairvoyance. Some even claimed to become filled with the Holy Spirit, undergoing an immediate moral and spiritual transformation. The mesmerists, it seemed, had tapped into the spirit of ultraism and gone the revivalists one better. In the twinkling of an eye they could effect a person's total renewal—physical, mental, and spiritual. And this was accomplished without asking persons to repent, to accept any formal doctrine, or to join any religious institution.

A short time after Poyen's lecture, another mesmerist by the name of Robert Collyer also came through Belfast demonstrating the extraordinary powers of the mind unleashed through the science of animal magnetism. Phineas Quimby, a thirty-six-year-old clockmaker, was hooked. Phineas had not been afforded a Brahmin upbringing.[19] His family was poor, forcing him to become a clockmaker's apprentice while still a boy and thus forgoing any formal education. What he did possess was the right personal temperament to question authority and invent ideas and practices that "worked" in the actual practice of life. Quimby's son, George, wrote that his father "had a very inventive mind, and was always interested in mechanics, philosophy and scientific subjects. . . . He was very argumentative, and always wanted proof of anything, rather than an accepted opinion."[20] Phineas resolved to master the theory and practice of animal magnetism and, in no time at all, he was launched on what was to be a twenty-eight-year career in mental healing.

It was Quimby's good fortune to meet up with a young man by the name of Lucius Burkmar. Lucius proved to be particularly adept at entering into the state of mesmeric trance. Quimby used Lucius to help him demonstrate the powers of mesmerism during his public lectures on the topic. He placed Lucius into the mesmeric state and then directed him to use his clairvoyant powers to diagnose people's illnesses. After completing his diagnosis, Lucius would prescribe medicinal remedies to rejuvenate a patient's vital fluids. On other occasions Quimby dispensed with Lucius' assistance and instead used classic mesmeric "passes" over his patients' heads. Quimby believed that this method allowed him to initiate the flow of magnetic energies into his patients' physical systems. The two methods were clearly distinguishable. The method using Lucius' trance-related abilities to diagnose illness led to the prescription of remedies that basically conformed to the era's standard medical treatments. The other method relied solely upon Quimby's abilities to create the conditions permitting an influx of animal magnetism into the patient's physical system. Yet, to Quimby, both rested upon his belief that "the phenomenon was the result of animal magnetism, and that electricity had more or less to do with it."[21] Quimby's muddled explanations notwithstanding, cures abounded. Newspapers began to take notice, and soon the magnetic doctor from Belfast was being touted as the world's leading mesmerist.

Over time Quimby became skeptical whether animal magnetism could really be responsible for all of his therapeutic successes. Most of the remedies that Lucius prescribed were innocuous substances that seemed to produce results regardless of the actual physical ailment. On one occasion Quimby actually substituted a less expensive prescription for the costly one Lucius had suggested—and the patient recovered just the same! It dawned on Quimby that Lucius might not be diagnosing the patients' ailments at all. Quimby thought

Mental Healer and Pioneer of "Psychological Spirituality"
Credit: Devorss and Company

it more likely that Lucius was instead using his telepathic powers to discover what patients already believed to be the cause of their troubles. He wasn't so much diagnosing illness as reading minds. Lucius' "accurate" diagnoses so astonished patients that they put their full faith in his curative powers. And thus even though the herbal remedies Lucius prescribed had little effect on patients' actual physical disorders, they worked wonders on patients' beliefs.

Other mesmerists had surmised that their patients' beliefs played an important role in their rapid recoveries. But Quimby arrived at a more radical conclusion. He deduced that their beliefs and ideas had caused their illnesses in the first place. He said that our minds are the sum total of our beliefs, and that if a person "is deceived into a belief that he has, or is liable to have a disease, the belief is catching and the effects follow from it."[22] Quimby moved mesmerism one step closer to modern psychiatry by identifying faulty ideas—not magnetic fluids—as the root cause of both physical and emotional disorders. In Quimby's words, "all sickness is in the mind or belief . . . to cure the disease is to correct the error, destroy the cause, and the effect will cease."[23]

It is important to note that Quimby's theory of human illness was not the fully psychological explanation for which many of his interpreters have mistaken it. He viewed patients' beliefs as intervening variables. He held that the real source of human health was the magnetic fluid, or vital force, flowing into the human nervous system from some deeper level of the mind. Beliefs function like control valves or floodgates: They serve to connect or disconnect the conscious mind and its unconscious depths. "Disease," Quimby insisted, "is the effect of a wrong direction given to the mind."[24] When persons identify themselves solely in terms of outer conditions, they place their minds at the mercy of constantly fluctuating external stimuli. As long as the mind is directed outward, it is unreceptive to the inflow of magnetic forces; and, depleted of its proactive energies, the body eventually lapses into disease.

According to Quimby, health can be achieved only to the degree that we overcome self-defeating attitudes. It followed that "the theory of correcting diseases is the introduction to life."[25] If he could just show his patients "that a man's happiness is in his belief, and his misery is the effect of his belief, then I have done what never has been done before. Establish this and man rises to a higher state of wisdom, not of this world, but of that World of Science . . . the Wisdom of Science is Life eternal."[26]

Quimby's gospel of mind cure had a beautiful simplicity about it. Right beliefs channel health, happiness, and wisdom out of the cosmic ethers and into the individual's mental atmosphere. If we can control our beliefs, we will control the shunting valve that connects us to psychological abundance. Quimby's ability to break metaphysical piety down to a set of practical beliefs prompted Steward Holmes to label him the "Scientist of Transcendentalism." By this Holmes meant that Quimby "demonstrated visibly, on human organisms, the operational validity of Emerson's hypotheses. . . . While Emerson arrived at his theories deductively and never submitted them to anything approaching laboratory proof, Quimby forged his theories—and thence his view of ultimate reality—from years of patient experiment with individual persons; something lawful and orderly occurred when he applied his technique."[27]

Quimby's work wasn't really scientific in the normal sense of a fully inductive enterprise. But it surely "worked" in people's lives. A major reason was that many of his patients suffered from the era's predominant religious views: "Religious creeds have made a large class of persons miserable, but religion like all creeds based on superstition must give away to Science. So superstition in regard to religion will die out as men grow wise, for wisdom is all the religion that can stand, and this is to know ourselves not as man, but as part of Wisdom."[28]

What troubled Quimby most about the Protestant theology of his day was its emphasis upon sin—a belief that he traced to a good deal of the nervousness and illness found in his patients. Quimby therefore devoted a fair amount of time to showing his patients how their religious beliefs stood in the way of their ability to live a God-filled life. It was necessary, he thought, for him "to destroy the false opinion in order to relieve the patient."[29] In Quimby's view the Bible offered only a distorted view of the true Wisdom called God. Quimby believed that as much as half of all the diseases he treated stemmed from the fear of death caused by the Bible. To dissolve these fears, Quimby was forced to show his patients just how crude and misleading the Bible could be. For their own highest good he was forced to show his patients "that they have been made to believe a wrong construction. My arguments change their minds and the cure comes. This is my excuse for what I have said upon the scriptures."[30]

Slowly but surely, Quimby formulated conceptions of God and Christ that he found more in keeping with a progressive spirituality. God, he wrote, is not to be thought of in human form. Like the Transcendentalists, he envisioned God as an impersonal spirit pervading the universe. He often referred to God as Wisdom, "an invisible wisdom, which fills all space, and whose attributes are all lift, all wisdom, all goodness and love . . . [which] lets man work out his own salvation."[31] The concept of Christ, for Quimby, was a way of symbolizing "the God in us all." Indeed, Quimby insisted that "every man is a part of God, just so far as he is wisdom."[32] It followed that Jesus should be understood as "a man of flesh and blood, like anyone else. The difference between him and other men was called Christ. . . . Christ is the God in us all."[33] Again, like the Transcendentalists, Quimby envisioned Christ as the great example—not the great exception—of humanity's potentials. Jesus, to a degree greater than most any other human being, demonstrated the life that results from opening oneself inwardly to a higher Wisdom.

Quimby frequently used the words Wisdom and Science to refer to the higher awareness achieved by attaining the "right direction" of thought. He used these words in diverse, and not wholly consistent, ways. His message was nonetheless clear: the human mind is capable of connecting with a more-than-physical reality that is as yet unacknowledged by either our current science or our current churches. In this metaphysical reality "lie all the causes for every effect visible in the natural world, and that if this spiritual life can be revealed to us, in other words, if we can understand ourselves, we shall then have our happiness or misery in our own hands."[34]

Quimby died in 1866. His disorganized set of written notes remained unpublished. Yet he had healed hundreds, perhaps thousands of patients who returned home talking about what he had variously termed Science of Health, Science of Life, or Christian Science. A few of his patients stayed in close contact with Quimby and became students of his Science. It was through these former patients that Quimby's religious views gradually exerted influence on American religious life. The best-known of Quimby's student-disciples was Mary Baker Eddy. She had arrived at Quimby's doorstep in 1862 a desperate patient (sent by her second husband, the dentist Daniel Patterson). The crafty mesmeric healer worked wonders on her and in the process introduced her to an entirely new philosophy of life. Once healed, Mrs. Eddy (the last name of her third husband, Ada Gilbert Eddy) resolved that she, too, could take up a career in mental healing. Soon thereafter she gave her first public lecture, titled "P. P. Quimby's Spiritual Science Healing Disease as Opposed to Deism or Rochester-Rapping Spiritualism." Unfortunately, no sooner had she begun to master her role as dispenser of metaphysical truths, than Quimby suddenly passed away.

Quimby's death temporarily robbed Mary Baker Eddy of her newly found confidence. No longer able to rely on the support of her mentor, she had no other choice but to put her faith in the interior powers which he had awoken in her. She paid her final respects in a poem titled "Lines on the Death of P. P. Quimby, Who Healed with the Truth that Christ Taught in Contradistinction to All Isms." She then resolved to carry the message forward by herself. All she had left was a disorganized collection of notes that she had copied from Quimby's unpublished writings and vague memories of his many attempts to describe the principles of the system he variously referred to as Science of Health or Christian Science. From that point until her death in 1910, Mrs. Eddy worked incessantly at giving literary, theological, and eventually even ecclesiastical embodiment to the science of mental healing.[35]

Mary Baker Eddy's church, the Church of Christ, Scientist (commonly known as Christian Science) became one of the largest native-born churches in American history. Along the way, however, she denounced Quimby and his teachings as "mere mesmerism," and proclaimed total originality for all her important insights. In 1875 she published her most important work, *Science and Health with Key to the Scriptures*. While Quimby's influence is profound, Eddy reworked his ideas and gave them more explicit connection to scriptural passages. Her basic thesis was that God creates all that is, and all that God creates is good. It follows that evil, sickness, or limitation are not rooted in God and thus do not really exist. They are the false constructions of "mortal mind." Illness and health are thus spiritual, not physical conditions. The key to full spiritual living is to discard mental error and to adhere steadfastly to only those thoughts based squarely on metaphysical understanding. Eddy's teachings apparently struck a responsive chord. She lived to see *Science and Health* sell over 400,000 copies and her church attract over 100,000 members. Today Christian Science appears to be declining in membership. But its role in introducing Americans to metaphysical spirituality has been enormous.

Three of Quimby's other patient-disciples proved equally capable of ensuring that his teachings would have a permanent influence on American religious thought. Anetta Dresser, her husband Julius, and Warren Felt Evans all contributed to the evolution of Quimby's teachings into what became known as the mind-cure movement (and eventually known as the New Thought movement). Evans and the Dressers set up healing practices in the Boston area. They eagerly expanded upon what they had learned from the Belfast mesmerist by latching on to almost every metaphysical notion they happened across. Their enthusiasm proved contagious. Cured patients turned into pupils eager to participate in this bold new philosophical quest. The Dressers organized their followers into informal metaphysical discussion groups, which later developed into structured classes. They started charging tuition and awarding credits toward eventual certification in the theory and practice of mind-cure.

Upon graduation, mind-cure students found a new profession awaiting them. Practitioners were able to charge up to five dollars per visit, and the more successful rapidly developed a coterie of followers willing to sign up for course instruction. Boston soon reached the saturation point, prompting many to move westward in search of new clients. Metaphysical clubs sprang up in scattered locales around the country, including New York, Chicago, Kansas City, and finally Los Angeles.

More than 95 percent of those attracted to the study of metaphysical healing lived in urban areas.[36] Many of them had only recently arrived from smaller towns and were still seeking strategies for adjusting to the complexities of their new surroundings. Their names reflect little ethnic diversity, with most suggesting white, Anglo-Saxon, Protestant backgrounds. It also seems safe to infer that the majority belonged to the middle or upper-middle classes, since new recruits were inclined toward attending lectures and setting aside large blocks of time for independent reading. Moreover, mind cure appealed to women over men by a ratio of almost two to one. Middle-class women in the late nineteenth century had more leisure time and far fewer constructive outlets for their energies than did their male counterparts. It is also possible that their social and cultural positions made them more prone to the psychosomatic ailments that could most effectively be cured through mind-cure techniques. In a period in which neither businesses nor churches encouraged women to aspire to roles of leadership, mind cure was a new field in which they might express their otherwise uncultivated potential.[37]

A study conducted in 1890 explored the reasons for public interest in mind-cure. Its major conclusion was straight and to the point: "We have abundant experimental proof of the value of mental practice for the cure of disease . . . we are convinced that it is impossible to account for the existence of these practices if they did not cure disease, and if they cured disease it must have been the mental element that was effective. It is not a thing of the day; it is not confined to a few; it is not local."[38] Nor was it a thing of only medical interest. Those interviewed for this study waxed eloquently concerning their new spiritual outlook:

Knowledge of the creative power of thought stood before me as the one great truth needed to cure the woes of the world. But the supra-naturalism of the church and the materialism of science made and still make both hostile to such a philosophy. A feeling of at-one-ment with the Universal Goodness may be systematically cultivated and may be depended upon to displace all opposites. I became convinced that these things are all law, as exact as any law of physics or chemistry.

I learned to lean upon the ALL WITHIN myself. . . . I listen to the Kingdom of the ALL WITHIN me for the wisdom that never fails. This is the most essential thing I have learned in Mental Science, and this has the greatest influence upon my life. There are millions and millions of forces awaiting our recognition and if we hold ourself receptive to this truth, there is no limit to our growth.[39]

Converts to metaphysically based healing philosophies believed that they were on the verge of a new age in the world's spiritual evolution. They were at last discovering the lawful principles governing the deepest workings of the universe. Mind-cure writers such as the Dressers and Warren Felt Evans were helping them think their way to new understandings of God, human nature, and Christ. The metaphysical interpretation of these concepts was intended to help them unlock the secrets to unlimited spiritual evolution. The movement's most successful writer, Ralph Waldo Trine, made it clear that the mind cure movement was meeting the era's spiritual needs. Americans were crying out for a "religion that makes for everyday life—adequacy for life. Adequacy for everyday life here and now must be the test of all true religion. We need an everyday, a this worldly religion."[40] To Trine, and the more than two million persons who bought his book, the test of all true religion was whether or not it produced psychological results. More specifically, it must enable us to live "in tune with the infinite." Trine inked the New Thought's rallying cry when he proclaimed:

The great central fact in human life is the coming into a conscious vital realization of our oneness with the Infinite Life, and the opening of ourselves fully to the Divine inflow. In just the degree that we come into a conscious realization of our oneness with the Infinite Life, and open ourselves to the Divine inflow, do we . . . exchange dis-ease for ease, inharmony for harmony, suffering and pain for abounding health and strength. To recognize our own divinity and our intimate relation to the Universal, is to attach the belt of our machinery to the power-house of the Universe.[41]

Trine and others in the New Thought movement viewed mental healing as irrefutable proof that "thoughts are forces." Thoughts generate a vibratory field of energy that can be strengthened so that they might become a causal influence upon natural conditions. Trine further described that "in the degree that thought is spiritualized, does it become more subtle and powerful . . . this spritualizing is in accordance with law and is within the power of all."[42] More to the point: "Within yourself lies the cause of whatever enters your life. To come into the full realization of your awakened interior powers, is to be able to condition your life in exact accord with what you would have it. . . . The realm of the unseen is the realm of effects. . . . this is the secret of all success."[43]

New Thought philosophy thus had important connections with its metaphysical forerunners, Transcendentalism and Swedenborgianism. New Thought writers espoused belief that the individual mind is a potential vessel for an indwelling divinity; that the transcendentally awakened persons are the masters of their own destiny; that our inner selves correspond to nature's deeper powers; and that all is well even now if we but expand our spiritual vision. The parallels between these movements attest to the often-obscured symmetry between highbrow and middlebrow cultures. New Thought psychology provided American reading audiences with a kind of reified doctrine of correspondence. The microcosm, or subconscious mind, is in a predetermined harmony with the powers that activate the macrocosm. Students of mind cure, by learning to establish a rapport between their subconscious selves and "the Infinite," could in turn learn to direct powerful cosmic forces.

What the New Thoughters and the Transcendentalists studiously avoided, however, was making any reference to the existence of angels, spirits, or any other kind of personal entities who might be residing in higher metaphysical realms. Most of them considered such belief to be crass superstition, wholly incompatible with their progressive and co-scientific spiritual outlook. But not everyone who found mesmerism to be a royal road to the metaphysical heavens agreed. A young man from Poughkeepsie, New York, began dabbling in mesmerism only to discover that it transformed him into a channel for messages originating in the spirit world. A new avenue of metaphysical exploration had been opened.

THE POUGHKEEPSIE TRANCE CHANNELER

Andrew Jackson Davis was born in Blooming Grove, New York, in 1826.[44] His father, Samuel Davis, was an uneducated farmer, weaver, and shoemaker. The family was poor and young Andrew received only a few weeks of formal education before being apprenticed to a shoemaker in nearby Poughkeepsie. As a youth he attended a Presbyterian church, where he was taught of a "God clothed in Calvinist attributes, also in His eternal decrees of election and reprobation and also in many other points of faith ascribing unamiable qualities to the Deity."[45] Whether out of curiosity or cantankerousness—or both—Davis took it on himself to quiz his religious teachers about the evidence supporting their oppressive religious doctrines. His queries were stifled. He was admonished that it must be a very depraved and hell-bent boy who would dare to question the ways of God as described in the Bible. Davis' dissatisfaction with Calvinism led him to investigate other Protestant denominations. Unfortunately, he fared no better with the Methodists. Their "program for prayer and conversion" failed to satisfy his craving for experiential insight into divine truth. It soon became apparent that no ready-made system of doctrines could contain Davis' spiritual restlessness. He relates that "by another year I was introduced to Universalism. Its teachings were more congenial with my better nature . . . [but] I couldn't believe the Universalist system of theology as a whole."[46]

A quirk of fate rescued Davis from a life of spiritual impoverishment. In 1843 an itinerant mesmerist passed through Poughkeepsie giving lecture-demonstrations on the science of animal magnetism. Davis was fascinated and began experimenting, with the help of a local tailor, William Levingston. As it turned out, Davis possessed extraordinary aptitude for attaining the deepest levels of the mesmeric trance. When mesmerized, Davis performed such feats as reading from books while blindfolded, telepathically receiving thoughts from those in the audience, or traveling clairvoyantly to distant locales. Davis proved so adept at entering the mesmeric trance that he hired himself out as a professional subject and for a time toured New England, exhibiting his miraculous powers (especially that of diagnosing and prescribing cures for illness).

After several months of repeated journeys into the recesses of his mind, Davis abruptly declared that mesmerism had activated "some of the many powers which we know to rest in the soul's deep bosom."[47] The mesmeric trance state opened Davis for a sacramental encounter with "higher realities." Using language invoking the metaphysical concepts of correspondence and influx, Davis explained that "when an individual human mind . . . reaches nigh unto the spirit-world, then spiritual enlightenment and direction flow into the soul's affections and understanding."[48] Visionary experiences followed. In one such vision he met the spirit of Galen, who gave him a magic staff and charged him with the mission of healing (something that Davis made central to his peculiar ministry until his death in 1910). Of far greater importance, however, was the appearance of the spirit of Emanuel Swedenborg, who promised Davis that he would instruct and guide him as he continued to open himself to spiritual enlightenment. From that time forward Davis learned to enter into special revelatory trance states on his own, without the aid of a mesmeric operator. And, while in these states, he was guided by Swedenborg to discover the grand secrets of the universe.

In 1845 Davis traveled to New York, where he teamed up with Dr. Silas Lyon, a physician with an interest in mesmerism, and Rev. William Fishbough, a Universalist minister with an extraordinarily eclectic range of philosophical interests. During a period extending almost two years he entered into a self-induced mesmeric trance and delivered metaphysical lectures that he believed were dictated from the spirit world. Numerous persons came to observe this curious communication with the spirit world. Among them were Edgar Allan Poe (who later mused that "There surely cannot be more things in Heaven and Earth than are dreamt of in *your* philosophy"), the utopian spiritualist and communitarian Thomas Lake Harris, and the Swedenborgian-inspired professor George Bush. The Rev. Fishbough oversaw the transcription of these lectures and, in 1847, fifty-seven of these lectures delivered "by and through Andrew Jackson Davis, the 'Poughkeepsie Seer' and 'Clairvoyant'" were published in a two-volume work entitled *The Principles of Nature, Her Divine Revelations, and A Voice to Mankind*. The book contained an encyclopedic overview of sundry cosmological issues and set the agenda that Davis would

Spiritualist and Advocate of the Divinity of Every Person
Credit: American Antiquarian Society.

continue to pursue in the more than thirty books that would follow. Perhaps the most important of his other books was the five-volume treatise, *The Great Harmonia*. Here Davis supplemented the metaphysical scheme sketched out in *The Principles of Nature* and announced his own utopian vision, which seemed to be a combination of mesmerist psychology, Swedenborgianism, Transcendentalism, and the communitarian ideals of Charles Fourier.

Davis' revelations depicted a universe that is both structured and lawful.[49] The basic principles of the universe, not surprisingly, are correspondence and influx. It seems that there is a series of concentric "spheres" of increasing beauty and wisdom. These spheres are ordered hierarchically. At the top of the hierarchy is God, the source of all life and force. God is the source of all vital influences that radiate outward through the various levels or spheres, finally reaching our earthly sphere. God's influence permeates the universe, drawing us onward and upward toward higher spiritual attainment. Davis described God as a "Spiritual Magnet," the "irresistible Magnet which attracts upward the human soul."[50] Divine influence surrounds us, communicated through an electricity-like ether that serves as "the vehicle or medium of divine vitality." God uses this ultrafine spiritual substance "as a medium of communication to all parts and particles of the universe."[51]

Occupying the spheres between earth and God are spirit beings of progressively higher levels of spiritual attainment. Each of these spirit beings is on his or her own spiritual journey toward perfection and increasing proximity to God. They receive spiritual influences from above and, in turn, pass them on to those below them in the hierarchy. Humans, who occupy the lowest sphere, can avail themselves of wisdom and support from spirit guides immediately above them in the cosmic order. Upon death, humans ascend to a higher spiritual sphere in direct accordance with the spiritual progress achieved during their earthly life.

Three features of Davis' harmonial cosmology deserve special consideration. The first is the glorified role it accords science. Every sphere along the cosmic scale operates according to lawful principles that are in basic correspondence with those operating in all other spheres. Thus truth could be found within (through direct mystical experience) or without (through scientific inquiry). Religion thus has nothing to fear from science. True spirituality should embrace science as a way of extending our understanding of spiritual law and beauty. Second, Davis' cosmology emphasized the principle of spiritual progress. The whole purpose of creation, both in this life and those following our physical death, is to present us with opportunities for growth and progress. Davis contrasted his metaphysical vision of spheres with traditional Christian views of heaven and hell. Whereas Christian doctrine breeds fear or despair, his cosmology points persons in the direction of hope and ongoing spiritual aspiration. Davis had "perfect faith in the divinity of every man" and envisioned the universe as the great training ground where that divinity progressively manifested itself. Third, Davis' universe is populated with spirit beings who yearn to provide us with comfort, guidance, and wisdom. These spirits are responsible for the "special providences" we receive from time to time. Communication with them thus provides proof of life after death (and that this afterlife consists of endless opportunities for eternal spiritual progress). It also provides direct and immediate assistance with the vexing details of human life. Davis, and the spiritualist movement that followed him, introduced a "personal" element to American religion. American Protestantism repudiated belief in the efficacy of prayer to saints or the Virgin Mary. The God depicted by Protestant denominations was, furthermore, typically seen as distant and remote. American Protestants thus had to face life's rigors without the consolation that Catholics found when they sought intercession from the quasi-human personages of Mary and the saints. Even the metaphysical traditions of Transcendentalism, mesmerism, and Christian Science postulated an impersonal deity (and criticized those Swedenborgians who proclaimed belief in angels). Spiritualism's belief in the existence of spirit guides who take a personal interest in our lives (and who are in a position to mediate on our behalf) was thus an appealing alternative to either conventional Protestant theism or rational metaphysics.

Davis' belief in ongoing spiritual progress committed him to concrete programs of social reform. He used his influence in both the New York Spiritual Association and the National Association of Spiritualists to prevent them from becoming solely focused on the phenomenon of mediumship. He desired instead to organize spiritualists into volunteer activities that would help usher in a new age of worldly and spiritual attainment. In 1863 Davis formed the Children's Progressive Lyceum, which he designated "an association for the mutual improvement of children of all ages, and both sexes, from two years to eighty."[52] Davis believed that spiritualists were in a special cultural position to oversee programs for educating children without imposing traditional Sunday-school moralism upon them. His lyceum was designed to develop healthy bodies and stimulate the reasoning faculties in such a way as to foster "the progressive unfolding of the social and divine affections by harmonious methods."[53] Davis later organized the Moral Police Fraternity as a social service agency dedicated to reducing crime, instructing the uneducated, providing aid to the poor, and helping the unemployed find suitable work. In addition to his concern for progressive social reform, Davis retained a life-long interest in spiritual healing. Disease, in his view, is a direct consequence of spiritual disharmony. Cure thus requires restoring a person's harmony with the laws of nature. Davis enrolled in a school of medicine in New York that was sufficiently eclectic to allow him to pursue his interest in combining spiritual and scientific perspectives on healing. Earning his doctorate in medicine in 1883, Davis opened a medical office in Boston and, until his death in 1910, practiced an irregular form of medicine that relied upon his clairvoyant abilities for diagnosing disease and prescribing medicine.

It is clear that Davis saw himself a prophet of a new stage in humanity's religious consciousness. This new stage could come into being, however, only when the tyranny of existing religions had been fully overcome. In a steady stream of publications Davis railed against the abuses of his era's religious institutions. "Institutionalism," he argued, stifles our human spirit and forces us to abandon our individual conscience in order to conform to man-made doctrines. His second wife, Mary Fenn Davis, put the matter even more forcefully when she argued that when "ecclesiastical regulations merge into customs; individualism ceases; and men become automatons, and exist for centuries on a dead level of mental slavery and conservatism."[54] Davis and other spiritualist leaders devoted considerable energy to attacking the institutional church. Davis was also an outspoken critic of the Bible, going so far as to organize an anti-Bible convention in Hartford, Connecticut, in 1853. The harmonial philosophy underlying early spiritualism emphasized ongoing spiritual progress, leaving no need for the doctrine of vicarious atonement central to orthodox Christianity. The person of Jesus, then, was irrelevant to Davis' theological concerns. Making a distinction between the person of Jesus and the concept of Christ, Davis predicted the coming of an age in which every person would act upon the "Christ-Principle," which he described in terms of "loving forgiveness, womanly gentleness, and a hospitality of the soul."[55] These, he proclaimed, would be the distinguishing marks of all who follow the eternal principles of "Association, Progression, and Development" and studied the "fixed laws of Science and the immortal principles of Philosophy."[56]

Davis' writings attracted considerable attention among intellectuals. His books were reviewed widely and generated discussion among those inclined to metaphysical speculation. But Davis' work would probably never have had a wider impact had it not been for the popular spiritualist movement that had its roots in the activity of the Fox sisters. In 1847 (four years after Davis commenced his career), John D. Fox, his wife, and six children moved to a new home in Hydesville, New York. Shortly after moving in, they claimed to hear mysterious rapping noises. Two daughters, Maggie and Kate, became brave enough to clap their hands and snap their fingers in an effort to elicit these knocking sounds. A series of raps responded to their initiative. Soon a simple code of communication was set up between the Fox sisters and the invisible spirit who apparently resided in their home. With time Maggie and

Kate learned that the spirit who made these rapping noises was that of a murdered peddler whose remains were buried in the cellar of their home. News of the Fox sisters' sensational communication with the spirit world traveled rapidly. They had, it seemed, stumbled upon dramatic proof of life after death. Within months they were national celebrities.

The Fox sisters understood the commercial value of their newfound ability to make contact with the spirit world. They charged admission to their seances and in no time at all spiritualism proved to be a lucrative enterprise. Other spirit "mediums" followed their lead and attracted audiences eager to pay for the right to witness this fascinating spectacle. The spiritualists' seances were part sideshow entertainment, part shaman-like encounter with awesome supernatural powers. Some mediums were able to produce slates on which spirits had written special messages. Others used their spirit contacts to perform feats of telepathy and clairvoyance. All offered solace to those who came hoping to hear that departed loved ones were safe in their new heavenly existence.

Andrew Jackson Davis found himself the official philosopher of the early spiritualist movement. His harmonial cosmology was, with minor modifications, taken as canonical among the thousands attracted to this new religious outpouring. Davis, however, wasn't completely comfortable with his role. He claimed that most spirit mediums were too interested in the "outer" aspects of spiritualist phenomena. Many were, and for understandable reasons. A large number of those drawn to spiritualism believed that they were in a position to demonstrate the existence of life after death in a thoroughly scientific manner. They consequently sought to establish communication with the spirit world as an objective, empirical fact. For this reason they had little sympathy for "inner" or "subjective" states of mind. And, of course, there were always other spirit mediums who were interested almost exclusively in the entertainment aspect of the whole séance phenomenon. Davis chided those who were only concerned with the sensational elements of mediumship. He was also critical of those who focused almost exclusively on establishing empirical evidence of the existence of spirits. All of this was of relatively minor significance to him. Indeed, the main purpose of spiritualism to him was philosophical and religious. Its concern was not with establishing objective evidence of higher spiritual realms but with "individual improvement and spiritual communion."[57]

Davis opened up intellectual and religious lines of thought that, in retrospect, can be seen as the most liberal, progressive, and liberating of his generation.[58] His new religious ideology reflected the spiritual yearnings of a wide spectrum of Americans dissatisfied with the existing religious establishment. Foremost among these were women who were tired of religious institutions dominated by male clergy. Spiritualism emerged at a time when no churches ordained women and forbade them to speak aloud in church. In contrast, the spiritualist movement offered women equal authority, equal opportunities for positions of leadership, and equal access to divine inspiration. Spiritualism was, furthermore, sensitive to women's interest in religious language that emphasized their relationship with God. Spiritualist leaders paved the way for innovations in the way we describe God so as to balance male and female imagery. Another contingent of early spiritualists consisted of persons eager to reconcile religion and science. Most middle-class Americans admired science and accepted its growing cultural prestige. They were, however, unsettled by its materialistic tendencies. Those who embraced spiritualism argued that it would at long last furnish empirical evidence for the basic truth of religion—that there is more to the universe than can be detected with the senses alone. Spiritualism thus promised to move religion past reliance on either blind faith or a literal interpretation of the Bible. Instead, spiritualism freed persons to explore the spiritual spheres of life in the same way that science investigates the world of nature. Curiosity and free-thinking inquiry could now be affirmed as the keys to a genuine spirituality.

When all is said and done, however, the main reason for spiritualism's popularity (then or now) is that it contained a thrilling experiential element. Attending a séance is an eerie, awe-inspiring experience. It promises to bring one face-to-face with supernatural entities who possess mysterious powers. Such encounters are exhilarating. They suggest that there is far more to our universe than is being taught by either science or religion. All this is in stark contrast to the "extraordinary dullness" that most converts to spiritualism associate with established churches. Andrew Jackson Davis thus succeeded in pioneering a movement that to this day inspires many Americans to adopt a starkly metaphysical religious outlook. Even though Emerson despised the kind of spirit communication that Davis engaged in, spiritualism was probably more effective than Transcendentalism in bringing basic metaphysical themes to the attention of the general public. From the early spirit mediums to today's "trance channelers," spiritualism has introduced millions to such enduring metaphysical beliefs as the immanence of God, the spiritually destructive nature of orthodox Christianity's message of sin, and the need to seek God both in nature and within the self.[59] These beliefs also became prominent in the liberal religious thought that was to dominate mainstream Protestantism at the dawn of the twentieth century. And, too, they were prominent in the single most creative thinker in the history of American philosophy, psychology, and religion—William James.

ℰ

Liberals, Conservatives, and Unchurched Seekers

The Legacy of William James

THE LATE NINETEENTH CENTURY WAS A TUMULTUOUS PERIOD in American religious life. Social and intellectual change seemed to outpace religious innovation. Culture lag set in, forcing religion to play "catch up" as Americans adjusted to wholly new ways of living and thinking. These conditions prompted historian Arthur Schlesinger to label the final decades of the century "the critical period in American religion." Between 1875 and 1900 the churches struggled "to adjust to the unprecedented conditions created by rapid urban and industrial growth. American Protestantism, the product of a rural, middle-class society, faced a range of problems for which it had neither the experience nor the aptitude."[1]

Adjustments eventually came. The first major response was the rise of theological liberalism. The liberal or modernist stance embraced the new cultural climate and modified Christian doctrines to suit the progressive temper of the age. Inevitably, however, others would call the new America into question and reaffirm the fundamentals of biblical faith. This second response, the rise of fundamentalist theology, sharpened the theological debate between opposing groups of Christians. To this day American Christians, Protestant or Catholic, must eventually locate themselves somewhere on the religious spectrum spanning the great distance between the liberal and fundamentalist positions. Jews have similarly aligned themselves along a continuum ranging from modernist (Reform) to traditional (Orthodox) understandings of faith. Yet even as American religion divided between the liberal and fundamentalist positions, a third response to the modern cultural situation was emerging. It embraced the importance of personal spirituality, but rejected the need for membership in a church or adherence to a specific theological creed. This response, the decision to be "spiritual, but not religious," would be championed by one of the greatest thinkers that America has yet produced, William James.

THE NEW SOCIAL CLIMATE

Immigration, urbanization, and industrialization combined to launch post – Civil War America along a new and vaguely defined path. From 1865 to 1900, more than thirteen million immigrants arrived on American shores. Another nine million came in just the first decade of the twentieth century. Given the fact the nation's population in 1865 was only thirty million, this influx of foreign-born citizens completely reconfigured the cultural landscape. Of further significance was the fact that a large number of these immigrants had languages, customs, and religious affiliations that differed from their Yankee "hosts." In 1850 only 5 percent of the total population was Roman Catholic. But, beginning in 1870, continuing waves of Irish, German, and Italian Catholic immigrants began to erode the hegemony formerly enjoyed by Anglo-Saxon Protestants. By the first decade of the twentieth century, one out of every three church members in the country was Catholic. New Protestant groups also appeared, threatening to rearrange the nation's traditional power structure. Lutherans poured in from Germany and Scandinavia, soon overtaking Presbyterians and Congregationalists to become the third largest Protestant group in the nation (behind Baptists and Methodists). Jews, too, began to immigrate in sizable numbers. While there were as few as 250,000 Jews in the United States in 1880, that number increased almost tenfold in the span of just three decades.

Most of the immigrants who arrived on American shores headed straight for the cities. There they joined the growing influx of native-born citizens who migrated to the cities in search of economic opportunity. The thirty years immediately following the Civil War saw almost every urban center in the Northeast triple in size. They were no longer large towns but massive metropolitan complexes. This transition from landscape to cityscape thrust American culture onto untested ground. Slums, crime, political conflict, and a myriad of logistical problems cluttered the American cityscape. Social blight served as a constant reminder that the realities of American life were a far cry from the cherished vision of the nation as a land of kindred spirits working toward common goals. The loss of social homogeneity proved to have a profound impact on the country's self-interpretation. For better or worse, white, Anglo-Saxon Protestants and their way of life were being displaced from the center of the national experience. Many among the WASP mainstream began pointing fingers at those they held responsible for eroding inherited patterns. A Methodist minister in New York, for example, singled out a few of the culprits by compiling a long list of what he described as the "forces opposed to the extension of Protestantism." At the top of the list were urban crowding, saloons, Romanism, and "a foreign element" that refused to be assimilated.[2] This list is, in retrospect, a kind of sociological epitaph of WASP moral and spiritual leadership. The increasingly pluralistic character of American society made it increasingly difficult for Protestants to impose their pattern upon American life. Whether Protestantism's gradual loss of religious hegemony should have been celebrated or bemoaned, one thing was apparent to most: the United States seemed a society without a core, lacking centers of authority and information that might have given order to such swift social changes.[3]

The problems of urbanization went hand in hand with those of industrialization. The factory soon replaced the farm as the symbol of the nation's productivity, leaving wage earners utterly mystified. An agrarian economy provides individuals with a relatively simple vision of economic opportunity:

success is a function of the expenditure of time and energy. An industrial order, however, doesn't permit such straightforward calculations. Few nineteenth-century Americans had the vision to see something objectively "out there" around which to set their sights and harness their energies. They lacked rules for reducing their complex world into manageable proportions. And without ready-made guides for action, many floundered. All the while American society was dividing into three main groups: (1) the definitely victorious, who were regarded as cultural heroes; (2) the definitely defeated, who were without hope of rising above the urban slum; and (3) the middle group, who were ceaselessly searching for the right set of beliefs to guide them through the maze of modern life.

It would be no exaggeration to say that the "glue" that had previously bonded American society together had evaporated. The United States was less a melting pot of world cultures than a grab bag of divergent peoples. One of the era's church spokespersons, Washington Gladden, lamented that American society had splintered into "scattered, diverse, alienated, antipathetic groups." Gladden was sensitive to the fact that intensified conflict over economic resources had eroded the very basis of community feeling.

> It is not very many years since society in this country was quite homogenous; the economical distinction between capitalist and laborer was not clearly marked. . . . But our national process has given full scope to the principle of differentiation. . . . Anyone can see that progress, under a system like ours, must tend to the separation of men, and to the creation of a great many diverse and apparently unrelated elements. Under this process men tend to become unsympathetic, jealous, antagonistic; the social bond is weakened.[4]

American culture was losing its organicity. What Gladden called the "centrifugal motion" of modern life was intensifying our human tendencies to be unsympathetic. A major challenge to American religion would be to evolve new ways of cultivating empathy for the social "other." In truth, many churches have never learned to do this well. Religion in America remains divided along racial, ethnic, and socioeconomic lines. Fortunately, a few voices have spoken out about these divisions and have suggested new spiritual patterns that address matters of race, gender, and class. We will revisit these issues and explore two such revolutionary voices in the next chapter.

THE NEW INTELLECTUAL CLIMATE

The last two decades of the nineteenth century witnessed a remarkable shift in Americans' understanding of themselves and their place in the wider universe. Science was rapidly altering the way that educated people thought about the forces affecting their lives. The scientific method focused upon the observable laws of cause and effect; it had no room for ideas that could not lend themselves to empirical confirmation. This method demonstrated its superiority over competing intellectual systems on an almost daily basis. The technological advances ushered in through scientific achievement gave humans control over areas of life that were formerly thought to be governed by fate or by the whims of God. By comparison, religion appeared anemic. Belief in miracles or supernatural intervention seemed the stuff of ancient folklore.

Darwin's theory of biological evolution became the focal point of the cultural clash between science and religion. In the academic world, Darwin won. By 1880 virtually every important scientist in the United States had been converted to the new worldview. This new scientific view filtered into the educated public's awareness in a surprisingly brief period of time. The theory of evolution, after all, meshed perfectly with Americans' progressivist and forward-looking character. It seemed almost ideally suited to an optimistic people eager to learn that progress and development were intrinsic to the very laws of nature. Yet the challenge that evolutionary science presented to religion was both blunt and unavoidable. The theory of evolution by itself doesn't invalidate the possibility of taking a religious perspective upon the world. But it does force people to acknowledge that the Bible does not contain factual information. This discrepancy between two competing avenues to truth, science and biblical religion, caused an entire generation of American college students to experience an acute tension between head and heart, rationality and faith. Most had no choice but to choose what all their rational faculties showed them to be the most intellectually defensible: science. Many who in earlier eras would have chosen careers in the ministry instead opted for careers in science, philosophy, or the newly founded fields of psychology and sociology.

Evolutionary science did more than undermine belief in the literal truth of the Bible. It also eroded the entire foundation of evangelical Christianity: the view that God created humans to be perfect, but through willful disobedience they fell into the condition of sin. The biblical worldview presupposes that humans are fallen due to perverse self-centeredness and stand in need of redemption. Evolutionary science, however, provides a very different view of human nature. It shows humans to be an integral part of the larger web of life on this planet. True, the human genetic code does include a variety of instinctual tendencies that are aggressive and "animalistic." But a relatively large cerebral cortex gives humans the potential to act in creative, environment-transcending ways. It is even possible from a scientific perspective to be guardedly optimistic about humanity's potentials for even greater progress, growth, and development.

The challenges that science presented to religious belief were matched by those emerging from the field of modern biblical scholarship. While the most penetrating biblical scholarship would come a few decades into the twentieth century, the basic outlines of its attack on conventional piety were already clear before the turn of the century. Academic scholars began using the techniques of scientific history and careful linguistic analysis to examine the origins and authorship of Jewish and Christian texts. Their sophisticated analyses established beyond scholarly dispute that the Bible was the work of numerous authors who collected, edited, and arranged their source materials according to their own conceptions of religious truth. Modern scholarship therefore made it impossible to view the Bible as a "delivered once and for all" revelation from God. The Bible was instead now seen to be a collection of ancient writings whose original purpose was to witness to its authors' personal faith, not to convey factual information. It is, after all, difficult to defend the doctrine of biblical inspiration when confronted with irrefutable evidence that the supposed "books of Moses" were written by several different writers at different times in history. Educated persons were similarly dissuaded from simple biblical literalism when they learned that the accounts of Jesus' life included in the New Testament were not eyewitness accounts. Indeed, scholarly studies of the New Testament reveal that the accounts of Jesus' life were written between thirty and seventy years after his death. Viewed in historical context, these accounts appear to be far less concerned with providing an objective biography than with proclaiming the faith of the believing community.

A further blow to confidence in the "absolute truths" of biblical religion came from increased awareness of other cultures. Previous generations of Euro-Americans had enjoyed the luxury of being fairly ignorant about the non-Western world. The Jewish and Christian bibles make it natural to think that God is especially interested in Jews and Christians, making them the recipients of His true plan for humanity. By the twentieth century, however, Americans had to learn to confront the "other" and the possibility that cultural conditioning accounts for why each part of the world has its own "one true religion." The study of comparative world religion brought this point home in a particularly vivid way. The Transcendentalist writer James Freeman Clarke published the *Ten Great Religions* in 1871, encouraging readers to find spiritual edification in Eastern faiths such as Hinduism, Buddhism, and Confucianism. Clarke's volume found a receptive audience and eventually went through twenty-one editions. Walt Whitman furthered Americans' interest in nontraditional forms of mysticism in such works as *Leaves of Grass* and *Passage to India*. In 1892 the World's Parliament of Religions was held in Chicago in connection with the Columbian Exposition. The event attracted more than 150,000 visitors to exhibits and lectures offering sympathetic introductions to the teachings of the world's great religions. The event was also covered in almost every newspaper and popular magazine, helping a wider reading audience discover that Judaism and Christianity did not possess a monopoly on lofty religious teachings. Confucius, after all, taught the Golden Rule nearly 500 years before the birth of Jesus. Global awareness brought the stark realization that every religion has a sacred text that it considers divinely revealed. Thus, depending upon the part of the world in which persons are born, they will in all likelihood learn to proclaim the Hindu Vedas, the Buddhist Lotus Sutra, or the Muslim Quran as "the one true scripture." Thoughtful people have found it increasingly difficult to pledge blind allegiance to any one religious tradition.

Yet another challenge to conventional religious faith came from the new academic disciplines of psychology and sociology. The growth of science in the late nineteenth century created interest in the academic study of "psychology without a soul." The first generation of academic psychologists were, almost without exception, former seminary students or sons of Protestant ministers.[5] They had grown uncomfortable with biblical religion. They were instead inspired by the era's progressivist spirit and set themselves to the task of describing "the good person" and "the good life" on a purely academic and scientific basis. Early sociologists, too, eschewed biblical faith and instead studied the nature of "the good society" through an empirical study of human behavior. The cumulative effect of these two disciplines on American culture has been considerable. Whereas earlier generations often turned to a minister of the Bible for guidance in times of personal distress, today persons are more likely to look to a psychologist or pick up a self-help book based on social scientific models of personality adjustment.

Leading theorists in the burgeoning disciplines of sociology and psychology argued that religion is a retrogressive social force. Karl Marx (1818-1883), an economic historian, believed that religion diverts our attention away from the actual forces that determine human happiness. He argued that religion induces us to ignore the real social and economic forces that affect the quality of human life by causing us to focus instead on such intangible things as a heaven or an afterlife. Marx realized that belief in an afterlife comforts people in their misery by reassuring them that they will be compensated for their suffering when they reach heaven. But such comfort, according to Marx, works in the same way that opium does. It gives suffering persons an illusory feeling of well-being but does absolutely nothing to improve the conditions that actually cause this misery. Marx's message was clear. If we wish to better the condition of humankind, we must first give up the unproductive kinds of thinking fostered by religion and instead tackle our problems in a rational, technical manner.

Sigmund Freud (1856-1939) also viewed religious belief as an outmoded, superstitious form of thinking. He acknowledged that life is hard to endure. We are powerless in the face of natural disasters, accidents, disease, and death. The prototypical human response to our fundamental weakness is "to humanize nature"—to envision supernatural beings who have the power to help and protect us if they are so inclined. Once we believe the world to be governed by beings similar to ourselves, we are no longer entirely helpless. We can hope to gain at least some control by attempting to bribe, appease, or cajole these supernatural beings much the way we would persons in our daily lives. Freud further observed that we tend to visualize these supernatural beings in the image of a father figure who, though stern, can be implored to watch out for and protect his family. We thus find ourselves yearning for a heavenly father who will protect us if we beg and flatter (i.e., pray and worship). The idea of God, then, is not based upon any empirical evidence or rational process. The idea of God has its origins in the human wish for protection against the dangers of existence. Yet a belief that is held only because we want it to be true is nothing more than an illusion. It rests on nothing other than wishful thinking. Freud thus used modern psychology to portray religion as a form of psychological weakness. However understandable the psychological need for religion, it stands in the way of us taking a more rational, problem-solving approach to life. Freud believed that only scientific rationality can lead us to a more productive future. Fully mature persons must therefore abandon the illusion of religion and face life in a fully rational manner.

Freud didn't publish his psychological critique of religion until the 1920s. By this time, however, American psychologists had long since been using social scientific concepts to debunk the conversion experience.[6] Conversion, they argued, can be fully explained as an exaggerated instance of normal developmental processes. The implication was that even the "best" part of the older biblical view of the world had now been subsumed under this scientific, progressive academic discipline.

Many "free thinkers" around the country felt emboldened by the modern intellectual climate and set off on a pilgrimage from religion to science. The best known of these, Robert G. Ingersoll, became the nation's leading agnostic. A lawyer living in Peoria, Illinois, Ingersoll had been raised the son of a conservative Protestant minister. The father's hellfire and brimstone religion fueled his son's later iconoclasm. In 1877, Ingersoll made his first transcontinental lecture tour, earning him the reputation as the revivalist of Free Religion. For the next thirty years large audiences paid for the right to hear him lambaste the religious establishment. Ingersoll's printed lectures, *The Gods* (1872), *Some Mistakes of Moses* (1879), and *Why I Am an Agnostic* (1896) extended the reach of his attack on Christian faith. Suffused throughout Ingersoll's rebellion against institutional religion was his faith in human nature. He, like many of the period's nonbelievers, had confidence that worldly progress was inevitable once the shackles of religion are fully discarded.

Biblical religion had come under full assault from the forces of modernity. The cultural battle lines had been drawn and few could escape the pressure to commit themselves to one side or the other.

THE RISE OF RELIGIOUS LIBERALISM

By the last two decades of the nineteenth century many church leaders concluded that religion must accommodate itself to the new social and intellectual climates or risk becoming irrelevant. The liberal or modernist impulse in American religious thought emerged to help the churches adjust to the new cultural order.[7] The most prominent liberal clergyman of the era, Henry Ward Beecher (1813-1887), was keenly aware that the churches were in danger of being left behind by "the intelligent part of society."

> There is being now applied among scientists a greater amount of real, searching, discriminating thought . . . than ever has been expended . . . in the whole history of the world put together.

> If ministers do not make their theological systems conform to the facts as they are, if they do not recognize what men are studying, the time will not be far distant when the pulpit will be like a voice crying in the wilderness.

> The providence of God is rolling forward in a spirit of investigation that Christian ministers must meet and join.[8]

Liberal theologians embraced the basic tenets of modern biblical schol-arship. They no longer adhered to a literal reading of scripture. Instead, they made a distinction between what might be called the "verbal inspiration" and the "personal inspiration" of the Bible. Belief in the verbal inspiration commits one to accept a literal reading of the Bible as the inerrant, infallible words of God. Belief in the "personal inspiration," however, entails believing that biblical authors were indeed inspired by God but that their attempt to communicate these insights were necessarily colored by their personal and historically limited knowledge of the world. The liberal view of scripture thus retains faith in the revelatory nature of scripture while nonetheless permitting modern readers to move from a literal to a symbolic interpretation of passages that conflict with contemporary culture.

Once freed from a literal reading of the Bible, liberally minded church members adjusted their beliefs to fit the progressive spirit of the age.

Ironically, it was precisely the era's evolutionary and psychological sciences that furnished the principal imagery used to make religion relevant to modern understandings of the world. In such influential works as John Fiske's *Through Nature to God* (1899), Lyman Abbott's *The Theology of an Evolutionist* (1897), and John Bascom's *Evolution and Religion* (1897), evolution became the new paradigm for Christian cosmology. God was increasingly described in pantheistic imagery. Abbott, for example, contended that God was no longer to be understood as a separate entity residing in a celestial kingdom, but as "the Infinite and Eternal Energy from which all things proceed."[9] Fiske defined God as "the Power which is disclosed in every throb of the mighty rhythmic life of the universe."[10] When Fiske proclaimed that "evolution is God's way of doing things," he was simultaneously opening up new ways of viewing humanity's role in furthering divine providence. He and other theistic evolutionists believed that humans are inwardly linked with God's providential spirit. He declared that "the lesson of evolution is that . . . [the soul] has been rising to the recognition of its essential kinship with the ever-living God."[11] Abbott amplified this important implication of religious liberalism when he declared that the "foundation of spiritual faith is neither in the church nor in the Bible, but in the spiritual consciousness of man."[12] It follows that whatever contributes to the development of humanity's "spiritual consciousness" furthers the progressive evolution of our universe.

Denominations whose members were most likely to have college educations, such as Congregationalists, Episcopalians, and Presbyterians, gradually drifted to moderate theological positions. They no longer charged their members to read the Bible literally. Many church members thus came to hold liberal (i.e., nonliteral) views about such issues as biblical miracles, the Virgin Birth, or the likelihood of a literal Second Coming. Even within such traditionally conservative groups as Roman Catholics, Baptists, and Lutherans, theological divisions emerged. Thus, for example, American Baptists are rarely as conservative as Southern Baptists. Members of the Evangelical Lutheran Church of America are far less likely to hold strict biblical views as are members of the Missouri Synod Lutheran Church.[13]

Something along the lines of a theological spectrum emerged, differentiating religious denominations according to their theological outlook. Unitarians (renamed the Unitarian-Universalist Association in 1961) occupy the far left or liberal end of the spectrum. Then, in rough order from left to right come the Congregationalists, Presbyterians, Methodists, Disciples of Christ, Episcopalians, ELCA Lutherans, American Baptists, Roman Catholics, Missouri Synod Lutherans, Holiness and Pentecostal churches, and Southern Baptists. By the mid-twentieth century this liberal-conservative split became the most important factor in American religious identity. That is, it is now far less important which specific denomination a person belongs to than whether he or she takes a more liberal or more conservative approach to that denomination's teachings.

The first few decades of the twentieth century were receptive to the liberal religious stance. It is estimated that by 1920 liberal ideas had become accepted in more than a third of all Protestant pulpits in the country.[14] The liberal outlook was even more predominant in theological journals and monographs, accounting for at least half of all the formal writing done by church scholars in the early twentieth century. Other kinds of liberal expressions abounded. For example, many denominations embraced the emerging discipline of psychology as a tool of effective church ministry. Seminaries offered training in various kinds of pastoral counseling, adopting the dominant therapeutic models of secular psychology.[15] Many pastors, as would later be exemplified in the best-selling books of Rev. Norman Vincent Peale, actually incorporated psychological theories into their theological message concerning human wholeness and well-being.[16]

Another expression of religious liberalism was the "social gospel" movement. The social gospel had its origins in nineteenth-century evangelicalism's emphasis upon born-again persons joining voluntary organizations aimed at the renovation of American society. Societies were created for such causes as prison reform, urban renewal, and aid to the poor. These voluntary organizations paved the way for later efforts among liberal church leaders to replace "creeds" with "deeds" as the center of Christian faith. Washington Gladden, for example, placed such strong emphasis upon the Golden Rule that Christian commitment was soon seen to include concern for the rights of labor. Walter Rauschenbusch transformed his experiences as a pastor among poor immigrants in New York City into an articulate theology of social action. He steadily developed a "Christian socialism" that called persons of faith to commit themselves to the concrete task of building the Kingdom of God. The titles of his major books reflect his conviction that religious faith entails serious commitment to social causes: *Christianity and the Social Crisis* (1907);

Christianizing the Social Order (1912); and *A Theology for the Social Gospel* (1917). Other liberals were even more influenced by the era's secular thought and urged a more "scientific" approach to worldly activism. These progressive thinkers embraced the modern social sciences as the key to meaningful religious action in the world. All in all, liberals were turning attention from the afterlife to this life; from reliance upon the miraculous intervention of God to the concerted efforts of humans; from worshipping Jesus as God incarnate to emulating Jesus as a model for ethical living.

Liberalism manifested itself differently in Judaism. Since ancient times Jews have found themselves a religious and ethnic minority. They have characteristically lived apart from the broader population, sometimes by choice and sometimes by governmental coercion. Even when they have lived among Christians they have preserved their identity as a "separate" people by adhering to Talmudic customs. In the United States, however, the situation has been slightly different.[17] American Jews have always been a religious and ethnic minority (in 1800 there were only about 2,000 Jews in the United States), but they have never been forced to live in isolation as they often had to in Europe. Because Jews were free to assimilate into American life, many came to regard the ancient Talmudic laws as irrelevant to the modern world. Thus, when the American Jewish population steadily grew to 150,000 by 1860, many were thus quite receptive to the Reform movement that began in Germany in the 1840s.

The leader of Reform Judaism in America was Isaac Wise (1819-1900). After immigrating to the United States in 1846 he was first a rabbi in Albany, New York, and then relocated to Cincinnati (which to this day is the major center for training Reform rabbis). Wise founded and edited a paper, the *American Israelite*, which disseminated Reform views. Wise encouraged American Jews to affirm the possibility of the ongoing development of Jewish faith. This entailed distinguishing between the Torah (the first five books of the Bible) and the Talmud (the collection of ancient moral and religious practices). Reform Judaism believes that the Talmud reflects the customs of an ancient culture and thus possesses no authority upon modern Jews. Reform Jews, therefore, are free to disregard kosher dietary laws and need not wear the yarmulke (prayer hat). Wise and other Reform leaders also discarded belief in a personal Messiah who will lead Jews back to the land of Palestine. They neither expected nor desired such a return to ancient Israel, professing

PROPORTIONAL DENOMINATIONAL STRENGTH AMONG
JUDEO-CHRISTIANS IN THE UNITED STATES: 1890

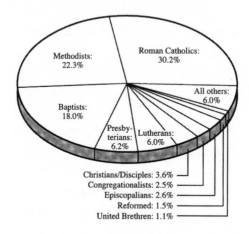

instead loyalty to the nation to which they belonged by birth or citizenship.
And, even more boldly, Reform Jews teach the equality of rights for women
(including the right of ordination as a rabbi), substitute English for Hebrew
in weekly worship services, and hold Sabbath worship on Friday evening
rather than on Saturday.

What distinguishes Reform Judaism as "liberal" is thus more than theological outlook. It also entails a greater willingness to accommodate to the
wider culture. Reform Judaism was the most dominant form of Judaism in the
early twentieth century. Immigration patterns after 1940, however, brought
an increasing number of Orthodox Jews to America. Both Orthodoxy and the
third expression of Judaism, Conservative Judaism, appeal to those Jews
seeking greater continuity with historic traditions. Both have witnessed
considerable growth in size and influence during the past twenty years. It is
difficult to arrive at an accurate statistical breakdown of American Judaism.
One recent survey of religion in America, for example, suggests that as few
as 5 percent of all American Jews are Orthodox, 40 percent are Conservative,
and 55 percent are Reform.[18] Yet another recent study suggests that approx-

imately 40 percent of all synagogues are now Orthodox, with the remaining 60 percent about equally divided between Reform and Conservative.[19]

Those religious organizations that incorporated liberal elements became known as "mainline" denominations. What distinguishes a group as mainline is that its theological outlook permits its members to participate fully in the wider sweep of American life—its basic patterns of entertainment, academic thought, and lifestyle. Denominations that have a significant presence of liberal elements thus readily fit the designation of being mainline. Their members embrace religious beliefs in a way that enables them to feel very much at home in American culture. Congregationalists, Presbyterians, Episcopalians, Lutherans, and Methodists are the clearest examples of mainline denominations. Although the term is most commonly used to designate Protestant denominations, Roman Catholics, Reform Jews, and Conservative Jews also embrace religion in ways that permit full accommodation to American culture. Of course some members of all these denominations (especially some conservative-leaning Presbyterians, Methodists, and Missouri Synod Lutherans) might be at greater theological odds with certain social trends, but the denominations as a whole fit part and parcel with the broader American way of life. Baptists should probably be considered at the boundary of mainline religion. Although most Baptist groups probably conform to the basic patterns of Americans, others—notably Southern Baptists, the largest Protestant denomination in the country—are sufficiently clear about their rejection of modern culture that they exist outside the mainline configuration.

Members of mainline denominations have traditionally occupied positions of considerable power and influence in American society. They tend to be better educated and to earn more income than those who belong to more conservative religious groups. Episcopalians, Presbyterians, and Congregationalists, for example, are three times more likely to appear in *Who's Who in America* than their actual percentage of the national population. In the early twentieth century it appeared to most observers that liberal trends would eventually dominate American religious life.

A trial held in Dayton, Tennessee, in July of 1925 came to symbolize the apparent triumph of liberal religion and culture. John Scopes, a young biology teacher fresh out of college, was charged with violating Tennessee's statute making it illegal to teach "any theory which denies the theory of the Divine creation of man as taught in the Bible, and to teach instead that man is descended from a lower order of animals." The "Scopes Monkey Trial," as it came to be known, attracted worldwide attention from the press, whose coverage totaled over two million published words. The judge barred testimony on the validity of the Darwinian theory of evolution. The sole question at issue was whether Scopes had, or had not, actually taught Darwin's theory. Scopes' guilt should have taken only a minute or two to ascertain. Instead, the trial lasted eleven days and came to resemble a prize fight more than a legal process. Famed criminal lawyer Clarence Darrow defended Scopes, while the equally famed politician William Jennings Bryan assisted the prosecution. The climax of the trial was Darrow's articulate cross-examination of Bryan, during which he revealed that Bryan was profoundly ignorant of both biological science and the Bible. Scopes was found guilty and fined $100, but public sentiment went resoundingly against the conservative cause, which came across to the nation as backward and intolerant.

Most liberals—both those belonging to mainline churches and those in secular culture—assumed that ultraconservative religion was destined to whither away. Members of mainline churches were, after all, far more likely to be among the country's political and economic elite. It thus appeared that hard-line conservatives were restricted to the "culturally deprived" residing in places such as the backwoods of Kentucky or the hollows of Tennessee. Yet nothing could have been further from the case. Conservative religion was poised to stage a dramatic comeback. The remainder of the twentieth century would witness remarkable gains for conservative-leaning denominations and a serious loss of membership for most mainline groups.

THE CONSERVATIVE REVIVAL

Religious conservatives continued to make up a share of every American denomination (with the exception of Unitarian-Universalists). It wasn't until liberalism emerged, however, that conservatives had specific issues around which to define themselves. By the second decade of the twentieth century conservatives were in danger of being displaced from center stage. They would need a new theological strategy if they were to avert being forced to the margins of American life. Many did precisely this by self-consciously refusing to accommodate to the new sources of cultural authority and prestige. They emphatically reaffirmed the fundamentals of Christian faith over and against current intellectual trends. What we today call fundamentalism represents the conviction among conservative Christians that modernism needs to be resisted in the name of biblical faith.[20]

In the broadest sense, fundamentalism refers to concern with evangelism and biblical values such as has been found historically in conservative Protestant religion. Yet in a narrower sense, fundamentalism must be considered as a distinct subset of conservative, Bible-oriented faith. It was Curtis Lee Laws, editor of a Baptist paper, *The Watchman Examiner*, who coined the word "fundamentalists" and used it to denote those who were ready "to do battle royal" for the fundamentals of faith.[21] What distinguishes fundamentalism from other expressions of conservative religion is thus its self-conscious opposition to the influences that modernism has had within both the church and the wider scope of American culture.

The "over and againstness" that fuels fundamentalist convictions is reflected in its emphasis upon four interconnected themes: biblical inerrancy, premillennialism, evangelism, and separatism. The insistence upon biblical inerrancy was a rallying cry in the war against liberalism. The Bible was to be affirmed as true in everything it touches upon, including the details of the origins of life on earth. Belief in the inerrancy of the Bible was also a way of drawing renewed attention to the prophecies contained in Daniel and Revelation. Daniel and Revelation are apocalyptic texts. That is, they describe the events that are predicted to occur as the forces of God conquer the forces of evil at the end of the world. These texts prophecy an impending final judgment and vividly describe the eternal paradise awaiting faithful Christians and the horrible punishment awaiting their modernist adversaries. This theological outlook came to be known as "premillennialism" because it predicts the Second Coming of Christ before a thousand-year period during which the world will be rejuvenated. Premillennialists thus embrace the cultural chaos surrounding them, remaining confident that the forces of Christ will eventually triumph over all sinners and doubters.[22] Belief that the "end-times" are near heightens the sense of expectancy and encourages all-out, unquestioning fervency. It also provides the reassurance that, in the twinkling of an eye, the tables will be reversed; the faithful will suddenly find themselves in control of a new world order while the enemies of Bible-believing Christians will be vanquished from the earth.

The groundswell of popular support for the fundamentalist cause came in part from the continued success of revivalism. Dwight L. Moody (1837-1899) adapted revivalism to the new urban environment. Born in Northfield, Massachusetts, Moody moved to Chicago, where he became a successful businessman at an early age. He then became involved with the local Y.M.C.A., where he began perfecting his skills as an evangelist and organizer. Teaming up with a song leader, Ira Sankey, Moody transformed old-fashioned revival meetings in such a way as to ensure their success in large urban areas. Moody's preaching style was warm and inviting, but the substance of his message was stern. He believed in biblical infallibility, taught the imminence of Christ's return to judge the wicked, and called for Bible-believing Christians to separate themselves from the sinful world. Moody's lasting achievement was the new level of organization he brought to the revivalist enterprise. He left nothing to chance. He formed committees well in advance of his revivals to plan advertising campaigns and begin fundraising efforts. Moody also created committees that would ensure a successful follow-through, including one in charge of preparing "decision cards" that newly converted persons could fill out in order to receive follow-up calls from local pastors. Moody's successes in large cities and on college campuses encouraged others to follow his pattern. The twentieth century witnessed a steady parade of successful urban revivalists, including Billy Sunday, Billy Graham, Jack Van Impe, Jimmy Swaggart, and Pat Robertson.[23]

Revivalism probably hasn't been very successful at convincing either secularists or liberals to abandon modern cultural thought in favor of simple Bible-based teachings. But it has reinforced the faith of those who were already committed to the conservative outlook. The conservative cause became increasingly self-confident as the twentieth century progressed. Thus, for example, during the 1970s both Missouri Synod Lutherans and Southern Baptists began ejecting liberal-leaning theologians from their seminaries and resolved to stake their futures to the cause of conservative religion. They, and other groups like them, were rewarded for their efforts. Throughout the second half of the twentieth century, most mainline denominations lost membership.[24] Congregationalists (The United Church of Christ), Presbyterians, Episcopalians, Methodists, and Disciples of Christ all lost upwards of 20 percent of their memberships over the past several decades. Meanwhile, conservative churches prospered. Baptists grew over 20 percent.

Roman Catholicism, partially owing to immigration and large families, held to its conservative teachings and also grew about 20 percent. And the nation's fastest growing groups were the most conservative of all: Seventh-Day Adventists, the Church of Jesus Christ of Latter-day Saints, the Church of the Nazarene, and the Assemblies of God. All are ardently fundamentalist and are characterized by their adherence to biblical inerrancy, premillenni-alism, separatism, and evangelism.

Churches belonging to the Holiness and Pentecostal movements provide the most dramatic example of the rise of conservative religion during the twentieth century. The United States was introduced to what might be called "the Wesleyan impulse" in the early nineteenth century. John and Charles Wesley, founders of the Methodist denomination, emphasized that the experience of salvation is not sufficient without the further commitment to a life of ongoing sanctification. Sanctification entails a life concerned with personal holiness. "The Wesleyan impulse" thus predisposed a sizable number of Americans to equate personal piety with a well-ordered life that demon-strates commitment to ongoing moral perfection. This includes separating oneself from the secular world and its sinful amusements such as drinking, swearing, dancing, or card-playing. The Wesleyan impulse thus inclined many Americans to equate true Christian faith with a willful desire to dedicate themselves solely and completely to ongoing moral perfection, sinlessness, and personal piety.

At first the Methodist denomination embodied the basic characteristics of this quest for personal holiness. Yet, over time, the Methodist denomi-nation gradually moved toward mainstream adaptation to the broader American way of life, leaving those interested in this Wesleyan style of personal piety to gravitate to new religious groups. A cluster of these groups, known collectively as Holiness Churches, now have a combined member-ship of over two million members. Principal examples are the Church of God (Anderson, Indiana), Church of God (Cleveland, Tennessee), and Church of the Nazarene. They are all strongly fundamentalist. They have a strong interest in the Second Coming of Christ (and the need to prepare for final judgment by separating themselves from worldly vices). And, importantly, they believe that Christians must be concerned with more than the initial blessing of salvation. They must also open themselves fully to the Holy Spirit so that they might receive a distinct second blessing, the power needed for a life of ongoing sanctification. It is believed that such openness to the Holy Spirit may also lead to a distinct third blessing, the blessing of charismatic gifts.

A second cluster of religious groups born of the Wesleyan impulse is known as the Pentecostal movement. Closely related to the Holiness movement, Pentecostal churches emphasize this third blessing—the external and visible signs of the Holy Spirit known as charismatic gifts. Pentecostals believe that they are fulfilling Jesus' promise that his followers would be baptized with the spirit and with fire.[25] The Book of Acts records that ten days after the ascension of Christ, on the Jewish holiday of Pentecost, a small group of Christ's followers were filled with the Holy Spirit. It is written that they began to "speak in tongues"—a form of divinely inspired prophecy that can be interpreted only by persons also under such direct contact with the Holy Spirit. This speaking in tongues, also known as glossolalia, is only one of the charismatic gifts mentioned by Paul. Other such gifts of the spirit include prophecy, new interpretation of the Bible, the power of healing, and the recognition of spirits.

The Pentecostal experience does not center on speaking in tongues per se. It is instead concerned with fully opening one's life to the Holy Spirit. Being filled with the Holy Spirit automatically gives rise to the external and visible display of one or more of the charismatic gifts. The Pentecostal experience is exhilarating. It encourages individuals to open themselves to a felt encounter with God's gracious spirit. Pentecostalism promises that by opening ourselves to the inflow of the Holy Spirit we can expect miraculous transformations in our lives.

Pentecostal enthusiasm is scattered across many conservative Protestant churches. It also appears in Roman Catholicism, where it is known as the Charismatic Movement (though the movement is not nearly as conspicuous today as it was in the 1970s). Yet as many as three million Americans belong to churches that distinguish themselves by overtly emphasizing the Pente-costal experience. Most Pentecostal churches are locally organized, bearing names indicating their commitment to the "full gospel" or the experience of being "fire baptized." There are also several denominations set up around the centrality of the Pentecostal experience, including the International Church of the Foursquare Gospel and—one of the fastest-growing religious groups in the United States—the Assemblies of God.

Conservatism manifests itself somewhat differently in Roman Catholicism and Judaism. A key issue in American Catholicism is the authority of the church to speak on matters of faith and morals. "Liberal" Catholics believe that individual members of the church must be free to follow their own conscience, especially on issues of personal morality. A significant minority of American Catholics quietly opt for liberal theological ideas in a manner similar to their Protestant counterparts. But what draws most attention in Catholicism are observable instances (e.g., the use of birth control, failure to attend mass regularly, divorce and remarriage) of ignoring the dictates of priests, bishops, and the pope. The late twentieth century witnessed a flurry of liberal protest from such well-known clergy as Daniel Berrigan, John Dominic Crossan, Charles Curran, Edward Schillebeeckx, and Hans Kung. Yet for all the sympathy that liberal-leaning lay Catholics have had with such maverick theologians, the majority of American Catholics have apparently opted to remain committed to papal authority and the hierarchical structure of the Church. Many continue to dissent quietly and on a personal level, but the conservative tone of the larger Church has prevailed into the twenty-first century.

Reform Jews rose to the forefront of American Judaism precisely because their members integrated so well into mainstream American life. In the 1930s and 40s, however, a new influx of Jewish immigration began bringing Jews who were deeply committed to traditional theology and cultural practices. Orthodox synagogues began to multiply, first in the greater New York metropolitan area and eventually spreading to other urban centers throughout the country. Orthodox Jews continue to use Hebrew in services, to hold Sabbath services on Saturday, to keep men and women separate during religious functions, to restrict the rabbinate to males, to abide by kosher dietary rules, to have males wear the yarmulke at all times, and to follow the intricacies of Talmudic law. Yet a third branch of Judaism, Conservative Judaism, stakes out something of a middle ground between the Reform and Orthodox modes of observance. Conservatives believe that religion does change over time, but choose to honor most traditional Jewish beliefs and customs. It is possible that the Conservative movement has benefited from the Reconstructionist Movement headed by Mordecai Kaplan in the 1930s. Kaplan had emphasized the importance of Jewish traditions and ceremonies even for those who were not religiously inclined, encouraging American Jews to find meaning in their cultural heritage. Conservative Judaism has been far more interested in preserving traditional elements of Jewish culture than has Reform Judaism. Thus, for example, Conservatives observe kosher dietary principles (but in a more relaxed manner than do Orthodox Jews). They use some English in their services. Conservative males typically wear the yarmulke at worship services, but not at other times. The Conservative approach to Judaism seemed to become more popular during the last few decades of the twentieth century. Many young Jewish families made a conscious effort to recapture their religious and cultural heritage and consequently embraced Conservative Judaism. Again, while it is difficult to obtain precise figures, some estimates suggest that as many as 40 percent of all synagogues in the United States are Orthodox; with an additional 32 percent being Conservative.

The last several decades, then, have seen conservative religion thrive. While scholars had long predicted that the modern intellectual and social climates would lead to the gradual secularization of American culture (as it had in Europe), the opposite turned out to be the case. A loyal liberal contingent persists, but conservative religion continues to dominate the nation's religious institutions. All the while, however, a third style of American spirituality has gone almost unnoticed. The "seeker style" has steadily prospered to the point where it now exerts tremendous influence on American religious life. Its most eloquent spokesperson, William James, helped Americans carve out a path where they might pursue a vital personal spirituality, but remain aloof from the doctrines and rituals of institutional religion.

THE LEGACY OF WILLIAM JAMES

William James (1842-1910) was born into a family that assured his early introduction to the modern intellectual climate.[26] He later studied science at Harvard and the challenges facing religious thought in the modern world. Although trained as a scientist, he rejected scientism—the view that the physical sciences can exhaustively account for the universe. William James possessed a tremendous sense of curiosity. It was as though he was fated to spend his life wrestling with the great questions concerning the ultimate origins and meaning of life. He asked, for example, Why are there so many forms of religious belief, when each religious system proclaims the one, universal truth? And, for personal reasons, he asked, Does religious belief make any practical difference in our lives?

William James always seemed to have more religious questions than answers. He deeply longed for a spiritual philosophy that he could have intellectual confidence in. He insisted, however, that any system of ideas worthy of our allegiance must be grounded in scientific fact. James spent his entire lifetime piecing together a spiritual outlook that bypassed both the liberal and conservative religious positions that most of his contemporaries felt forced to chose between. Instead, he struck out in a third direction—the path of being spiritual at a personal level, yet having no affiliation with organized religion.

William's father, Henry James Sr., had inherited a sufficient fortune to devote his energies to philosophical and theological investigations. He was a close friend of many of the era's most progressive thinkers, including Emerson, who frequently visited the James home to engage in lively discussion. Henry became enamored of the era's metaphysical religious systems, particularly Swedenborgianism, with its central doctrines of correspondence and influx. He even expanded upon Swedenborg's ideas in his own, largely ignored publications. He was determined that his children would make original contributions to the world, and provided them with expensive educations, private tutors, and numerous trips to European cultural centers. One son, Henry Jr., became a gifted novelist. But it was the oldest son, William, who was destined to emerge as one of the greatest intellectuals in American history.

After a brief stint as an artist, William knew he had to pick a more conventional career. His father's example gave him little help. His father had made a habit of dabbling in grandiose metaphysical theories, seizing upon elaborate theoretical schemes that seemingly explained the entire universe. Unfortunately, William was unable to affirm any such "once and for all" system of truth that might help him figure out what direction he should follow. He was an especially sensitive young man and soon began to crumble under the weight of trying to know what one, true vocation and meaning his life was to have. He developed nervous disorders that were to plague him the rest of his life. Chronic insomnia, eye trouble, digestive problems, and back pains were cruel reminders that his upbringing had done little to help him come to grips with the physical world. He had no direction in life and his despair continued to worsen. At a deep emotional level he yearned for religious relief. Unfortunately, he had long before ceased believing in a God "up there" who hears our prayers and who occasionally chooses to intervene miraculously on our behalf.

William James was in many ways a prototype of modern individuals who yearn for a grand spiritual dimension to their life, yet feel alienated from conventional religious beliefs. He was destined to have to fight his way to an original religious outlook that moved beyond—not ignored—modern intellectual difficulties with organized religion. By gradually assembling a spiritual philosophy that helped him restore his sense of personal vitality, William James—as the psychologist Erik Erikson has said of Martin Luther—was able "to lift his individual patienthood to the level of a universal one and try to solve for all what he could not solve for himself alone."[27] The first step on this pilgrimage was his humble recognition that "if we have to give up all hope of [depending upon God] as vain and leading to nothing for us, then the only thing left to us is will."[28] He needed a more stable reality to lean upon than conventional religion could provide. James demanded a religious humanism; that is, a religious outlook grounded solely on what humans can truthfully claim to know, what they can achieve, what they can willfully accomplish with their own mental and emotional abilities. He worked gradually at building a new spiritual outlook, beginning with shreds of evidence from the natural sciences, from psychology, and from philosophy. Only in this way could he develop a spirituality that could stand up to the modern social and intellectual climates.

James eventually earned a medical degree from Harvard and joined its faculty to teach physiology. A few years later he opened up a laboratory for the study of psychology. The next several years of his career were devoted to the new field of scientific psychology. And, eventually, he published what is heralded as the finest textbook in the history of American psychology.[29] Science, however, bored William. His desire was to develop a philosophical system that would synthesize his scientific and religious interests. He subsequently left the field of psychology for philosophy (although retaining interest in psychological issues). He helped pioneer one of the only philosophical systems to originate in the United States—pragmatism. Pragmatism sought to ground philosophy in the evolutionary outlook that dominated American intellectual circles. It views all human activities in terms of our

Pioneer of Unchurched Spirituality
Credit: Harvard University Archives

ongoing struggle to adapt to our environment. Pragmatism consequently interprets ideas in terms of their ability to guide us to productive relationships with our surroundings. A form of modern relativism, pragmatism is skeptical about all claims of "absolute truth." Pragmatism focuses solely on the human attempt to fashion sensory information into ideas that can orient us toward satisfying activity. Ideas and beliefs are hypotheses that need to be tested in the ongoing stream of human experience. Hence pragmatism's only concept of truth is "what works best in the way of leading us, what fits every part of life best and combines with the collectivity of experience's demands, nothing being omitted."[30]

James had never been brought up to believe in the Bible. He thus never understood how so many of his contemporaries were able to accept these ancient writings as factually reliable information. Nor was he able to believe in Christianity's basic message that salvation was made possible through Jesus and Jesus alone. James viewed most of what passed for religion in his day as the product of social conditioning. He didn't, however, want to throw out the baby with the bath water. He was convinced that a truly comprehensive philosophy of life must address the great mysteries of the nature and meaning of life. And, although he was not a mystic himself, he was especially curious about mystical experiences. He once confessed that there was something "in me" that "makes response" when hearing mystics describe their experiences of a reality undetected by our present sciences. The possibility that we live in a wider, spiritual universe led him to conclude that science alone is an insufficient guide "to the collectivity of experience's demands, nothing being omitted."

James devoted a significant portion of his life to the task of constructing a philosophy that might combine the best of both science and religion. He believed that a modern spiritual philosophy must—like science—be built from the "ground up." It must have a factual basis that will distinguish it from the superstitions of "revealed religion." But where might we begin looking for the factual evidence that might support a spiritual outlook on life?

The first place that James turned was the scientific investigation of psychic phenomena.[31] He joined the American branch of the Society for Psychical Research, even serving a term as its president. James devoted considerable amounts of time and energy investigating psychics and trance mediums. He and his colleagues used contemporary scientific procedures to investigate alleged instances of spirit communication, telepathy, and clairvoyance. They were able to show that the vast majority of these cases were nothing more than examples of simple deception or outright fraud. Yet a few cases baffled them. James pointed out that even a single confirmed case of paranormal activity would be sufficient to show the limitations of modern science and force even the toughest-minded intellectuals to acknowledge the existence of metaphysical realities. As he put it, "If you wish to upset the laws that all crows are black, you mustn't seek to show that no crows are; it is enough if you prove one single crow to be white."[32] James was confident that he at last came upon one such white crow. A trance medium by the name of Mrs. Lenora Piper was able to give him information that he knew could not have been obtained through fraud or deceit. He obviously couldn't be certain that Mrs. Piper received the information from a "spirit" in the spirit world as she claimed. There were other possible explanations such as some form of telepathy. The incident was nonetheless an important beginning point for him to think his way back to religion. He believed that he now had positive evidence that there was more to the universe than can be accounted for in our current scientific models. This was enough to inspire him to continue to investigate experiences that occur at the margins of ordinary human awareness.

While engaged in his work for the Society for Psychical Research, James came across the work of the British investigator W. F. Myers. Myers had extended the early mesmerists' study of the unconscious mind and proposed his own theory of "subliminal consciousness." According to Myers, "each of us is in reality an abiding psychical entity far more extensive than he knows— an individuality which can never express itself completely through any corporeal manifestation. The Self manifests through the organism; but there is always some part of the Self unmanifested; and always, as it seems, some power of organic expression in abeyance or in reserve."[33] This unmanifested aspect of the self lies just beyond the margins of ordinary consciousness. The subliminal range of consciousness contains various kinds of information that are just out of the reach of everyday awareness: silly jingles, imperfect memories, inhibitions, etc. Myers and James believed, however, that there are further reaches of the subliminal Self that give rise to performances of genius. They also had reason to believe that at a level even further removed from ordinary awareness we connect with a "cosmic consciousness" extending far beyond our socially constructed self.

James had once experienced the subliminal reaches of consciousness on his own. One day while conducting research in his Harvard laboratory he inhaled nitrous oxide gas. He was instantly overwhelmed by a "tremendously exciting sense of an intense metaphysical illumination." Reflecting on this experience a few years later he observed:

> Some years ago I myself made some observations on this aspect of nitrous oxide intoxication, and reported them in print. One conclusion was forced upon my mind at that time, and my impression of its truth has ever since remained unshaken. It is that our normal waking consciousness, rational consciousness as we call it, is but one special type of consciousness, whilst all about it, parted from it by the filmiest of screens, there lie potential forms of consciousness entirely different.[34]

James was convinced that the concept of the subliminal reaches of consciousness provided the key to understanding religion. He accepted an invitation to deliver the prestigious Gifford Lectures in Edinburgh, Scotland,

and used the occasion to show how a "psychology of the unconscious" can lead to a spiritual philosophy that doesn't depend on the Bible, organized worship services, or an institutional church. He titled his lectures, "The Varieties of Religious Experience: A Study in Human Nature." With literary flair and philosophical precision, James carefully marshaled the evidence to support his view that the core of genuine spirituality is inner, mystical experience. To prove his point James gathered hundreds of diaries and autobiographies written by "articulate and self-conscious" religious leaders over the course of history. He was not particularly interested in "your ordinary religious believers, who follow the conventional observances of their country, whether it be Buddhist, Christian, or [Muslim]. Their religion has been made for them by others, communicated to them by tradition, determined to fixed forms by imitation, and retained by habit."[35] Ordinary religion, he contended, was arrived at secondhand from others. If he was to examine the real essence of religion he must turn instead to those who acquired religion firsthand, those for whom religion "exists not as a dull habit, but as an acute fever."[36]

James proceeded to walk his audiences step by step through the classic religious experiences recorded in history. He explored conversions, nature mysticism, theistic mysticism, and all sorts of spiritual rapture. The question was, How can we account for such a variety of religious experience? The answer, he contended, was that the root and center of religion is personal mystical experience. Theology, ritual, and institutional forms of worship are "secondary products, like translations of a text into another tongue."[37] The process of translation, however, inevitably colors the original experience with the translator's own culturally and historically conditioned terminology— thus adding "local and accidental" elements to the original experience that initially gave rise to these insights.

James argues that the varieties of religious experience constitute facts equal in importance to any other facts assembled about the human condition. These facts lead to particular conclusions about humanity's spiritual nature:

> The farther limits of our being plunge, it seems to me, into an altogether other dimension of existence from the sensible and merely "understand-able" world. Name it the mystical region, or the supernatural region, whichever you choose. . . . Yet the unseen region in question is not merely ideal, for it produces effects in this world. When we commune with it,

work is actually done upon our finite personality, for we are turned into new men, and consequences in the way of conduct follow in the natural world upon our regenerative change.[38]

James' scientific inquiry into the further reaches of human consciousness had thus led him a long way. It convinced him of "the continuity of our consciousness with a wider spiritual universe from which the ordinary prudential person (who is the only person that scientific psychology, so called, takes cognizance of) is shut off."[39] In exceptional moments the ordinary threshold of awareness lowers, the valve opens, and we become continuous with resources that conventional science never recognizes. What is more, the spiritual energies yield regenerative effects available in no other way. They bring inner-expansion and delight, opening up vistas of the universe that take our breath away. Moreover, they give us "another kind of happiness and power, based upon giving up our own will and letting something higher work for us, and these seem to show a world wider than either physics or philistine ethics can imagine."[40]

Personal spirituality—far from being a backward force of personality—could thus be seen as necessary to a fully vital life. James knew that many intelligent persons actually refuse to hold religious beliefs because there isn't compelling evidence to support them. He countered that we should not avoid religious beliefs just because "pure reason" cannot establish their validity. Beliefs of many kinds are absolutely necessary in the "doing" of life (the task of "practical reason"). There are important moments in which we must act without rational certainty. Deciding whether to accept a religious attitude toward life is one of these occasions. Our rational intellect alone cannot give us complete certainty. In such an instance, however, we are philosophically justified in adopting (at least tentatively) those beliefs that promise to bring us into productive relations with our surrounding environments. James points out that in many cases beliefs actually produce the very confirming evidence that will support them. Consider, for example, coming across another person in a room and trying to decide whether they are friendly and will reciprocate a handshake. If we believe they won't respond amicably and refuse to initiate a greeting, we will produce that very result. If, on the contrary, we extend our hand we are likely to generate the very results that will confirm this belief. James observes that "there are, then, cases where a fact cannot come at all unless a preliminary faith exists in its coming. And when faith in a fact can help create that fact, that would be an insane logic which would say that faith running ahead of scientific evidence is the 'lowest kind of immorality' into which a thinking being can fall."[41]

Religious beliefs, James argued, support the fullest expression of human nature. They interpret the world in ways that elicit our energetic action. Religious views of life open up an infinite perspective, helping us to think in terms of a longer time frame (eternity). They also encourage us to cooperate with God's world-building, wholeness-making activity. If we look objectively at world history it is hard to escape the conclusion that the highest flights of charity and service have soared on the wings of religious faith. Thus even though James thought that all the actual beliefs proclaimed by existing religious institutions were intellectually absurd, he nonetheless acknowledged that they often perform important functions in our lives. The basic problem with religious beliefs, James cautioned, is that we tend to forget that they are merely hypotheses. Their purpose is to guide us toward meaningful activity in the world. They didn't appear magically from the heavens as absolute truths. Instead, we create them out of certain kinds of experience and we must continuously revise them as new experience warrants.

James reckoned that the actual facts of religious experience don't justify the many doctrines preached in our churches. In fact, all that religious experience actually warrants is the threefold belief (1) that the visible universe is part of a more spiritual universe from which it draws it chief significance; (2) that union or harmonious relation with that higher universe is our true end; and (3) that prayer or inner communion with the spirit thereof—be that spirit "God" or "law"—is a process wherein spiritual energy flows in and produces effects, either psychological or material, within the phenomenal world. Anything beyond this bare skeleton of belief takes us into the realm that James designates as "over-beliefs." Here psychological and cultural factors exert increasing influence upon our efforts to "translate" experience into coherent beliefs.

James argued on both psychological and moral grounds that the most interesting thing about a person is the kind of "over-beliefs" he or she holds. This is particularly true of a person's over-belief concerning the nature of God. The kind of God we believe in determines the overall stance we take toward life. James criticized the conceptions of God typically found in America's churches. Belief in an all-powerful God too easily fosters passivity on our part. The omniscient, omnipotent God of conventional theology induces us to rely upon divine intervention rather than exert our own self-initiated action. James countered that all that the actual facts of religious experience support is that the power we encounter is both other and larger than our conscious selves. This power need not be omnipotent. It need not be infinite.

James had sound moral and spiritual reasons for preferring to believe that God is finite. Whether God is finite or infinite makes pragmatically different ethical demands upon us. If we understand God as finite, then the ultimate outcome of the universe is truly undetermined. There can be real gains and losses. The final outcome might well depend upon our actions. In a very real sense, then, we and God have business with one another. By opening ourselves to divine influence we regenerate our personal energies, rekindle our identification with other living beings, and reinvigorate our action on behalf of the wider cause of life. Yet the future is still up for grabs. The final outcome is dependent upon the strength and appropriateness of our worldly actions.

All of James' "over-beliefs" about God were predicated upon the fact that we live in an evolving universe. God, to him, must be understood pantheistically, as a power or directional urge pushing the universe toward greater wholeness and completion. Thus critical to any spiritual outlook on life is a firm belief in the melioristic character of our universe. Meliorism is the principle that the world is capable of improvement, progress. Belief in the possibility—but not inevitability—of improvement was to James the cornerstone of a vital spirituality. It was also the only real meaning that the concept of salvation had for him. "Meliorism," James wrote, "treats salvation as neither necessary nor impossible. It treats it as a possibility, which becomes more and more of a probability the more numerous the actual conditions of salvation become."[42] We, and we alone, have responsibility for seeing that these "actual conditions" of wholeness and unification are brought into concrete existence. And thus, James observes, "one sees at this point that the great religious difference lies between those who insist that the world *must and shall be*, and those who are contented with believing that the world *may be*, saved."[43] Embracing our role as co-creators of an evolving universe demands intelligence, planning, and effort on our part. This mode of spirituality demands courage. It means adopting beliefs without absolute certainty. It requires committing ourselves to the ongoing amelioration of life without total assurance of the final outcome.

James, then, steered a middle course between the competing worldviews of science and religion. The universe he envisioned was wild and woolly. Throughout his entire life he remained open to the possibility of genuine "paranormal" phenomena. He had personally witnessed too many possible instances of extrasensory perception, mental healing, and trance mediumship to exclude the metaphysical contours of experience. And, of course, he had observed his own white crow—forever impressing upon him that science cannot be the sole and ultimate dictator of what we may believe. But James was not gullible. He never surrendered his critical, questioning intellect. He knew that it is human nature to jump to beliefs that at the moment appear convincing, but that do not hold up under sustained scrutiny. Group consensus and social reinforcement predispose us to adopt beliefs in a way that almost inevitably leads to sheer superstition, intolerance, or sectarian antagonism. James expressed hope that a "science of religion" will one day emerge to help eliminate the tribal and accidental elements from religious belief. It is possible, he thought, to abandon dogmatic reasoning in religion and, instead, create a co-scientific spirituality based upon critical, inductive methods of reasoning.

James was a daring religious thinker. He insisted that spirituality is not about churches or even about God, but about "the love of life." As he put it, "Not God but life, more life, a larger, richer, more satisfying life, is in the last analysis the end of religion. The love of life, at any and every level of development, is the religious impulse."[44] James was therefore suggesting that anyone moved by the love of life, eager to contribute to its development "at any and every level" is expressing a spirituality as vital—if not more vital—than that found in a formal worship service.

What is more, James was advocating a decidedly metaphysical and mystical spirituality. He thus responded to the spiritual needs of those of his contemporaries who yearned to establish intimate relations with a "spiritual More." The spirituality he envisioned was a thrilling, exciting one. It includes the possibility of finding ourselves inwardly "continuous with a MORE . . . which is operative in the universe outside of us, and which we can keep in working touch with."[45] Such encounters have a decidedly numinous, awe-inspiring quality to them. And, importantly, they need not be sought through the avenues defined by the institutional church.

William James succeeded in sketching the outlines of a spirituality that has become increasingly popular in recent decades. He encouraged modern, secularly educated Americans to continue to ask the question of their relationship to divinity and to humanity, but to do so in fully humanistic terms. One of the first to follow his lead was Bill Wilson, the founder of Alcoholics Anonymous and the Twelve Step tradition underlying so many of today's therapeutic systems.[46] Wilson was acutely aware that we do not contain the resources within ourselves needed to overcome profound personal distress. The only way to overcome serious inner division is essentially spiritual in nature, requiring us to develop a sense of what Wilson called "God-consciousness." Yet Bill W. (as he is called within the Alcoholics Anonymous movement) was wary of organized religion. He was particularly critical of the judgmental moralism associated with biblical religion. In his experience more alcoholics had been harmed than helped by institutional religion. He rejected traditional religious dogma and confessed that "in all probability, the churches will not supply the answers for a good many of us."[47] James' writings, however, inspired Bill W. to understand that spirituality need not entail entanglements with institutional religion. James prompted Bill W. to consider the possibility that certain experiences connect us with a MORE from which we might receive saving influences, yet these experiences might better be understand in psychological, rather than theological terms. Bill W. went on to describe A. A. as "a spiritual rather than religious program." This phrase has subsequently come to symbolize a distinctive modern spiritual orientation.

Today one out of every five Americans is spiritual at a personal level, but has no affiliation with a religious institution. William James is obviously not the only source of this strand of contemporary spirituality. An account of all the other historical roots of America's "spiritual but not religious" tradition would require a separate book.[48] Nineteenth-century metaphysical traditions such as Transcendentalism (Emerson), mesmerism (Quimby), spiritualism (Davis), all played a role. So, too, have various humanistic psychologists, advocates of alternative healing systems, and American enthusiasts of Asian religious and meditation traditions. Together they have given rise to a wide variety of unchurched forms of American spirituality. And, in so doing, they have created yet a third religious response to the modern social and intellectual climates that has made it possible for millions to proclaim themselves to be spiritual, if not fully religious.

ℰ

The Surfacing of Muted Voices

Paul Tillich, Mary Daly, and James Cone

THE UNITED STATES EMERGED FROM WORLD WAR II a confident nation. Democracy and the American way of life had triumphed over totalitarian regimes. Opportunities awaited the creative energies of a booming capitalist economy. Americans were eager to harness science and technology to the nation's relentless pursuit of progress.

This confident spirit seemed to spill over into American religious life as well. Americans seemed to agree that religious faith is critical to a democratic society. Shared beliefs help forge unity among otherwise disparate peoples. Writing in 1955, Will Herberg observed that America had succeeded in creating a religious melting pot.[1] Herberg's study, *Protestant-Catholic-Jew*, revealed that although American culture encourages religious membership, it embraces a spectrum of Judeo-Christian faiths. The nation's main denominations teach different sectarian creeds, but they serve the same overall cultural function of orienting persons to the broader American way of life.

Mainline denominations prospered. Consensus religion prevailed. Unity seemed to be prevailing over and against difference. In 1950 representatives from twenty-nine denominations (with combined memberships of over thirty-one million) came together to organize the National Council of Churches. The NCC was a mostly symbolic organization. Its main purpose was to provide a forum to express the hope for greater ecumenical, or interfaith, unity. Church attendance in the United States hit a historic high during this era. A full 47 percent of the population attended church on any given weekend. And most, it seems, preferred to emphasize what Christians (and to a lesser extent Jews) had in common rather than the doctrinal differences that might otherwise separate them.

This was an especially vibrant time for American Roman Catholics. Catholics had historically been accustomed to being a minority in the predominantly Protestant United States. Slowly but surely, however, they grew into the largest religious group in the country. What is more, they had long outgrown their status as an immigrant faith. By the late 1950s Catholics were just as likely to attend college or to hold professional-level positions as their Protestant counterparts. And, in 1960, John F. Kennedy was elected president of the United States—symbolizing the fact that American Catholics had come of age. Then, in the early 1960s, Pope John XXIII convened the Second Vatican Council so that church authorities might explore "how we ought to renew ourselves." Vatican II resulted in several changes that, though small in themselves, had the cumulative effect of breathing new life into the Catholic church. The council urged Catholic leaders to engage in open dialogue with modern intellectual thought. The Index of Prohibited Books was abolished. Priests and laity alike began to discuss the likes of Darwin, Freud, and Marx in an open manner that was unprecedented in church history. Vatican II also charged church leaders with taking a deepened sense of responsibility to society. The Catholic church was not to live in isolation from the world, but to redirect its ministry of love to help alleviate the hunger and poverty that dehumanize a sizable percentage of the world's population. Another initiative arising from Vatican II was a renewed interest in interfaith relationships (recognizing the truth contained in Protestant

PROPORTIONAL DENOMINATIONAL STRENGTH AMONG JUDEO-CHRISTIANS IN THE UNITED STATES: 1990

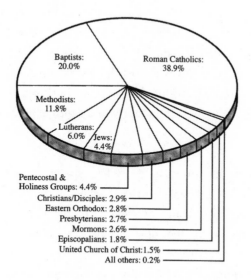

Baptists: 20.0%

Roman Catholics: 38.9%

Methodists: 11.8%

Lutherans: 6.0%

Jews: 4.4%

Pentecostal & Holiness Groups: 4.4%
Christians/Disciples: 2.9%
Eastern Orthodox: 2.8%
Presbyterians: 2.7%
Mormons: 2.6%
Episcopalians: 1.8%
United Church of Christ: 1.5%
All others: 0.2%

Christianity and the truths expressed in non-Christian religions as well). Vatican II called for a more democratic church structure, initiated a host of liturgical changes (including changing the language of worship from Latin to the vernacular language), relaxed church discipline, and invited the laity to assume a greater role in the church. All in all, Vatican II unleashed a heady spirit of progress and change. As the century would wear on, however, many Catholic leaders concluded that Vatican II had caused the pendulum of change to swing too far to the liberal side. Pope John Paul II went on record as opposing many of Vatican II's proposals. Much of John Paul II's long term in office was devoted to urging Catholics back toward a more conservative expression of faith. The Catholic church has thus vacillated in recent years. The more liberal spirit that had seemed consistent with Catholics' participation in American culture has been dampered. Catholicism's historic conservatism has, at least for the present, reasserted itself and Catholics now seem uncertain how to address their most pressing issues (e.g., the celibacy of priests, women in the priesthood, birth control, divorce, democracy within the Catholic church).

By the mid 1970s the theological climate in the United States suddenly became more conservative. Many mainline denominations began declining in membership. For some (e.g., Congregationalists, Episcopalians, Presbyterians, Disciples of Christ, Methodists) this decline continues and may threaten their long-term viability.[2] One symbol of America's steady turn toward conservative theology during the last few decades of the twentieth century was the career of the evangelist Billy Graham. Graham was born in 1918, the son of a North Carolina dairy family. At the age of sixteen he was converted to fundamentalist Christianity at an old-fashioned revivalist tent meeting. The conservative subculture in which he grew up rejected the modernist elements that had seemingly become associated with consensus religion in America. Evolutionists, Social Gospelers, and liberals of every stripe were heretics in Graham's world. It seems that just below the media's radar screen there existed an enduring core of religiously conservative Americans who quietly resisted most of what was transpiring around them. Bible-believing Christians were poised to reassert their dominance in American life. Graham emerged to champion this silent majority's cause.

Graham began his career in 1947 as a minister with an organization called Youth for Christ.[3] Two years later he gained widespread attention by converting three minor celebrities (a local television personality, a former Olympic athlete, and a notorious racketeer). He was soon traveling from city to city conducting revivals and winning conversions. Graham's message was simple. He ignored changing cultural conditions and instead reasserted a traditional, backward-looking biblical message. A part of his success stemmed from his ability to alert audiences to the cultural crises that surrounded them. We are living in the latter days, he warned them, and the moment of judgment is near. Yet even as we await the return of our Lord, Satan seems to be gaining the upper hand. Graham had no difficulty identifying the troubles instigated by Satan in his last desperate assault on this world: juvenile delinquency, wives who don't submit to their husbands' authority, disobedient children, big labor, communists, the welfare state, the United Nations, unpatriotic citizens, and ecumenical groups that were watering down the authority of the Bible. America, he warned, was in danger of falling apart at the seams due to the influence of godless liberals. Graham's solution to this impending crisis was simple and straightforward: we must each make an immediate decision for Christ and thereby save our own souls and rescue America.

In certain respects, Graham's ministry was an inclusive one. He tried to avoid aligning his message with any one denomination. He hoped to achieve a fellowship of all born-again Christians and consistently offered pleas for unity among believers. His conservatism was never so strident as to alienate mainline church members. Indeed, Graham boldly envisioned an America unified in belief and values. He even went so far as to equate "true" Christianity with "true" Americanism. Throughout the Cold War that he saw pitting Christian America against the godless Soviet Union, he preached that Christianity's very survival depended on American military might and the power of economic capitalism. Yet, he argued, the ultimate source of America's strength is its biblical faith. Graham thus felt perfectly at ease proclaiming that "If you would be a true patriot, then become a Christian. If you would become a loyal American, then become a loyal Christian." No wonder, then, that Graham became the "minister to the presidents." Eisenhower, Kennedy, Johnson, and Nixon all courted his advice and support. Graham urged Americans to live up to their biblical heritage and resist all those who would dare subvert it. Otherwise, he warned, God will eventually punish America for straying from His will. He urged us to realize that it is not yet too late for the nation to return to traditional faith: "America cannot survive, she cannot fulfill her divine purpose, she cannot carry out her God-appointed mission without the spiritual emphasis which was hers from the outset." Bible-based conservatism, far from being obsolete, was Graham's and other evangelists' prescription to restore unity, order, and national progress.

The kind of inclusiveness envisioned by Graham and other conservative religious voices could never extend to the whole nation. Non-Christians, for example, were marginalized. Jews, Hindus, and Buddhists—let alone atheists or unchurched "seekers"—had no role to play in America's traditional religious systems. Also marginalized were women, who were restricted to the sidelines by virtue of their gender. And while many black Americans continued in their conservative Protestant faith, others came to the conclusion that the unity envisioned by consensus white culture would never fully include them. Many of the most vocal black leaders of the period (e.g., Malcolm X and Muhammad Ali) finally severed ties with what they deemed to be a hopelessly racist Christianity and instead embraced the faith of Islam. A series of events (Little Rock in 1957, Selma in 1965, the 1965 riots in Watts, and the assassination of Martin Luther King in 1968) drew attention to the stark reality that America was far from achieving cultural unity.

The persisting problems of race and gender in the United States exposed the cracks in traditional efforts to forge religious and cultural unity. Too many voices had been excluded. Unity—without inclusiveness—is an unobtainable objective. Intellectuals whose insights threatened adherence to "the one truth" had been relegated to the cultural sidelines. Women were as yet not taken seriously as men's theological equals. And though there were weak efforts to integrate blacks into white-dominated cultural systems, there was as yet no theology that clearly connected faith with racial issues. It was time for these previously muted voices to be heard.

PAUL TILLICH: THE SHAKING OF FOUNDATIONS

By the late twentieth century many educated persons were tempted to abandon religion in favor of a purely rational, secular approach to life. They asked any number of questions for which their churches had no answers. Can someone exposed to scientific thinking still believe in God? In an age of space exploration, how can we believe in a God or heaven that exists "up there"? If we no longer believe in Thor, Zeus, or Osiris, why should we believe in the God of the Bible? Isn't religion really an accident of birth? If I had been born in India, wouldn't I have grown up believing in Hinduism? Why should I believe that Jesus is the only route to salvation? Am I wrong to pick reason over faith? Can a person with honest doubts about God and the Bible still be a Christian?

These are precisely the kinds of questions that Billy Graham and other conservative-leaning religious leaders evaded. They called for unswerving loyalty and implied that we should repress any lingering doubts. Faith in the Bible, they maintained, is a prerequisite for becoming a true Christian. Those who question the foundations of Christianity do so at the risk of eternal life.

It is in this context that we can appreciate the phenomenal response— both among scholars and the general public—to the writings of Paul Tillich (1866-1965). Tillich was born in Germany, the son of a Lutheran minister.[4] He attended some of the leading universities in his native country, earning a doctorate in philosophy and a licentiate in theology. He went on to teach theology and philosophy at several universities before his opposition to the

Nazi party caused Hitler to order him removed from his faculty position. He fled to the United States, where he taught at Union Theological Seminary, Harvard, and the University of Chicago. By the end of his career he had obtained almost celebrity status in the United States. His picture appeared on the cover of *Time* magazine in 1959. The article heralded Tillich's ability to deliver "a kind of shock treatment" to the American religious world. Noting that Tillich's theology gave completely new meaning to traditional Christian terminology, it quoted one of his critics, who called Tillich "the most dangerous theological leader alive." When *Time* celebrated its fortieth anniversary in 1963, its publisher invited all living celebrities who'd been on the cover to attend a gala celebration. The two major speakers for the banquet were to be President John F. Kennedy (who had to decline at the last moment) and Paul Tillich. Tillich's death in 1965 was reported on national radio and television networks, and the obituary that appeared on the front page of the *New York Times* stated that religion in the United States had become "profoundly different" due to his thought-provoking writings.

What distinguished Tillich's thought was his conviction that theology must engage its "cultural situation." He maintained that traditional religion is becoming irrelevant. It asks persons to accept "revealed" truths that are said to be beyond investigation or doubt. Yet it is precisely these "truths" that modern persons have come to doubt. The Christian message, he argued,

> Cannot be a direct proclamation of religious truths as they are given in the Bible and in tradition, for the situation of modern persons is precisely one of doubt about all this and about the church itself. . . . It cannot be required of persons today that they first accept theological truths, even though [these truths concern] God and Christ. Wherever the church in its message makes this a primary demand, it does not take seriously the situation of the person of today and has no effective defense against the challenge of many thoughtful people of our day who reject the message of the church as of no concern for them.[5]

Tillich thought that it was impossible to turn back the clock of history. We can't ignore or pretend not to be influenced by modern secular thought. Instead of avoiding modern challenges to faith, religious leaders should welcome them as a stimulus to formulating an existentially relevant faith. In Tillich's view it

Interpreter of Religion in the Modern Intellectual Climate
Credit: The University of Chicago Divinity School

was time for a "shaking of the foundations." He even went so far as to propose that we cease using the word "God" for an entire generation. The word has become so linked with psychologically infantile and scientifically backward modes of thinking that it no longer connects with educated persons' conceptions of everyday life. Tillich was confident that the conception of "the ultimate" would gradually resurface in our reflections on life, but we would then truly understand what it signifies about our experience of the world.

Part of Tillich's appeal was that he utilized the vocabulary of depth psychology and existentialist philosophy. He sympathized with those who found that traditional religion no longer spoke to them, leaving them to hunt for meaning and truth on their own. Like Emerson some 120 years before him, Tillich urged persons to look for traces of God in the depths of human experience. Like

Emerson, Tillich asked his contemporaries to define religion not in terms of conformity with institutional churches but in terms of our relationship or sense of connectedness with the deepest currents of life.[6] And Tillich, like Emerson, strongly hinted of the mystical nature of the "depths" of human awareness. Each of us is susceptible of "a feeling for the inexhaustible mystery of life, the grip of an ultimate meaning of existence, and the invincible power of an unconditional devotion."[7] We have intuitions of the holy and the sacred, an awareness of the unconditional, the numinous, and the ecstatic. That is, we connect with life in ways that cannot be reduced to purely secular categories. Experience reveals that "within itself, the finite world points beyond itself."[8]

In one of his most forceful books, *The Dynamics of Faith*, Tillich argued that authentic spirituality has virtually nothing to do with institutional religion. It is, rather, a state of existential relationship to the universe. The word "faith" designates our human encounter with the "ultimate depths" of the universe. The problem with organized religion, Tillich contends, is that it too often presents faith to us as a set of doctrines that we must accept out of obedience and loyalty. In Tillich's view faith has nothing to do with making up for a lack of evidence with an act of will. Nor is it trust in authority or agreeing to believe in something that has a very low amount of evidence to support it. Instead, faith is experiential and relational. It is the state of being grasped by and oriented to the ultimate horizon of human experience. Here Tillich drew upon the theology of Friedrich Schleiermacher, who defined faith in terms of the feeling of absolute dependence (that is, our creaturely awareness that we are dependent upon the "absolute" source of life and meaning). In Tillich's terms, faith is the state of being ultimately concerned. It emerges as we find ourselves in relationship to the ultimate source of all existence. Revealing the mystical overtones of his understanding of human experience, Tillich contended that faith emerges in experiences in which we "are grasped by and turned to the infinite."[9]

Of further interest is Tillich's analysis of the role of doubt in genuine religious faith. Faith, in his view, is rooted in our awareness of the infinite mystery undergirding human existence. This mystery, however, can never be reduced to doctrinal statements that have the character of factual knowledge. Religious language is symbolic only. Symbols point to, and in a certain sense participate in, the infinite. But they do not convey factually certain propositions. The only certainty of faith is the experiential certainty that we have had an immediate awareness of an ultimate horizon of human existence. Yet faith will always contain an element of doubt because we can never put unconditional trust in our human-made formulations. In Tillich's words, "Faith is certain in so far as it is an experience of the holy. But faith is uncertain in so far as the infinite to which it is related is received by a finite being. This element of uncertainty in faith cannot be removed, it must be accepted."[10] The human condition is such that certainty in matters of faith can never be ours. A spirituality befitting our modern age must therefore live in a creative tension between faith and doubt.

Unlike the Billy Grahams of consensus religion, Tillich realized that God was not the answer to modern spiritual doubts. The whole concept of God was itself part of the question, part of the reason for modern doubt. Western culture had long since outgrown the supernatural concepts the Bible uses to depict God. The Bible describes God with metaphors drawn from the ancient world's understandings of a male authority figure: shepherd, king, father, ruler, or judge. The Bible thus portrays God as a being somewhat like ourselves, only somehow of supernatural proportions. He is said to be a supernatural person, a being who rules our universe from on high. Yet in Tillich's estimation this is precisely the concept that thoughtful persons can no longer accept. Modern persons go about their everyday lives utilizing technology and interpreting life with conceptual categories that have no connection whatsoever to biblical supernaturalism. Traditional beliefs about God can only be held by compartmentalizing them, holding them in complete separation from the thinking style we otherwise use to make sense of life. No wonder, then, that so many people gradually realize that belief in God has become irrelevant. Educated persons simply can't avoid wondering whether God, like the Easter Bunny and Santa Claus, is—like Freud suggested—a belief we have held to because we want it to be true even though it can't be supported by any evidence or reasoned argument.

It was Tillich's awareness of the inadequacy of traditional concepts of God that led him to propose that we think of God in terms of "depth" rather than height. The metaphor of depth was intended to be understood in two ways. First, it meant that faith in God must be deep rather than superficial or shallow. But more important, it meant locating God within—not beyond—our connection with the universe. Tillich was well versed in depth psychology and existential philosophy. With these in mind he urged his contemporaries to think about God as "the ground of being." By this he meant the creative source out of which life emerges. He was invoking the concept of the First or Ultimate Cause of the universe, but doing so in a way that emphasized its dynamic connection with our lives. God, Tillich proposed, must be understood as "the creative ground of all natural objects."[11] Understood this way, God is a central concept in any thinking person's reflection about the origins, meaning, and purpose of life. If you care deeply about truth and about life, you must care about the infinite and inexhaustible ground from which these emerge.

> The name of this infinite and inexhaustible depth and ground of all being is God. That depth is what the word God means. And if that word has not much meaning for you, translate it, and speak of the depths of your life, of the source of your being, of your ultimate concern, of what you take seriously without any reservation. Perhaps, in order to do so, you must forget everything traditional that you have learned about God, perhaps even that word itself. For if you know that God means depth, you know much about him. You cannot then call yourself an atheist or unbeliever. For you cannot think or say: Life has no depth! Life is shallow. Being itself is surface only. If you could say this in complete seriousness, you would be an atheist; but otherwise you are not.[12]

Tillich's conception of God—like Emerson's, Quimby's, Davis', and James'—was somewhat pantheistic. Although he went to great efforts to suggest that God is not less than personal, and that God contains a personal element, he tended to describe God as an impersonal spiritual power. His conception of God as the "ground of being" had further implications for how the concept of sin is to be understood. For traditional Christianity, sin means disobedience to the commands of a father-figure deity. The Heavenly Father gives moral commandments, and humans break them, thereby forfeiting eternal life. For Tillich, however, sin was not something that we commit. It is better, he argued, to think of sin as a state of estrangement from our true self. The human condition is such that we are ordinarily estranged from our creative ground and power. Our capacity to express life is thus seriously curtailed, creating fragmentation and brokenness.

Christianity's answer to the problem posed by sin is its testimony concerning the life and saving work of Christ. For traditional Christianity, this has to do with Christ's death and resurrection, which mysteriously atoned for humanity's disobedience or sin. Yet in Tillich's view traditional beliefs about Jesus presuppose a supernaturalist worldview that the educated public abandoned several generations ago. Conventional Christologies that describe Jesus as a half-man, half-God superperson no longer speak to modern persons who are searching for ways to overcome their estrangement from God. Tillich argues that the crucial message of Christianity should not be that Jesus *was* God, but that he became so completely united with the ground of his being that he *expressed* this infinite and creative power of life. The biblical account of Jesus is thus to be understood existentially as a depiction of a person in whom estrangement with the ground of being is overcome. As Tillich put it, "In the picture of Jesus as the Christ we have the picture of a man who . . . became completely transparent to the mystery he reveals."[13]

Tillich's unorthodox reinterpretations of God and Christ drew immediate and heated response. Many criticized him for abandoning almost every traditional Christian belief. But Tillich was unfazed. He believed that Christianity could not continue to be a vital system of belief in the modern era if it remained wedded to outmoded ways of thinking. He knew that his thought was both creative and daring. He had always lived on the boundary: the boundary between his native Germany and his adopted country, the United States; the boundary between philosophy and theology; the boundary between the academic world and the church; and, most important, the boundary between the finite and the infinite. Living on these boundaries meant that he never belonged fully in any one world. But it also made it possible for him to see these worlds more creatively than those who belonged exclusively to just one.

Tillich's most lasting contribution to his era's understanding of religion was that he—like Jefferson, Emerson, Quimby, Harris, and James before him—severed spirituality from any necessary connection to a church. "Religion," he wrote, "is not a special function of our spiritual life, but it is the dimension of depth in all its functions."[14] By this he meant that what makes an aspect of our life religious is not that it relates to a heavenly being called God, but that it engages our quest for the ultimate meaning of life. Authentic spirituality is thus not confined to the life of theological institutions. It is instead an element of any activity that discloses to us what, at the level of its deepest mystery, is the creative reality and ultimate significance of our lives.

We therefore find genuine spirituality in a wide variety of human activities: art, sport, helping professions, love, and intellectual development.

God, Tillich wrote, is deeply connected with the ongoing creativity manifesting itself in the evolutionary process. In this Tillich was influenced by process theologians such as Charles Hartshorne and Alfred North Whitehead, and—above all—the evolutionary spirituality of Pierre Teilhard de Chardin. Following their lead, Tillich suggested that God prompts us to participate in this "Divine Life" of ongoing creativity. God's mode of influencing life, however, is not that of intervening from above, but of luring us into life-affirming activity from within. The key to spiritual living is to open ourselves to this directing activity of God and, in so doing, add our own creative achievements to the Divine Life.[15]We do this, however, not in a church but in whatever cultural activities enable us to push beyond superficial concerns and become transparent to the infinite and inexhaustible power of the Divine Life.

Religious studies scholar Amanda Porterfield has recently drawn attention to Tillich's role in cultivating a distinctive spiritual style among college students. She notes that at Harvard, where Tillich taught between 1955 and 1962, the student newspaper investigated Tillich's popularity. A survey conducted by the *Harvard Crimson* revealed that the "undergraduate speculation about religion" Tillich had stimulated did "not represent a return to the faith in which [students] or their forefathers were raised."[16] The paper further noted that students' revitalized spirituality was far more evident "in campus discussion that in church attendance." They tended to describe church activities as "trivial," "mundane," and "unworthy of a religious person's interest," while at the same time showing intense interest in philosophical inquiry of religious issues. The final effect of Tillich's teaching, the paper concluded, seems to be one of "reshaping" students' beliefs. This influence obviously extended well beyond Harvard, reshaping the conception of religion at college campuses across the country over the span of at least three decades.

There is a certain irony to Tillich's lasting influence on American religious life. He had hoped to embrace the doubts that many modern Christians have and, in so doing, prevent them from rejecting Christianity altogether. His goal was thus to make it possible for educated persons to sustain their relationship with the Christian tradition (albeit a reinterpreted version of this tradition). Tillich had no effect whatsoever on the conservative wing of American religion that considers the kinds of doubts he struggled with to be the opposite of a God-centered life rather than the starting point. He did, however, have a significant impact on persons from mainline traditions. Indeed, many clergy in these traditions were greatly influenced by Tillich and incorporated the style and substance of his thought into their ministries. Laypersons were encouraged upon learning that they weren't the only ones who felt out of step with conventional religion. It was a great relief to learn that respected scholars had the same doubts, the same difficulties in proclaiming "absolute truths" in the face of the modern intellectual climate. Yet Tillich's message did little to keep mainline baby boomers in the church. It was the children of mainline churches who were most likely to be exposed to Tillich's thought. And thus an unexpected consequence of his career was that he emboldened many who might otherwise have joined these churches to pursue new, and unchurched, spiritual interests.

One of the individuals who was greatly influenced by Tillich's thought was a Roman Catholic theologian by the name of Mary Daly. Tillich's conceptions of God as "ground of being" and of faith as "the state of being ultimately concerned" led her to develop new ways of addressing women's religious concerns. But Mary Daly was destined to grow beyond her early source of inspiration, and open up entirely new lines of theological reflection. The previously muted voice of women was to find a powerful new advocate.

MARY DALY: BEYOND GOD THE FATHER

Tillich had dazzled reading audiences with his bold rejection of traditional theism. He had affirmed that finding the "courage to be" requires dispensing with the god of biblical theism. He encouraged twentieth-century Americans to think in ontological rather than theological terms. Spirituality was not about obeying a Heavenly Father, but about participating in Being. To be spiritual was to be engaged in the ongoing creation of the universe. This meant being willing to forego the psychological comforts of a protective Supreme Being. It required courage, a desire to embrace life as a creative agent who must face life with no moral or religious absolutes. For many this was profoundly liberating. It enabled them to cease pretending to believe in biblical doctrines that they intellectually knew weren't true (at least in any literal sense). It also meant freeing themselves from the authority of the church, which many had come to see as an oppressive cultural institution. But Tillich's ontologically phrased message said very little about either the racist or sexist oppression that religion had traditionally done more to perpetuate than to remedy.

The women's movement that surfaced in American life during the 1960s and 70s focused attention on a variety of issues concerning the relationship of women and religion.[17] Some studies examined the historical role of women in the formation of religious movements. Anne Hutchinson, Ellen White, and Mary Baker Eddy are prime examples of women who have had a significant impact on American religious life. Yet many other women have exerted considerable influence on American spirituality and have nonetheless been overlooked by standard histories. This concern with the role of women in American religious history led directly to a second area of interest, the controversy surrounding the ordination of women. Although women out-number men in virtually every religious organization in the United States, men have traditionally had the exclusive opportunity to preach from the pulpit, teach in seminaries, and publish in theological journals.

A third concern of women scholars is the revision of theology from a feminist perspective. Feminist theology is inherently liberal in orientation, incorporating modern, academic understandings of religion. Its basic assumption is that religion is an expression of culture (as opposed to consisting of delivered-once-and-for-all revelations containing absolute truth). Most feminist theologians affirm the essentially revelatory character of Judaism and Christianity, including their scriptures. They nonetheless insist that those who wrote the Bible were very much men of their time. Their writings therefore reflect the social customs, practices, and attitudes of their historical period. What is unfortunate is that once these customs, practices, and attitudes became embedded in scripture, they subsequently became viewed as part of "revealed truth" and perpetuated down to our own day. Feminist theologians thus believe it is now time that thoughtful persons learn to distinguish between the essence of their faith and the blatant cultural accretions with which it is tainted. Their goal, then, is to replace outmoded ways of religious thinking with new ways that give meaning and vision to the experience of all people.[18]

The most influential feminist theologian has been Mary Daly. She was born in Schenectady, New York, in 1928 and raised in a Roman Catholic family. Daly recounts that when she was about nine years old, a boy in her Catholic elementary school taunted her, bragging that he was an altar boy and that girls were never allowed to serve Mass.[19] As it turned out, this would only be the first in a long line of experiences that would drive home the message that the doors of the church are never fully open to women. After graduating from college she realized that no graduate schools of philosophy and theology offered scholarships to women. She came across an ad for a newly opened School of Sacred Theology at St. Mary's College in Notre Dame, Indiana. The school's president, Sister Madeleva, had set out to remedy the problem that in the early 1950s there was not a single university in the country that would admit women to study Catholic theology at the doctoral level. Sister Madeleva not only admitted Daly to the program, but offered her a scholarship that made it possible for her to earn a doctorate in this rigorous program of philosophical theology by the age of twenty-five.

Daly continued her theological education by earning two more doctorates at the University of Fribourg in Switzerland. She was now ready to begin her career as a university professor. In 1966 she joined the theology faculty at Boston College, a Jesuit-run university with a reputation for having a liberal academic bent. Just two years later she published her first book, *The Church and the Second Sex*. The book appears fairly tame from current academic perspectives. But in 1968 it was perceived as an outright assault on the authority of the Roman Catholic church. Daly had been inspired by the French feminist philosopher Simone de Beauvoir, who had boldly proclaimed that "Christian ideology has contributed no little to the oppression of women." Daly concurred. Her book offered a sustained reflection on what she identifies as the shocking contradiction between "Christian teaching on the worth of every person and the oppressive, misogynistic ideas arising from cultural conditioning."[20] Daly was particularly critical of Christianity's perpetuation of the myth of the "Eternal Feminine." Doctrines about Mary envision the ideal woman as passive and self-sacrificing, finding fulfillment only through motherhood.

The Church and the Second Sex argued that Christianity needs to exorcise the images that haunt women and limit their potential. Daly noted that the theological "root of such distortions as antifeminism is the problem of conceptualizations, images, and attitudes concerning God."[21] Attitudes

Feminist Who Exorcised Religion of Gender-based Oppression
Credit: Gail Bryan

relegating females to a secondary status are "reinforced by the fact that God is called Father, that Christ is male, that the angels, though they are pure spirits, have masculine names."[22] The Christian identification of God as a sin-haunted masculine being implicitly assigns negative connotations to matter, sexuality, and women.

At this stage in her life, Mary Daly had hope that Roman Catholicism would enter a new theological era. Vatican II had seemingly set the liberating spirit of reform into motion. She called upon Christian leaders to end discrimination against women in the ministry and to eliminate the barriers that isolate nuns from the world. Daly expressed faith that the presence of God would propel Christianity forward, helping it to be an agent of progress that would liberate women so that they might express their full human potential. It was time, she proclaimed, for Christianity to admit its past sins and devote its energies to the creation of a world in which men and women might work together on all levels:

It is only by this creative personal encounter, sparked by that power of transcendence which the theologians have called grace, that the old wounds can be healed. Men and women . . . will with God's help mount together toward a higher order of consciousness and being, in which the alienating projections will have been defeated and wholeness, psychic integrity, achieved.[23]

Mary Daly wasn't prepared for the strong and immediate reaction to her book. On the one hand, many female scholars and lay women enthusiastically embraced its arguments. But the male faculty and administration of Boston College thought otherwise. Daly was summarily fired. Fortunately, the student body spoke out in support of Daly's academic freedom. An estimated 1,500 students demonstrated on campus. Nearly 2,000 signed a petition in support of her cause. Her plight received national coverage. Several months later the administration reconsidered and somewhat surreptitiously offered her tenure and promotion. Yet although she now had her teaching position back, Mary Daly was forever changed. Her views of academe, Roman Catholicism, and Christian theology altered drastically. From that moment on she "moved into an invisible counter-university—the Feminist Universe."[24]

It slowly dawned on Daly that her previous theological assumptions were wrong. She had proceeded under the assumption that there is a revelatory core at the base of Christian teachings that had somehow been contaminated by patriarchal attitudes. Now she realized that Christian teachings were patriarchal to their very core. Institutional religion was irreversibly misogynist. Why, she wondered, would she or any other woman even want equality in the Christian church? After all, a woman asking for equality in the church is equivalent to a black person demanding equality in the Ku Klux Klan. She concluded that the religious conservatives had been right all along. Attempts to liberalize Christian teachings weren't really returning the church to some mythical moment in the past when its doctrines were pure and true. Christian teachings were oppressive from the very start. Indeed, that is why Christianity developed in the first place. This realization signaled a new stage in Daly's spiritual journey. She cut ties with the institution in which she had been raised and set off alone to explore the possibilities of a post-Christian feminist spirituality.[25]

Daly's next book, *Beyond God the Father* (1973), challenged the very premises of traditional religion. "The entire conceptual system of theology and ethics," she argued, "have been the products of males and tend to serve the interests of sexist society."[26] Daly realized that any attempt to revise theology from a feminist perspective would be viewed as deviant by male church authorities. She noted that "the beginning of liberation comes when women refuse to be 'good' and/or 'healthy' by prevailing standards. To be female is to be deviant by definition in the prevailing culture. To be female and defiant is to be intolerably deviant. This means going beyond the imposed definitions of 'bad woman' and 'good woman.'"[27]

Daly's first act of deviance was to call for an end to masculine identifications of deity. The image of "the divine Father in heaven" has supported cruel and oppressive behavior for centuries. The historical function of patriarchal images of God has been to foster necrophilia (the love of death, subordination, and oppression). In its place the women's movement seeks images of God that foster biophilia, the love of life. To suggest what such new God-language might be like, Daly explicitly invoked the ontological conceptions of three earlier religious revolutionaries—Ralph Waldo Emerson, William James, and Paul Tillich. Like Emerson, James, and Tillich, Daly found the word "God" too problematic to support a vital spirituality. While rejecting this word and its traditional connotations, she nonetheless embraced Tillich's ontological approach to conceptualizing God, and borrowed many of his guiding metaphors such as "the ground of being" or "Being itself." Yet Daly faulted the relatively static nature of Tillich's theological images, preferring more dynamic images that would lead to the actualization of women.[28] She thus advocated thinking of God as an active verb, as "Be-ing." This, of course, also aligned her with the pragmatic, evolutionary thought of William James. James, she noted, employed "God-language that soars beyond sexual hierarchy as a specific problem to be confronted in the process of human becoming."[29] Like James, she maintained that all conceptions of God should be measured by their ability to foster human becoming. And, like James, she emphasized that through our active thinking, believing, and willing we contribute to divine being itself.[30]

Tillich had already suggested new categories for Christian proclamations concerning Christ. Instead of emphasizing Jesus as God incarnate, Tillich had employed the more existentialist language of seeing in Jesus one who reveals the "New Being" made possible when we become transparent to the Ground of our Being through relationships of love. Daly borrowed this image of the New Being, reminding us of Emerson's observation that "historical Christianity has fallen into the error that corrupts all attempts to communicate religion. . . . It has dwelt, it dwells, with noxious exaggeration about the person of Jesus." Daly, too, spoke of the New Being as a possibility for anyone who finds the courage and convictions to live a life of authentic Be-ing. Yet, she offered, only radical feminism can open up human consciousness adequately to a truly life-affirming mode of being. And thus "the becoming of women may be . . . a doorway to a new phase in the human spirit's quest for God."[31]

Soon after publishing *Beyond God the Father,* Mary Daly moved even further away from traditional theological concepts. Her *Gyn/Ecology: The Metaethics of Radical Feminism* (1978) celebrates spiritual journeys geared exclusively toward the radical be-ing of women. This, she describes, is an Otherworld Journey, a journey taking women beyond the "foreground" myths and symbols of patriarchal culture. For centuries women have been the objects rather than the subjects of inquiry. Her play on the term gyn/ecology invoked the possibility of improvising a new "metalanguage" capable of exorcising all male-authored sciences of women. It is time, she argues, to exorcise religion of all the misogynist language and imagery that have been perpetuated by male-dominated institutions. *Gyn/ecology* invites women to journey to the Otherworld by embracing the myths and symbols of women's ancient past. Daly assures her readers that women's past contains a storehouse of woman-identified and woman-honoring spiritual symbols that they can appropriate in their own personal quests. Unlike the religious journeys of foreground religion that inevitably lead to domination and exploitation, the journey to the Otherworld is about "weaving world tapestries of our own kind. That is, about dis-covering, developing the complex web of living/loving relation-ships of our own kind. It is about women living, loving, creating our Selves, our cosmos."[32]

Daly helped chart the course of women's journeys to the Otherworld in subsequent books, including *Pure Lust* (1984) and *Quintessence* (1998). In these books she warns that the decision to reject our culture's foreground myths and travel to the Otherworld is a risky and sometimes frightening journey. It takes courage. It takes "wild women" who are willing to become "loose" and to ask "wild questions." It means choosing to step outside the accepted boundaries of patriarchal culture and accept the backlash or punishment for being named a "hag," "crone," or other names traditionally assumed to be derisive. One of Daly's strategies for affirming women's decision to express their moral outrage at patriarchal culture has been to examine what she defines as "the power of naming." The power of naming, she argues, has been stripped from women. Women find themselves objectified and labeled according to male-identified terminology. Women must reclaim this power of naming. Toward this end Daly has attempted to expose the deeper reasons why patriarchal culture is revolted by wild (i.e., untamed by men) and liberated women. Her later books, including her *Websters' First New Intergalactic Wickedary of the English Language* (1987), explore the etymological roots of words that have been used to subordinate women. In so doing she has been able to expose the exploitive motives underlying these evaluative words and thereby transform them into symbols of wild women's journey toward participation in Be-ing. Daly has, for example, come to describe herself as a "positively revolting hag," meaning "a stunning, beauteous Crone; one who inspires positive revulsion from phallic institutions and morality." She notes that the word "sin" is derived from the Indo-European root "es-," meaning "to be." She therefore encourages women to sin and to sin big. The courage of women to sin, and to sin big, may be the only hope this planet has of shaking off the culture of death and oppression that is threatening its final extinction.

The goal of this journey to the Otherworld is for women to rediscover their primordial life-affirming power. Daly describes this as a "biophilic participation in be-ing." It is with this in mind that Daly's writings have increasingly emphasized environmental and ecological concerns. A final test of religious thinking, in her view, is its ability to honor and protect the integrity of life. It is thus not sufficient for a biophilic spirituality to exorcise the life-hating imagery of traditional religion. It must also help us to discover and strengthen the threads of connectedness that make life whole.

Mary Daly, much like Joseph Smith, had an uncanny ability to adjust her theology to the needs of her audiences. Smith's doctrines of plural gods and eternal spiritual progress emerged in a symbiotic fashion as he intuitively responded to his community's spiritual needs. In a similar way both the substance and style of Daly's writings evolved to affirm women as they sought their own spiritual voice. Daly dared to explore questions that others preferred to ignore. Her efforts to make sure that women's voices would be heard met with much the same reaction that Anne Hutchinson's had in the seventeenth century: an attempt to banish her forever. But Mary Daly triumphed in a way that Anne could never have imagined. Her writings and public lectures have inspired an entire generation of women to seek out new modes of religious thought and expression. She has suggested an entirely new direction in religious thinking, one that replaces outmoded ways of religious thinking with new ways that give meaning and vision to the experience of all persons.

JAMES CONE: A THEOLOGY OF BLACK POWER

During the colonial period, slaves struggled to preserve elements of their African and Caribbean religious traditions amidst their forced acclimation to the Christian beliefs of white Americans.[33] Plantation owners welcomed Baptist and Methodist revivalist preachers, hoping they would spread the Christian gospel among the slave population. After all, the revivalists' promise of a future heavenly paradise diverted attention away from the injustices of the present social order. The otherworldly focus of the revivalist gospel also promulgated the ideal of the "suffering Christian servant." Those hoping to pass through the pearly gates were taught to accept life's hardships with humility rather than respond to injustice with defiance. We will, perhaps, never fully understand why evangelical Protestantism was so appealing to black slaves. But, by the end of the Civil War, most African Americans belonged to either a Baptist or Methodist church. To be sure, these were new Baptist and Methodist denominations (e.g., the National Baptist Convention, the African Methodist Episcopal Church, and the African Methodist Episcopal Zion Church) wholly separate from the Baptist and Methodist denominations that white persons belonged to. Even to this day, religion is the most segregated institution in American life. The experience of being a racial minority in a predominantly white church is a statistically rare phenomenon. Thus the vast majority of African Americans belong to Protestant congregations that are wholly separate from their white counterparts.

The most significant transformation in African American history was the shift in population from the rural South to the urban North. This migration was largely the result of sweeping technological changes in southern agriculture and the simultaneous expansion of industrialism in the North. The Depression contributed even more incentive for this massive change. Between 1910 and 1950, over a million-and-a-half blacks left the South. Between 1950 and 1960, yet another million moved northward. By 1965 three-fourths of the black population in the United States was living in cities, and about half was in the urban North.[34] The social and cultural context of African Americans' lives changed in the span of a single generation. A corresponding revolution was destined to occur in African Americans' religious thought.

The "black theology" that began to surface in the 1960s was not altogether new.[35] Since colonial times black churchmen had proclaimed that God is the creator of all humanity. They sustained faith in the belief that God is just and that His providential powers will someday usher in a just social order. Sermons delivered by black clergy frequently looked to the Book of Exodus as stirring proof that God acts decisively to liberate the oppressed. The gospels further attested to God's interest in the plight of the powerless, revealing that Jesus directed his ministry to those at the margins of society— the poor, oppressed, and downtrodden. As early as 1894 Henry McNeal Turner declared that "God is a Negro." A few years later Marcus Garvey, a forerunner of the Black Muslims, called for a black God and black Jesus.

The events in Little Rock, Selma, and Watts riveted Americans' attention on the Civil Rights movement. By the middle of the 1960s most Americans had been introduced to the voices of several black Americans who brought the resources of religion to bear on the most pressing issue of the day. The most important of these voices were those of Malcolm X (1925-1965) and Rev. Martin Luther King, Jr. (1929-1968). King is undoubtedly the better-known of these two progenitors of modern racial consciousness. His famous "I Have a Dream" speech ranks with Lincoln's "Gettysburg Address" as one of the most famous oratories in American history. He was named *Time's* "Man of the Year" in 1963 and won the Nobel Peace Prize a year later. A national holiday has been declared in honor of the moral and religious leadership he brought to the Civil Rights movement.

King was born the son of a prominent Baptist preacher in Atlanta.[36] The church then, as it is today, was the dominant institution in the religious, social, and political lives of many African Americans. The church served as the source of African American leadership and voiced the moral values that black leaders used in their fight for racial justice. Martin Luther King, Jr. grew up surrounded by middle-class southern blacks who believed that educational and economic success would eventually cause whites to accept them as equal partners in the American system. Martin adhered to this pattern, excelling at school and entering Morehouse College at the age of fifteen. He later decided to enter the ministry and earned a doctorate in theology at Boston University, writing a dissertation that compared the conceptions of God in the work of Paul Tillich and a process (i.e., a liberal form of theology that locates God as a dimension of the creative processes within nature) theologian by the name of Henry Nelson Wieman. Upon graduation from Boston, King became the pastor of a Baptist church in Montgomery, Alabama, that had a black, middle-class, educated congregation that was well known for its sophistication and service to the city's black community. He soon joined the NAACP and was extending his ministry to include active participation in causes concerned with social justice (which for King meant whites treating blacks with dignity and respect).

The phrase "American dream" appeared in King's public lectures as early as the 1950s. His understanding of this dream originated in two distinct sources: the American liberal democratic tradition, as defined by the Declaration of Independence and the Constitution, and the biblical tradition of the Old and New Testaments, as interpreted by Protestant liberalism and the black community.[37] It is important to remind ourselves that King spoke not only to audiences of middle-class blacks, but also frequently to the white public—the federal government, southern moderates, northern liberals, and religious communities. King assumed that whites' moral sensitivity would ultimately lead them to act upon the ideals of democracy and the moral vision of the Jewish and Christian faiths. As James Cone has observed, "King's articulation of the American dream, then, was primarily for the white public. He wanted to prick their consciences and motivate them to create a society and a world that were free of racial discrimination. . . . Martin was optimistic that his dream of a beloved community of blacks and whites, working together for the good of all, could be realized even in the most racist states in the nation."[38]

Malcolm X might as well have been born on a different planet than Martin Luther King, Jr. The America he experienced in the poor, urban North resembled a hate-filled nightmare more than a hope-filled dream. The seventh child of J. Earl Little, Malcolm would know mostly poverty and inhumane treatment from whites before he was ultimately arrested and put in prison at the age of twenty one. Earl Little was also a Baptist preacher, but unlike Martin Luther King, Sr. he never held a permanent pastorate. Earl rejected the integrationist model advocated by King and others who believed that whites would eventually permit blacks to integrate into America's social, economic, and political structures. Earl, instead, was an ardent nationalist. He argued that because America isn't for blacks, blacks must instead create a wholly separate culture. He became a dedicated organizer for Marcus Garvey's early nationalist organization, the Universal Negro Improvement association. Earl Little's activism got the attention of a white hate group that burned down his house in Omaha, forcing him to move his family to Lansing, Michigan.

Earl Little died in a street-car accident when Malcolm was only six. His mother was placed in a state mental hospital when he was just twelve. As a consequence, Malcolm was left to the care of white government social workers who treated him like the "nigger" they fully expected him to become. As a teenager Malcolm rebelled against both whites and the black middle class by entering the urban underclass world of street hustlers. After several years of drug use and minor crimes, Malcolm was finally arrested for burglary and sentenced to a prison term. As it turned out, this proved to be the turning point in his spiritual life.

While in prison Malcolm was introduced to the teachings of Elijah Muhammad and the fledgling Black Muslim movement. Elijah Muhammad rejected the goals of integrationist thinking and instead embraced an ardent form of black nationalism. Elijah Muhammad viewed Christianity as "white man's religion," and drew attention to its historic association with racism. He instead embraced the teachings of Islam: belief in a God of justice, belief in the equality of all persons before God, and strict moral principles— including both abstinence from alcohol and a strong commitment to family (entailing a prohibition against adultery). While the substance of Black Muslim faith was ostensibly that of Middle Eastern Islam, it nonetheless exuded the black underclass's hostility to their white oppressors. This was a message that spoke to the spiritual needs of someone like Malcolm, who had been a victim of the American system since the day of his birth. He embraced it wholeheartedly and, upon release from prison, became Elijah Muhammad's most promising protégé. Malcolm changed his last name from Little (a name derived from "the white blue-eyed devil") to X (a name symbolizing the "African family name that he could never know"). And, in almost no time, Malcolm X rose to the second-highest position within the Black Muslim movement.

Malcolm X's message was more strident than King's. Whereas King had embraced a philosophy of nonviolence modeled after the career of Mohandus Gandhi, Malcolm X's early life made it impossible for him to accept nonviolence as a philosophy of social change.[39] White hate groups had led (either directly or indirectly) to the death of his father, and the structural violence of the American system had led to the mental breakdown of his mother. When Malcolm spoke against the evils of white America, he engaged the frustrations and aspirations of the poor blacks of the urban North. Neither Malcolm nor his audiences shared much in common with the black professional class that King symbolized. Thus as Martin King's dream was influenced by his social origins, Malcolm X's nightmare was the product of his.

In Malcolm's view Christianity and Islam were diametrically opposed to one another. While Christianity enslaves and divides blacks, Islam liberates and unites them. While Christianity urges blacks to love whites and to be nonviolent toward them, Islam encourages blacks to love themselves, turn the other cheek toward each other, but to defend themselves against the violence of their enemies. Malcolm proclaimed that "it is time to throw aside the religious chains placed on our minds by Negro preachers and unite behind Muslim leader Elijah Muhammad, so we can stand up like men and protect our women and children."[40] He decried the otherworldly focus of traditional black Christianity. Spiritual integrity for blacks must begin by throwing off a white-dominated religious system that perpetuated the status quo:

> Now just bear with me, listen to the teachings of the Messenger of Allah, Honorable Elijah Muhammad. Now just think of this. The blond-haired, blue-eyed white man has taught you and me to worship a white Jesus, and to shout and sing and pray to this God that's his God, the white man's God. The white man has taught us to shout and sing and pray until we die, to wait until death, for some dreamy heaven-in-the-hereafter, when we're dead, while this white man has his milk and honey in the streets paved with golden dollars here on this earth.[41]

Malcolm X desired a faith that empowers individuals in the here and now. Religious faith, therefore, had to include commitment to social and economic justice. Efforts toward achieving such justice are thus spiritual; they advance God's will for the full realization of human life. Malcolm X understood that working for the realization of humanity's full potentials requires tremendous religious discipline and unwavering personal integrity. When he saw Elijah Muhammad waver from this discipline and integrity, Malcolm broke away from the Black Muslim movement. He was shot in Harlem a few months later, quite possibly by members of the organization he had just spurned.

Martin and Malcolm both died from the deep-seated hatreds they had devoted their lives to eradicating. They left Americans two contrasting visions of the spirituality it might take to at last succeed at this mission. Martin had made love his major emphasis; Malcolm had emphasized justice. Martin was an integrationist; Malcolm a black nationalist, stressing pride and affirmation of black culture. Martin believed that blacks must obtain equality through love of the oppressor (through nonviolence); Malcolm believed that love of black people was primary. Martin's faith was defined by the universality of his humanity; Malcolm's faith was defined by the particularity of his blackness.[42]

Both Martin Luther King and Malcolm X illustrate the religious creativity spawned by the racial tensions in American life. Yet although Malcolm will be remembered for his poignant critique of the existing racism in American culture, he never really advanced a constructive cultural or religious vision. King, meanwhile, was a social revolutionary but not really a religious revolutionary. He offered little or no critique of existing theological systems, pretty much grafting his concern with Civil Rights onto traditional biblical beliefs. For these reasons James Cone—though far less known—better symbolizes the change and creativity that racial tensions have spawned in American religious thought. Cone was born in Bearden, Arkansas, in 1938. It was there, in a rural community of 1,200, that he was initially taught what it means to be black and Christian.[43] He grew up attending segregated schools, drinking water from "colored" fountains, seeing movies from theater balconies, and only being permitted to approach the back door of white people's homes. Worse yet, he observed the overt contempt and brutality that white law meted out to any black who dared to question the racial boundaries that had been drawn for them.

In Bearden, like the rest of America, Sunday was the most segregated day of the week. Even though the town's blacks and whites attended Baptist or Methodist churches, read the same Bible, and worshipped the same God, they had virtually no religious or social dealing with one another. James's parents

belonged to the African Methodist Episcopal Church. There he first encountered Jesus through songs, prayers, and impassioned testimonies. And there he
was also exposed to a steady stream of sermons proclaiming that God had
created all people equal, that no person or group is better than any other. Cone
still remembers the biblical passages that preachers cited in support of this
claim. The prophet Malachi, for example, asks "Have we not all one father?
Hath not one God created us?" And Paul, who in his letter to the Galatians
proclaims that we are "all one in Christ Jesus," also preached that God "made
of one blood all nations of men." Yet all James needed to do was look outside
the church window to see the striking contrast between biblical teachings and
the actual order of things in the United States. The very politicians who
attended the Christian churches across town enacted the "Jim Crow" laws that
segregated and discriminated against blacks. White ministers seemed not to
notice that not one member of their congregations heeded Christian counsel
to "love thy neighbor" if that neighbor happened to have black skin. Theory
and practice bore no connection with one another in American Christianity.

After graduating from Philander Smith College in 1958, Cone went on
to graduate school at Garrett Theological Seminary and Northwestern
University, where he received a Ph.D. in 1965. Looking back at this time in
his life he realizes that the Civil Rights and Black Power movements of the
1960s "awakened me from my theological slumber." He reflects that "while
reading Martin Luther King, Jr. and Malcolm X, the blackness in my
theological consciousness exploded like a volcano after many dormant years.
I found my theological voice."

> Malcolm X taught me how to make theology black and never again to
> despise my African origin. King showed me how to make and keep
> theology Christian and never allow it to be used to support injustice. I was
> transformed from a *Negro* theologian to a *Black* theologian, from an
> understanding of theology as an analysis of God-ideas in books to an
> understanding of it as a disciplined reflection about God arising out of a
> commitment to the practice of justice for the poor.[44]

The assassination of Martin Luther King filled James Cone with an anger
that further awakened his black theological consciousness. In 1969 he
published *Black Theology and Black Power*, a book that has dictated the terms of

religious reflection on the issue of race ever since it first appeared. Black Power, Cone contends, means black people taking the dominant role in determining the black-white relationship in America. Black Power is, further-more, an *attitude*. It is an ardent demand for the complete emancipation of black people from white oppression by whatever means black people deem necessary.[45] This strident affirmation of Black Power might alone have elicited strong reaction. But Cone pushed the issue one step further. He announced that Black Power "is Christ's central message to twentieth-century America."

White Americans were understandably vexed by Cone's suggestion that Black Power is the central spiritual message of our time. Yet Cone offered a clear and cogent rationale for making Black Power the center of contemporary religious thought. The work of Christ, he argued, is essentially a liberating work. Jesus' ministry had, after all, been directed toward the oppressed and powerless. Since the gospel is a gospel of liberation for the oppressed, then Christ is where the oppressed are even today. It follows that if the church is to be a continuation of Christ's work, it must make a decisive break with the structure of this society and launch a vehement attack on the evils of racism in all forms. The church must become prophetic. It must demand a radical change in the interlocking structures of American society.[46]

Cone's theology of Black Power resonated more clearly with the message of Malcolm X than it did that of King's. Cone reasoned that "if integration means accepting the white man's style, his values, or his religion, then the black man must refuse."[47] Cone noted in this regard that "one cannot help but think that most whites 'loved' Martin Luther King, Jr. not because of his attempt to free his people, but because his approach was the least threatening to the white power structure."[48] It was further evident to Cone that white Christians were quick to tell blacks that nonviolence was the only appropriate Christian response to our world when they participated in—and perpetu-ated—a violently unjust socioeconomic system.

To Cone the most important task of black theology is to analyze the black person's condition in the light of God's revelation in Jesus Christ and provide the necessary soul to destroy white racism. The only way to understand Christ's saving work is to undrstand his presence in America's current racial struggle. White America, however, insists instead on creating Christ in its own image. And, in doing so, white Americans have become everything Christ is against; they have become the anti-Christ. Even the religious liberals who have proclaimed belief in a "raceless" Christ have failed to make the radical commitment that is required if we truly commit ourselves to Christ's saving work.

> The "raceless" American Christ has a light skin, wavy brown hair, and sometimes—wonder of wonders—blue eyes. For whites to find him with big lips and kinky hair is as offensive as it was for the Pharisees to find him partying with tax collectors. But whether whites want to hear it or not, Christ is black, baby, with all of the features which are so detestable to white society.[49]

Cone's proclamation that Christ is black was intended to be inflammatory. Cone was an angry prophet. He fervently desired to awaken us from our spiritual complacency. His rhetoric was geared to push every emotional button. He knew full well that some of the anger he aroused would be aimed at him. It was not, however, until the book's very last paragraph that he informed his readers that the terms "black" and "white" were not principally racial designations. He had used the word "black" to mean "that your heart, your soul, your mind, and your body are where the dispossessed are." In this special sense of the word, then, the only persons in America who are truly committed to Christ's liberating work are black. From a spiritual perspective, being black has nothing to do with the color of our skin. It instead refers to the color of our heart, soul, and mind. The real questions each of us must answer, then, are: Where is my identity? Where do my commitments really lie? Am I aligned with the oppressed blacks or with the white oppressors? Cone offered his "hope that there are enough to answer this question correctly so that America will not be compelled to acknowledge a common humanity only by seeing that blood is always one color."[50]

In subsequent books such as *A Black Theology of Liberation*, Cone clarified his use of the terms "black" and "white" to refer to moral perspectives rather than skin color per se. Cone was aware that many criticized his theological outlook as a form of reverse racism. Yet like Malcolm X, Cone was trying to make an important statement about what it means to break free from the values deeply entrenched in white American culture.

> In a society where blacks have been enslaved and segregated for nearly four centuries by whites because of their color and where evil has been

Combined Martin Luther King and Malcolm X to Create an
Inspiring Religious Vision
Credit: James Cone, Union Theological Seminary

portrayed as "black" and good as "white" in religious and cultural values,
the idea that "God is black" is not only theologically defensible, but is a
necessary corrective against the powers of domination. A just and loving
God cannot be identified with the values of evil people.[51]

It was with this in mind that Cone reiterated his intentionally disturbing
message that "to be black is to be committed to destroying everything this
country loves and adores." Cone deliberately agitated his audience, arguing
that black theology "will accept only a love of God which participates in the
destruction of the white enemy."[52] His point was that we cannot be faithful

to God without confronting our real values and motives. Mature religious faith requires moving past polite rhetoric and delving into our innermost commitments. If reading Cone doesn't disturb us, then we probably aren't quite getting what he has to say!

It is hardly surprising that Cone's writings drew heated response. Some black theologians roared with approval. Joseph Washington, for example, agreed that a "tough-minded" analysis of American culture leads to precisely the kind of vehemence and militarism found in Cone's theology of Black Power.[53] Others, however, accused Cone of substituting one form of racism with another. Deotis Roberts, Major Jones, and even James Cone's brother Cecil rushed into the fray and faulted Cone for abandoning the Christian faith for "the religion of Black Power."[54] Typical of these critical responses was Roberts' contention that a black Christ would be just as parochial as a red, yellow, or white Christ. While Roberts conceded that the image of a black Christ is liberating to a black American, he countered that the theological function of Christian symbols is not just to liberate but also to reconcile. His argument was that only the image of a universal Christ can lead us to reconciliation into a multiracial fellowship.

Cone was not easily deterred from pursuing his spiritual vision. He chided Roberts and others whom he felt were too quick to counsel blacks to forget the injustices perpetrated against them and to seek reconciliation with their white oppressors. The reconciliation he most hoped for was that of black people with each other. In his *God of the Oppressed* (1975) he maintained that "unless we can get together with our African brothers and sisters for the shaping of our future, then white capitalists in America and Europe will destroy us."[55]

The scope of Cone's theology of liberation grew over time. Although insisting that his basic theological views are the same as when he first issued *Black Theology and Black Power* in 1969, Cone concedes that his thought has grown in certain respects.[56] First and foremost, he admits that his previous failure to address the problem of sexism was a glaring omission. He believes that sexism, like racism, is a central problem of our culture and that any theologian who ignores this issue is guilty of distorting the gospel's central message. Second, Cone acknowledges that a theology of liberation needs to address oppression throughout the world. A full theology of liberation must also address the concrete situations of poverty, colonialism, and human rights in Asia, Africa, and Latin America. Third, Cone realizes that his earliest writings failed to address the role of economics and social class in creating widespread oppression. He now believes that a theological assessment of oppression must include an analysis of "the exploitive role of capitalism."

Cone's argument is that feminist philosophy, global politics, and economic analysis are central—not peripheral—elements of theological discourse. All three illuminate the concrete situations through which the forces of God must strive to bring forth the full potential of creation. As he reminds us, "Liberation is not an afterthought, but the essence of divine activity."[57] Mature faith must therefore move outside the walls of the church and engage the wider forces through which alone this divine activity can triumph over oppression.

Cone's major contribution to American religious life is that he has managed to keep the tension between King's and X's differing visions of race alive in the nation's theological debates. Early in his career Cone probably sided more with the strident vision of Malcolm X. Over time, however, he also came to appreciate the constructive possibilities of King's integrationist dreams. Cone never quit insisting on the "blackness of Christ," which, to him, means that "God has not ever, no not ever, left the oppressed alone in the struggle."[58] His increasing respect for the integrationist tradition in black thought was thus a cautious one, ever mindful of the pernicious racism deeply imbedded in both Christianity and American culture. The mistake that many contemporary black leaders had made was not that they embraced King's dream, but that they had too eagerly forgotten Malcolm X's nightmare. "We need them both," he writes, "as a double-edged sword to slay the dragon of theological racism. King and Malcolm X represent the yin and yang in the black attack on racism."

> Malcolm X teaches us that African-Americans cannot be free without accepting their blackness, without loving Africa as the place of our origin and meaning. King teaches us that no people can be free except . . . in a truly multicultural community. Malcolm X alone makes it too easy for blacks to go it alone and for whites to say "begone!" King alone makes it easy for whites to ask for reconciliation without justice. . . . Putting the two together enables us to overcome the limitations of each to build on

the strengths of both, thereby moving blacks, whites and other Americans toward racial healing and understanding.[59]

When James Cone began his career, few academic theologians were willing to address the ugly fact of racism in American culture. Cone opened up a religious discussion that forced the world of academic theology to realize that no one can be neutral or silent in the face of this great cultural evil. If any progress has been made toward racial healing, it is only because some bold revolutionaries such as Cone have dared to engage in open, honest dialogue.

🍂

SEVEN

Today's Seekers:

The Heritage of Revolutionary Religion

THE UNITED STATES is arguably the most religious nation on earth. Public opinion polls indicate that more than 90 percent of all Americans believe in some kind of Higher Power. This is considerably higher than most other economically developed nations. Furthermore, up to 60 percent of Americans belong to a church or synagogue. Participation in a formal religious organization thus continues to be Americans' principal way of "being religious." Roman Catholicism remains the nation's largest religious organization, accounting for about 23 percent of the entire population. The two largest Protestant denominations, the Baptists and Methodists, represent about 12 and 7 percent of the population, respectively. Yet despite the relative dominance of these three organizations, the American spiritual marketplace continues to be characterized by change and innovation. Several churches have experienced rapid growth over the past few decades. Among these are the Church of Jesus Christ of Latter-day Saints, Holiness churches such as the Church of the Nazarene, and Pentecostal churches such as the Assemblies of God. Common to these groups are a strongly conservative theology, strict adherence to biblical teachings, strong interest in the Second Coming of Christ, conservative moral principles, and a general wariness of the liberal tendencies found in popular culture. Their growth has seemingly come at the expense of mainline Protestant groups (e.g., United Church of Christ, Presbyterians, Episcopalians, Methodists, and Disciples of Christ) who failed to retain their traditional market shares among members of the baby boom generation. There will, in fact, soon be more Hindus, Buddhists, and Muslims in this country than members of some of these traditional mainline groups. The growing presence of these new immigrant faiths testifies even further to the dynamic nature of America's religious history.

Yet even as America's churches are collectively prospering, there is nonetheless a growing tendency for persons to report that they are wholly uninvolved in organized religion. Surprisingly, however, the majority of these unchurched Americans consider themselves spiritual at a personal level. Of the 40 percent of Americans who are unchurched, only about a fourth are completely unreligious. That means that the largest religious group in the United States is actually the unchurched. Some, of course, are only marginally religious. But a full 20 percent of the nation's population is concerned with spiritual issues but chooses to pursue them outside the context of a formal religious organization. It is among these contemporary Americans that we see a great deal of the creative spirituality engendered by the legacy of our nation's religious revolutionaries.

It has become common for this large group of unchurched Americans to describe themselves as "spiritual, but not religious."[1] That is, one out of every five Americans feels a tension between their personal spirituality and membership in a conventional religious organization. Most of them value curiosity, intellectual freedom, and an experimental approach to religion. They often find established religious institutions stifling. Many go so far as to view organized religion as the major enemy of authentic spirituality. For them spirituality has to do with private reflection and private experience—not public ritual. A recent survey showed that fully half of the nation's population has come to believe "that churches and synagogues have lost the real spiritual part of religion." One out of every three adults interviewed in this survey endorsed the still more radical view that "people have God within them, so churches aren't necessary."[2]

Unchurched spirituality is thriving. While many of those who consider themselves to be "spiritual, but not religious" are only marginally interested in their spiritual development, almost half can be considered highly active seekers. These "seekers" are individuals for whom spiritual and metaphysical concerns are a driving force.[3] They typically view their lives as a spiritual journey, hoping to make new discoveries and gain new insights on an almost daily basis. Religion isn't a fixed thing for them. They don't believe that any one religious organization or text has a monopoly on religious truth. They continuously read books, attend workshops, and experiment with new spiritual systems (e.g., vegetarianism, Eastern-style meditation techniques, breathing practices, alternative healing practices). And many self-consciously explore the kinds of spiritual styles opened up by the "religious revolutionaries" who blazed some of these trails before them.

TODAY'S SEEKERS

Today's religious seekers participate in a tradition of American spirituality that dates back at least to Emerson. Emerson had, after all, encouraged us to adopt revolutionary ideas about God and about God's presence within our own deepest selves. He also encouraged us to look beyond the confines of the Judeo-Christian tradition and draw upon the mystic wisdom of Eastern philosophies. And, too, Emerson taught that nature is the only "scripture" we will ever need. By opening ourselves fully to nature we become receptive to the in-streaming presence of an immanent divinity. Phineas Quimby was among those who followed Emerson's lead. His investigations of the spiritual possibilities available through the unconscious mind made it possible for many to believe that what separates us from God is not sin but limited self-understanding. Andrew Jackson Davis moved even further along this continuum of unchurched spiritual thought and practice. His eloquent messages urged middle-class Americans to seek their own, immediate connection with higher spiritual realms.

Emerson, Quimby, and Davis are only a few of the revolutionaries who have encouraged Americans to improvise new ways of being spiritual. One of America's many other religious geniuses was Madame Helena Blavatsky (1831-1891). Blavatsky immigrated to New York from her native Russia in 1872. She had traveled throughout the world, gravitating to people who dabbled in mesmerism, spiritualism, and other occult philosophies. In New York she earned a reputation as a trance medium, channeling messages from advanced spiritual teachers whom she referred to as the mahatmas (the Hindu term for "great souls"). In 1874, Madame Blavatsky met up with Colonel Henry S. Olcott (1832-1907), a lawyer who was deeply interested in the scientific and religious implications of spiritualism. A year later the two launched the Theosophical Society, a metaphysical organization dedicated to bridging the current gulf between science and religion through the study of mesmerism, spiritualism, and the universal ether.[4]

In 1877, Blavatsky published one of the most important books in the history of seeker spirituality, *Isis Unveiled*. Blavatsky claimed that her writing consisted of messages channeled through her from the mahatmas, members of the Universal Mystic Brotherhood who lived in the Himalayan mountains of Tibet. The mahatmas were spiritually evolved humans who had achieved the ability to travel and communicate psychically. Blavatsky had first met the mahatmas in her travels abroad and they had revealed to her that Hindu and Buddhist mystical teachings best express the core truth of all living world religions. With the help of the mahatmas, Blavatsky articulated what might be called an emanationist view of the world. This view explains that life originated with the emanation of a divine spark into the world of matter—a spark that is now gradually evolving back to its divine source. This cosmology enabled Theosophy to embrace Darwinian theories of evolution in a larger metaphysical synthesis. The physical sciences could thereby be affirmed as explaining the "how" of biological evolution, while metaphysics stepped in to provide seekers with insight into evolution's ultimate meaning and purpose.

Throughout *Isis Unveiled* and her later work, *The Secret Doctrine* (1888), Blavatsky sprinkled the Hindu concepts of reincarnation and karma. Belief in the principle of karma made it possible to interpret our personal lives against the backdrop of cosmic evolution. Each new challenge or struggle we face in daily life can be reinterpreted as an opportunity to further our spiritual growth. Blavatsky also contributed an intricate vocabulary that explains how we exist in a multidimensional universe. Borrowing from Asian mystical texts that describe the "subtle" layers of selfhood, Blavatsky taught that we exist simultaneously on seven levels or planes—including what she termed the astral and etheric planes. Other Theosophical writers have expanded upon this theme and taught that we possess seven subtle bodies. Our physical body is connected with these metaphysical bodies at the seven chakras (spiritual centers) located at various points along our spinal columns. Theosophy believes that meditation can open up our chakras and enhance our connection with these other planes of existence. Using a conceptual scheme reminiscent of Emerson's doctrines of correspondence and influx, Theosophy explains that by opening our chakras we make ourselves receptive to the inflow of subtle energies flowing from higher cosmic planes. This, Theosophy teaches, is the secret to physical health, emotional serenity, and even the cultivation of parapsychological abilities.

Even at the height of its popularity, Theosophy never had more than 10,000 members in the United States. Yet despite these relatively small numbers, Theosophy has probably exerted more influence on unchurched American religion than any other single metaphysical movement. Its literature reached a far wider audience than its actual membership numbers would indicate. *Isis Unveiled* has alone sold over 500,000 copies to date. And Theosophy's ideas, once put into general circulation, resonated clearly with the spiritual agenda of America's unchurched seekers. For one, it taught that there exist a few core spiritual concepts that comprise the inner truth of every living world religion. This enabled seekers to believe that they were not so much abandoning Christianity or Judaism as they were recovering the pristine truths that have somehow become obscured by our present-day institutions. Even more important was Theosophy's integration of Eastern religious concepts into the metaphysical vocabularies of unchurched Americans. Theosophy had not simply taught tolerance of Hinduism and Buddhism; it went further, suggesting that the more mystical wings of these religions possess superior spiritual insights. Theosophy was thus largely responsible for the fact that subsequent generations of seekers have freely latched on to such terms and practices as Yoga meditation, Zen *satori*, the Atman-Brahman unity, or the existence of "subtle energies" such as *kundalini, chi,* or *prana.* A high percentage of the alternative healing systems and the human-potential psychologies that seekers actively explore have intellectual histories that can be traced directly back to Theosophical teachings.

Theosophy's extension into popular American spirituality can also be traced through the writings of Jiddu Krishnamurti and D. T. Suzuki. While Krishnamurti introduced Americans to a Theosophy-colored version of Hindu religious philosophy, Suzuki whetted Americans' appetite for the rarefied teachings of Zen Buddhism. Suzuki embraced Theosophy's belief that the essence of true spirituality consists of an immediate, mystical experience of a transcendent reality. He became an eager spokesperson for Zen because he saw it as a pristine form of spirituality wholly removed from, and unaffected by, human culture. Suzuki taught that *satori*, or Zen enlightenment, reveals that the sacred is present in the here and now of everyday life. This insight, however, cannot be arrived at through logical thought or traditional religious ritual, but only through direct spiritual experience. Suzuki's writings about Zen had a powerful influence on the most important popularizers of Eastern thought: composer John Cage, novelist Jack Kerouac, poet Allen Ginsberg, Catholic monk Thomas Merton, psychologist Abraham Maslow, and eclectic philosopher Alan Watts.

It was the last of these, Alan Watts, who best illustrates the religious restlessness that has given rise to today's seeker spirituality.[5] Watts was a disillusioned Episcopal priest who had come to see the church's rituals as hollow. At a critical point in his personal spiritual journey he came under the tutelage of Christmas and Aileen Humphreys. The Humphreys were English Theosophists who had organized a Buddhist lodge in London. The lodge became a magnet for those embracing metaphysical philosophies. There Watts gained invaluable insight into the most exciting concepts of Vajrayana Buddhism, Daoism, Zen, Vedanta, Sufism, Christian mysticism, astrology, psychic research, magic, New Thought, and Jungianism.

Watts was not a particularly original thinker. Yet he succeeded brilliantly in reducing complex spiritual philosophies to simple insights that could inspire those who were disenchanted with organized religion. Many Americans, especially those who had spent time on college campuses, had come to blame Western religions for doing little to stem the tide of Western materialism. They yearned for a spirituality that would prepare them for an ecstatic experience of "cosmic consciousness." It was Watts' genius to take unconventional philosophies and repackage them in such a way that they spoke directly to these concerns. In his famous essay, "Beat Zen, Square Zen, and Zen," Watts depicted Zen as an elegant deconditioning agent. Zen, he proclaimed, "is the liberation of the mind from conventional thought."[6] Watts had a knack for mingling Eastern metaphysics with the therapeutic language of Western psychology. He invited his readers to acquire "an enlarged frame of mind" that would liberate them from the hum-drum world of everyday life. Once liberated, they would at last awaken to their own divine nature. Yet for all his advocacy of spiritual understanding, Watts remained wary of organized religion. He cautioned his readers that true spiritual insight "is nothing that can be organized, taught, transmitted, certified, or wrapped up in any kind of system."[7]

Feminism and ecological thought have also been prominent in recent American spirituality. We might recall that one of Mary Daly's favorite strategies was to provide audiences with a semi-whimsical examination of terms that males had for centuries applied to women who dared to break cultural molds. She put a new and positive spin on what it might mean to label oneself a wild woman, a hag, or a crone. Her goal was to expose the implicit oppression present in male-identified terms for women and to encourage women to fashion their own identities in the face of such oppression. In this she was not alone. Even before Daly began writing, there existed an almost imperceptible cadre of women who turned their back on Christianity and instead chose to honor goddess traditions. Many identified themselves as witches. They used this term strategically, knowing full well that it tends to elicit a negative reaction from those raised amid the patriarchal symbols of Christianity. One of the most influential modern witches, Starhawk, concedes that the term "witch" has negative connotations. She prefers the word rather than more acceptable alternatives (e.g., spiritual feminist, one who reveres nature) precisely "because the concept of a Witch goes against the grain of the culture of estrangement. It should rub us the wrong way. If it arouses fear or negative assumptions, then those thought-forms can be openly challenged and transformed, instead of molding us unseen from within our minds."[8]

Modern witches are self-conscious in their opposition to traditional imagery of God as a male Supreme Being. The God of biblical monotheism, witches say, has become a symbol of "power over." The biblical God is intimately connected with sexism, racism, ecological exploitation, and other cultural traditions that legitimate the exercise of "power over" others. Modern witchcraft seeks to help people turn instead to a "power-from-within." Witchcraft, like the larger pagan movement of which it is a part, is a religion of nature. Then trying to give a name to the divine energy present within nature, most witches use the term "goddess." As Starhawk explains,

There are many names for power-from-within, none of them entirely satisfying. It can be called spirit—but that name implies that it is separate from matter. . . . It could be called God—but the God of patriarchal religions has been the ultimate source and repository of power-over. I have called it immanence, a term that is truthful but somewhat cold and intellectual. And I have called it Goddess, because the ancient images, symbols and myths of the Goddess as birth-giver, weaver, earth and growing plant, wind and ocean, flame, web, moon and mild, all speak to me of the powers of connectedness, sustenance, and healing.[9]

The themes that characterize modern witchcraft and other neo-pagan philosophies are echoed in recent ecological spiritualities. Since the time of Emerson and the Transcendentalists, the concept of nature has factored strongly in unchurched American religion. Historian Catherine Albanese has gone so far as to argue for the existence of a long-standing tradition of "nature religion" at the periphery of our nation's institutional religious life.[10] Nature religion, however, comes in many forms. Some environmental activists, for example, use the term "deep ecology" to signify the radical new worldview required of us if we are ever to stop exploiting the natural environment. Deep ecology insists on the radical interdependence of life on this planet. It also invites us to see how each living organism both contains and expresses the creative force of evolution itself. Violating even a single organism is in this view more than an offense against the organic whole to which we all belong. It is also a violation of the sacred power of life.

Closely aligned with deep ecology is Green politics. Green politics refers to a set of loosely connected local, state, national, and international groups that aggressively promote environmental legislation. At one level, Green politics is associated with such causes as protection of wildlife, preservation of rain forests, elimination of nuclear power plants, and the search for renewable resources. But, at another level, Green politics is also about effecting a total change in human spiritual outlook. Sustainable systems of agriculture, economics, and technology must be undergird by a sustainable religion. A sustainable religion is one that focuses on the profound interconnectedness of life. It must trigger flashes of "God consciousness," which, in the vision of Green politics, can be defined as "awe at the intricate wonders of creation and celebration of the cosmic unfolding."[11]

Many of those attracted to an ecological spirituality cite James Lovelock's "Gaia hypothesis" that the earth behaves as a single entity, a living goddess.

Still others link their holistic beliefs with Buddhism or the "new physics." Indeed, the boundaries of nature religion—like other elements of contemporary unchurched spirituality—overlap with an eclectic array of spiritual interests. Thus when those interested in ecological spirituality turn to periodicals such as *Mother Earth News* or the *Whole Earth Catalog*, they learn about much more than camping or organizing recycling campaigns. As Catherine Albanese demonstrated in her study of nature religion, such journals also include articles on Western occult philosophies, yoga, Transcendental Meditation, Zen, Carlos Castenada's accounts of drug-induced ecstasy, astrology, the *I Ching*, tarot cards, and psychic healing.

The metaphysical beliefs that comprise today's seeker spirituality are widely diffused through American culture. So mainstream have metaphysical concepts become that a survey of church-going Americans revealed that 24 percent read their horoscopes every week, 20 percent believe in reincarnation, and 11 percent believe in trance channeling.[12] Books touting New Age religious principles such as *The Celestine Prophecy* and *The Road Less Traveled* have remained on the bestseller lists for years. The very phrase "New Age" is part of common parlance. The term has become a catchword for Americans' sustained interest in occult and metaphysical philosophies. Booksellers have responded to this considerable spiritual market with books on a wide range of unconventional religious topics: angels, astrology, holistic healing, ecospirituality, yoga, transpersonal psychology, trance channeling, out-of-body experiences, and numerous Eastern-inspired meditation techniques. Many of the themes covered in these books extend over into bestsellers stocked in the self-help psychology, business management, and leadership sections as well. Wade Clark Roof, who has studied the shifting patterns in baby boomer spirituality, notes that "words like *soul, sacred*, and *spiritual* resonate to a curious public. The discourse on spiritual 'journey' and 'growth' is now a province not just of theologians and journalists, but of ordinary people in cafes, coffee bars, and bookstores around the country."[13]

It is thus clear that the boundaries of American religion are being redrawn. Even though church membership (especially in churches that are theologically conservative) is at or near an all-time high, those who used to be casual attenders are joining the growing ranks of "seekers." The most important phenomenon in contemporary American religion thus seems to be the fact that the two ends of the religious spectrum are moving apart. The cleavage

between the churched and unchurched is widening.[14] Indeed, a full 20 percent
of the population now consciously reject the need to join a religious
organization yet nonetheless seek spiritual growth on a personal basis. What
is of even greater interest is the fact that many of the themes associated with
seeker spirituality have also begun to influence the personal piety of many
church members as well. It is too early to predict what long-term influence
"seeker spirituality" will have on America's churches. But for now it is safe to
assume that many persons already filter their church's teachings through a
wholly new set of personally chosen categories.

CREATIVELY RELIGIOUS:
THE LEGACY OF AMERICA'S RELIGIOUS REVOLUTIONARIES

Today's seekers freely choose within a wide-open spiritual marketplace. This
free and open religious environment is due in large part to the efforts of
Thomas Jefferson. The "wall of separation" Jefferson envisioned helped create
a religious democracy almost unrivaled in world history. This wall of
separation ensured that religion in the United States would be dynamic and
ceaselessly creative. American religious life is market-driven. Over the long
run supply will always follow demand. And thus while Jefferson was undoubtedly the least religious of the ten revolutionaries featured in this historical
narrative, he nonetheless made the greatest contribution to the nation's
heritage of creative spirituality.

The religious revolutionaries identified in this book were chosen primarily because they were iconoclasts, determined to break away from established
patterns. They perceived tensions and problems that most religious leaders
in their eras ignored. Their personal spiritual unrest prompted them to blaze
new paths—paths that over time have led others to more meaningful religious
lives. These ten religious revolutionaries were chosen because they help
illuminate themes of what being creatively religious has meant at different
times in American history. We must therefore not expect to find uniformity
among their personal religious commitments. Few beliefs or principles are
common to all ten. Yet we can nonetheless identify a number of themes that
they have collectively taught about what it means to be creatively religious.

Perhaps no commitment was more important to our religious revolutionaries than that of personal religious freedom. For them, however, this meant

far more than the right to choose one's own religious belief. The agents of change and creativity in American religious life steadfastly affirmed that it is not just the right, but even the duty of every person to establish her or his own criteria for religious belief. For Anne Hutchinson, this was the duty to follow biblical criteria even when doing so meant to disobey powerful church authorities. For Jefferson, it was the duty to follow the criteria of reason and common sense, even when doing so meant to repudiate most cherished religious beliefs. Smith looked to personal revelation as his guide to religious truth. Emerson, Quimby, Davis, and James found their criteria in certain kinds of mystical experience. Tillich demanded that humanity's encounter with the ultimate be made intelligible in culturally relevant terminology. Cone's and Daly's criteria were derived from principles of social justice. While the criteria vary from revolutionary to revolutionary, all reflect the judgment that spiritual integrity originates in the decision to be honest to the full range of one's life experiences. All of our religious rebels considered that wholesale acceptance of any existing church's teachings somehow lacks the integrity of "owning" one's own faith. Each chose to be honest *to* God by being honest in what they could in full intellectual conscience say *about* God.

Many of our religious revolutionaries followed their personal criteria to a point where they developed new and fairly unorthodox images of God. Joseph Smith and William James both emphasized that God is finite, changing and developing over time. In Smith's case, this doctrine emphasized that we, like God, are capable of ongoing spiritual progress—both in this life and for eternity. For James, belief in a finite God was meant to prevent us from moral complacency and to alert us to our responsibilities as co-creators of this evolving universe. Tillich and Daly, meanwhile, viewed God as alternatively the ground of Being and the power of Being. They, like Emerson, Quimby, Davis, and James, preferred to think of God in essentially pantheistic ways. Their intention was to emphasize the presence of God within all living things. These new conceptions of God invariably implied new understandings of what constitutes our moral and religious duties.

Our religious revolutionaries did not wholly agree on what constitutes "authentic" moral and religious duty. Anne Hutchinson, Joseph Smith, and James Cone all operated out of an essentially biblical understanding of our moral and religious duty to God. That is, each defined morality largely in terms of obedience to the commands of a Heavenly Father who watches over us from above. Cone, of course, emphasized the prophetic tradition that defines such moral obedience in terms of active concern for social justice. Our other revolutionaries, however, have embraced more pantheistic images of God and have consequently stressed the ethical importance of recognizing the presence of God within ourselves and others. In this view our moral and religious duty is to become active agents of God's ongoing creativity within this evolving universe. James and Daly are particularly eloquent in this regard. They emphasize the interdependent nature of life on this planet, hoping to sensitize us to the need for what Daly described as a biophilia—loving action on behalf of all living organisms. This view makes every form of exploitation a sin against the "god within." Because sexism, racism, and insensitivity to ecological issues thwart living beings from expressing their full divine potentials, they rank among humanity's most glaring sins.

If our religious revolutionaries have agreed on anything, it is the principle that our religious beliefs must be judged according to their ability to enhance this-worldly activity. This is in contrast to the more traditional practice of testing religious beliefs by their conformity to scripture or ecclesiastical tradition. Such conventional standards of belief foster conservatism and perpetuate the status quo. By placing the criteria of religious truth beyond human reason, they encourage persons to submit to even the most oppressive forms of religious authority. We simply don't know enough about Anne Hutchinson's religious views to know for certain where she might stand on this issue. Yet Joseph Smith's religious vision evolved through his concrete interactions with fellow Saints. Each successive revelation that came through him seemed perfectly suited to his followers' current life situations. Smith's revelations helped his followers to sense the spirit of God working in their lives and encouraged them to sustain a life aimed at continuing spiritual progress. Both Thomas Jefferson and James Cone made social justice the critical issue in discriminating between the value of competing religious systems. Cone was especially clear that religious beliefs must be tested by their ability to bring about social and economic equality. Emerson, Quimby, Davis, James, and Tillich were more psychological than Cone or Jefferson. All five would probably find that Emerson's notion of "Self-Reliance" provides an adequate model for understanding how inner spirituality empowers us to become effective agents of world-building and wholeness-making. And, finally, Mary Daly brought social and psychological perspectives together to show that religion must be tested by its ability to nurture the Be-ing of all persons (and, for that matter, of the natural environment). Thus with the possible exceptions of Hutchinson and Smith, our religious revolutionaries have identified growth, development, and healing as the goals of spiritual living—not humility or self-abnegation. The most eloquent expression of this principle came from William James: "Not God but life, more life, a larger, richer more satisfying life, is in the last analysis the end of religion. The love of life, at any and every level of development, is the religious impulse."[15]

Our religious revolutionaries have bequeathed us one final lesson about what it means to be creatively religious. All but Thomas Jefferson believed that any attempt to understand human life must finally take a religious or metaphysical form. In their view a purely secular or scientific perspective on life is incapable of illuminating the most significant features of human experience. We might remind ourselves that even Jefferson postulated an ontological correspondence between reason as it exists in the human mind and the reason that governs the universe as a whole. In this sense he had a pronounced faith in reason as the oracle through which we might discern, and then adapt ourselves to, the progressive laws that God has imparted to the world. Most of our religious revolutionaries were, however, more overtly metaphysical or supernatural. As James observed of the religious geniuses whom he studied when writing *The Varieties of Religious Experience,* "The world interpreted religiously is not the materialistic world over again, with an altered expression; it must have, over and above the altered expression, *a natural constitution* different at some point from that which a materialistic world would have. It must be such that different events can be expected in it, different conduct must be required."[16] This was clearly the case with Joseph Smith. For him the world was constructed such that new divine revelation might be expected at any and every moment. Prophecy and miracles are not restricted to an ancient past. They are imminent possibilities of our own lives as saints in the latter days. Emerson, Quimby, Davis, James, Daly, and Tillich were uncomfortable with the categories of biblical supernaturalism. But all embraced an overtly metaphysical view of humanity's place in the larger scheme of things. All six believe that we—even now—participate in a wider spiritual universe than is recognized by the ordinary person. And, although to a lesser extent in Tillich's case, all believe that we have inner access to energies and powers unimaginable in a purely secular vision of the universe.

These religious visions prompted them to embark on spiritual journeys aimed at establishing a deeply personal relationship with these higher levels of existence. Such journeys promise to be filled with ecstatic adventure. Our religious revolutionaries thought it possible to adjust our lives in ways that will help us achieve mystical communion with life-transforming powers. In this sense they heightened all of our sense of spiritual expectation. The spiritual life is for them an exciting adventure. It leads us to meanings and even ecstatic experiences that are qualitatively different than would be expected in a purely secular worldview.

The legacy of our religious revolutionaries lives on. Though often reviled by their contemporaries, these rebels stand out against the backdrop of American history as vivid examples of what it means to live a spiritually significant life. Their thoughts and actions have opened up new spiritual pathways. To this extent these rebels not only succeeded in helping to free their contemporaries from the religious past, but they also make it possible for us to be inspired by their historic efforts. The most important lessons to be learned from our religious revolutionaries are, therefore, not about our nation's religious history if by this we mean something belonging only to the past. The story of our religious revolutionaries is finally about how we, too, might learn to become creatively religious.

Notes

CHAPTER ONE

1. Another difficulty in generalizing about Native American religion is the fact that we have relatively few sources of historical information. Although the history of the people we commonly refer to as "Indians" spans nearly 20,000 years, we have written sources from only the last 400. And, unfortunately, the majority of these were written by Christian missionaries and settlers whose accounts are blatantly biased. A good beginning point for the study of Native American religion is Ake Hultkrantz, *The Religions of the American Indians* (Berkeley: University of California Press, 1967). See also Sam Gill, "Native American Religion," in Charles Lippy and Peter Williams, eds., *Encyclopedia of the American Religious Experience* (New York: Charles Scribner's Sons, 1988), pp. 137-152.

2. Bradford, *Of Plimouth Plantation*, quoted in Lois P. Zamora, "The Myth of Apocalypse and the American Literary Imagination," in *The Apocalyptic Vision in America: Interdisciplinary Essays on Myth and Culture*, ed. Lois P. Zamora (Bowling Green, OH: Bowling Green University Popular Press, 1982), p. 102.

3. A more complete discussion of how Christians, by claiming that Indians were the agents of Satan, justified their systematic destruction of Native American culture can be found in my *Naming the Antichrist: The History of an American Obsession* (New York: Oxford University Press, 1995), pp. 46-50.

4. I am relying here on an excellent discussion of "Who Migrates" in Roger Finke and Rodney Stark, *The Churching of America, 1776-1990* (New Brunswick, NJ: Rutgers University Press, 1997), pp. 32-39. Finke's and Stark's history of the "winners and losers in our religious economy" is one of the very best accounts of American religious history and served as a valuable resource for this book.

5. Bernard Baily, *Voyagers to the West: A Passage in the Peopling of America on the Eve of the Revolution* (New York: Knopf, 1986), p. 295.

6. As Roger Finke and Rodney Stark put it, "single women in New England during the colonial period were more likely to be sexually active than to belong to a church." In fact, whereas at best one in five belonged to a church, more than one in three became pregnant before marriage. See *The Churching of America*, p. 22.

7. Hector St. John de Crevecoeur, *Letters from an American Farmer and Sketches of Eighteenth-Century America*, ed. Albert E. Stone (New York: Penguin, 1981), p. 76.

8. See my *Spiritual, But Not Religious: Understanding Unchurched America* (New York: Oxford University Press, 2001).

9. See Jon Butler's excellent study of extra-Christian religiosity in America, *Awash in a Sea of Faith* (Cambridge, MA: Harvard University Press, 1990). Readers might also wish to consult Richard Weisman's *Witchcraft, Magic and Religion in 17th-Century Massachusetts* (Amherst: University of Massachusetts Press, 1984); Richard Godbeer's *The Devil's Dominion: Magic and Religion in Early New England* (Cambridge: Cambridge University Press, 1992); and Howard Kerr and Charles Crow, eds., *The Occult in America: New Historical Perspectives* (Urbana: University of Illinois Press, 1983).

10. Edmund Burke, *On Conciliation with the American Colonies* (1775), cited in Winthrop Hudson, *Religion in America* (New York: Charles Scribner's Sons, 1973), p. 7.

11. Peter Gay, *A Loss of Mastery* (Berkeley: The University of California Press, 1966), p. 16.

12. See J. F. Jameson, ed., *Johnson's Wonder-Working Providence* (New York, 1910), pp. 23, 25.

13. Samuel Danforth, cited in Perry Miller's highly acclaimed essay "Errand into the Wilderness" in *Errand into the Wilderness* (Cambridge, MA: Belknap Press, 1956), pp. 1-15.

14. John Winthrop, in Perry Miller, ed., *The American Puritans* (Garden City, NY: Doubleday, 1956), p. 82.

15. William Bradford, *Of Plimouth Plantation* (Boston: Wright and Potter, 1901), p. 110.

16. John Winthrop, quoted in Miller, *Errand into the Wilderness*, p. 6.

17. My accounts in this and the preceding paragraph are heavily dependent on discussions of congregational church polity in Sydney Ahlstrom, *A Religious History of the American People* (New Haven, CT: Yale University Press, 1972), pp. 146-147 and Perry Miller, *Errand into the Wilderness*, p. 157.

18. Paul Boyer and Stephen Nissenbaum, *Salem Possessed: The Social Origins of Witchcraft* (Cambridge, MA: Harvard University Press, 1974). Much of my discussion of Salem witchcraft follows their excellent account of the social drama enacted in the witchcraft trials. Readers should also consult Kai Erikson's excellent analysis of the witchcraft trials and dissension in Puritanism generally in his *Wayward Puritans: A Study in the Sociology of Deviance* (New York: Wilely, 1966).

19. Lyle Kohler, in *A Search for Power* (Urbana: University of Illinois Press, 1980), contends that the hysterical seizures precipitating the Salem witchcraft episode were based on sexual and gender hostility. Elizabeth Reis also emphasizes the role of "gender politics" in *Damned Women: Sinners and Witches in Puritan New England* (Ithaca, NY: Cornell University Press, 1999). John Demos' "Underlying Themes in the Witchcraft of Seventeenth-Century New England," *American Historical Review* 75 (1970): 1311-26, suggests that the underlying cause was generational conflict. Richard Slotkin, in *Regeneration Through Violence* (Middleton, CT: Wesleyan University Press, 1973), argues that demonic possession was a parody of the experience of captivity by the Indians. Linda Caporeal, in "Ergotism: The Satan Loosed in Salem?," *Science* (April 2, 1976), hypothesizes that a fungus infestation of rye bread produced the seizures and hallucinations that spawned the whole witchcraft episode. Readers might also want to consult David Thomas Konig's *Law and Society in Puritan Massachusetts* (Chapel Hill: University of North Carolina Press, 1979) for

his interpretation of how witchcraft enabled "opponents of the law" to find avenues for gaining extralegal power.

20. Boyer and Nissenbaum, p. 170.

21. Ibid., p. 174.

22. Cotton Mather, *The Wonders of the Invisible World* (Boston, 1692; reprinted Mount Vernon, NY: Peter Pauper Press, 1950), p. 6.

23. Ibid., p. 14.

24. Ibid.

25. Ibid., p. 15.

26. Brief accounts of Roger Williams' role in American religious history can be found in Winthrop Hudson's *Religion in America* or Sydney Ahlstrom's *A Religious History of the American People.* A more complete account can be found in Clark Gilpin's *The Millenarian Piety of Roger Williams* (Chicago: University of Chicago Press, 1979).

27. The most lively and illuminating discussion of Anne Hutchinson's disputes with the New England authorities can be found in Kai Erikson's *Wayward Puritans.* Much of the following account is based on Erikson's analysis. Readers might also wish to consult the account of Anne Hutchinson's life in Richard A. Hutch, *Religious Leadership: Personality, History and Sacred Authority* (New York: Peter Lang, 1991). Other accounts of the Hutchinson episode include those by Edmund S. Morgan, *The Puritan Dilemma* (Boston: Little, Brown, 1958); David Hall, ed., *The Antinomian Controversy, 1636-1638: A Documentary History* (Middletown, CT: Wesleyan University Press, 1968); and William Stoever, *"A Faire and Easie Way to Heaven": Covenant Theology and Antinomianism in Early Massachusetts* (Middletown, CT: Wesleyan University Press, 1978).

28. Quoted in Erikson, p. 94.

29. Ibid., p. 101.

30. Two excellent sources of demographic and statistical information concerning the historical growth (or decline) of religious groups in the United States are Edwin Scott Gaustad and Philip Barlow, *New Historical Atlas of Religion in America* (New York: Oxford University Press, 2001) and Finke and Stark, *The Churching of America, 1776-1990.*

31. Cotton Mather, quoted in Ahlstrom, p. 164.

32. Almost every general history of American religion highlights the First Great Awakening as one of the most important episodes in American religious history. Most historians identify a Second Great Awakening that erupted in the western regions of the expanding nation during the first three decades of the nineteenth century. William McLoughlin, in one of the most insightful histories of American religion ever written, contends that there have been four such great awakenings (with the third transpiring from 1890 to 1920 and the fourth from 1960 to 1990). His *Revivals, Awakenings, and Reform: An Essay on Religion and Change in America, 1607-1997* (Chicago: University of Chicago Press, 1978) argues that awakenings are the result of "disjunctions in our self-understanding" occurring in periods of cultural change and serve the purpose of reinterpreting older religious beliefs in new terminology that better adapts persons to changing social realities. More recent studies have argued that McLoughlin's and other accounts of such alleged awaken-

ings do not bear up under close scrutiny of statistical and documentary evidence. For a helpful review of this debate, see Finke and Stark, *The Churching of America, 1776-1990*, pp. 87-92.

33. Quote from Stephen A. Marini's excellent article, "The Great Awakening" in Lippy and Williams, *The Encyclopedia of the American Religious Experience*, p. 782. Readers might also wish to consult Stuart Henry's article, "Revivalism" in Lippy and Williams, 799-812.

34. Jonathan Edwards, "Sinners in the Hands of an Angry God," quoted in William McLoughlin, *Revivals, Awakenings, and Reform*, p. 46.

35. One of the best overall treatments of Edwards' thought can be found in William Clebsch's brilliant *American Religious Thought* (Chicago: University of Chicago Press, 1973). This book articulates Clebsch's argument that Jonathan Edwards, Ralph Waldo Emerson, and William James together constitute the creators and bearers of a distinct American spirituality.

36. Jonathan Edwards, *The Works of Jonathan Edwards*, 4 vols. (New Haven, CT: Yale University Press, 1957), 2:95.

37. Perry Miller, "From Edwards to Emerson" in *Errand into the Wilderness*, p. 192.

38. Jonathan Edwards, *Works*, 2: 254-255. Emphasis mine.

39. Miller, p. 192.

CHAPTER TWO

1. Scholarly works on the religious roots of the American Revolutionary War and American patriotism include Jerald Brauer, ed., *Religion and the American Revolution* (Philadelphia: Fortress Press, 1976); William McLoughlin's "The Role of Religion in the Revolution: Liberty of Conscience and Cultural Cohesion in the New Nation," in Stephen G. Kurtz and James Hutson, eds., *Essays on the American Revolution* (Chapel Hill: University of North Carolina Press, 1973); Conrad Cherry, ed., *God's New Israel: Religious Interpretations of America Destiny* (Englewood Cliffs, NJ: Prentice-Hall, 1971); Catherine Albanese, *Sons of the Fathers: The Civil Religion of the American Revolution* (Philadelphia: Temple University Press, 1976); and Cedric B. Cowing, *The Great Awakening and the American Revolution* (Chicago: University of Chicago Press, 1971).

2. A concise overview of the role that apocalyptic thinking played in the American Revolutionary War can be found in my *Naming the Antichrist* (New York: Oxford University Press, 1995), pp. 68-73.

3. George Duffield, *A Sermon Preached in the Third Presbyterian Church* (Philadelphia, 1784), quoted in Nathan Hatch, *Sacred Cause of Liberty: Republican Thought and the Millennium in Revolutionary New England* (New Haven, CT: Yale University Press, 1977), p. 22.

4. Alexander Pope, cited in Thomas Greer, *A Brief History of the Western World* (New York: Harcourt Brace Jovanovich, Inc., 1982), p. 362.

5. John Locke, cited in Kerry S. Walters, *Benjamin Franklin and His Gods* (Urbana: University of Illinois Press, 1999), p. 32.

6. See Kerry S. Walters' discussion of Enlightenment thought in *The American Deists: Voices of Reason and Dissent in the Early Republic* (Lawrence: University Press of Kansas, 1992), pp. 5-10. See also John Corrigan's excellent overview of the influence of the Enlightenment in American religious thought in "The Enlightenment" in Charles Lippy and Peter Williams, eds., *Encyclopedia of the American Religious Experience* (New York: Charles Scribner's Sons, 1988): 1089-1102.

7. Cited in Kerry S. Walters, *The American Deists*, p. 1.

8. Ibid.

9. See the discussion of this issue in Sidney E. Mead, *The Lively Experiment* (San Francisco: Harper & Row, 1963), p. 63.

10. Kerry S. Walters, in *Benjamin Franklin and His Gods*, p. 128.

11. Benjamin Franklin, cited in Kerry S. Walters, *The American Deists*, pp. 92-93. Emphasis added.

12. Walters, *Benjamin Franklin and His Gods*, pp. 86-87.

13. Benjamin Franklin, cited in Walters, *The American Deists*, p. 104.

14. Ibid., p. 111.

15. Walters, *Benjamin Franklin and His Gods*, p. 133. Emphasis added.

16. Franklin's clever use of humor in connecting his hobby of theological speculation with his hobby of indulging in wine can be found in his argument that only Divine Providence could account for the location of the human elbow. After all, had God placed the elbow either lower or higher on the arm, we would not be able to life our wine glass directly to our mouths. Having previously mused that wine is "a constant proof that God loves us, and loves to see us happy," Franklin concluded that "from the actual situation of the elbow, we are enabled to drink at our ease, the glass going directly to the mouth. Let us, then, with glass in hand, adore this benevolent wisdom;—let us adore and drink." Franklin also toyed with the notion that wine might also be the conduit through which God reveals His wisdom to us:

> *In vino veritas*, say the wise men,—Truth is in wine. Before the days of Noah, then, men, having nothing but water to drink, could not discover the truth. Thus they went astray, became abominably wicked, and were justly exterminated by water, which they loved to drink. The good man Noah, seeing that through this pernicious beverage all his contemporaries had perished, took it in aversion; and to quench his thirst God created the vine, and revealed to him the means of converting its fruit into wine.

See my *Religion and Wine: A Cultural History of Wine Drinking in the United States* (Knoxville: University of Tennessee Press, 1996), pp. 17-18.

17. Among Franklin's most famous aphorisms is "A fool and his money are soon parted." This observation accentuates the humor in Franklin's account of how one of Whitefield's sermons moved him to donate funds on behalf of the orphanage Whitefield had founded in Georgia: "I happened soon after to attend one of his sermons, in the course of which I perceived he intended to finish with a collection, and I silently resolved he should get nothing from me. I had in my pocket a handful

of copper money, three or four silver dollars, and five pistoles in gold. As he proceeded, I began to soften and concluded to give him the coppers. Another stroke of his oratory made me ashamed of that and determined me to give the silver; and he finished so admirably that I emptied my pocket wholly into the collectors dish, gold and all." Cited in Roger Finke and Rodney Stark, *The Churching of America, 1776-1990* (New Brunswick: Rutgers University Press, 1992), p. 50.

18. Thomas Jefferson, cited in Walters, *The American Deists*, p. 107.

19. Thomas Jefferson, letter to Margaret Bayard Smith (August 6, 1816), cited in Walters, *The American Deists*, p. 131.

20. Thomas Jefferson, cited in Edwin Gaustad's *Sworn on the Altar of Reason: A Religious Biography of Thomas Jefferson* (Grand Rapids, MI: Eerdamans Publishing, 1996), p. 29.

21. Thomas Jefferson, from a letter to Edward Dowse (April 19, 1803) and "Notes on the State of Virginia," cited in Charles B. Sanford, *The Religious Life of Thomas Jefferson* (Charlottesville: University Press of Virginia, 1984), p. 23.

22. Thomas Jefferson, cited in Gaustad, p. 37.

23. Thomas Jefferson, letter to John Adams (April 8, 1816), cited in Sanford, *The Religious Life of Thomas Jefferson*, p. 86.

24. Ibid., p. 93.

25. Thomas Jefferson, cited in Sanford, p. 86.

26. Thomas Jefferson, letter to William Short (April 13, 1820), cited in Sanford, p. 105.

27. Thomas Jefferson, letter to Peter Carr (August 10, 1787), cited in Walters, *The American Deists*, p. 117.

28. Thomas Jefferson, letter to John Adams (April 11, 1823), cited in Sanford, p. 111-112.

29. Thomas Jefferson, letter to Justin Pierre Plumard Derieux (July 25, 1788), cited in Sanford, p. 88.

30. Thomas Jefferson, letters to Benjamin Rush (April 21, 1802) and Charles Thomson (January 9, 1816), cited in Walters, *The American Deists*, pp. 120, 129. Slightly edited.

31. Thomas Jefferson, cited in Sanford, p. 105. In a letter to John Adams on October 12, 1813, Jefferson wrote that the essential teachings of the New Testament must be freed from the crass conceptions appended to them by followers who gave "their own misconceptions as his dicta, and expressing unintelligibly for others what they had not understood themselves. . . . I have performed this operation for my own use, by cutting verse by verse out of the printed book, and arranging the matter which is evidently his, and which is as easily distinguishable as diamonds in a dunghill."

32. Thomas Jefferson, letter to John Adams (October 12, 1813), cited in Walters, *The American Deists*, p. 123.

33. Thomas Jefferson, letter to Magaret Bayard Smith (August 6, 1816), cited in Walters, *The American Deists*, p. 131.

34. Thomas Jefferson, letter to Miles King (September 26, 1814), cited in Sanford, p. 146.

35. Thomas Jefferson, from *Notes on Virginia*, cited in Walters, *The American Deists*, p.112.

36. Thomas Jefferson, from "An Act for Establishing Religious Freedom," cited in Walters, *The American Deists*, p. 115.

37. A helpful summary of the arguments associated with Jefferson's Act for Establishing Religious Freedom can be found in Sanford, pp. 27-34.

38. See the excellent discussion of America's struggle to define the terms of religious freedom in Sidney Mead's essay "Thomas Jefferson's 'Fair Experiment'—Religious Freedom" in *The Lively Experiment*, pp. 55-71. Another helpful overview of the course leading to religious freedom can be found in Winthrop Hudson's *Religion in America* (New York: Charles Scribner's Sons, 1973), pp. 99-105.

39. Thomas Jefferson, letter to the Danbury, Connecticut Baptist Association on January 1, 1802, cited in Sidney Mead, *The Nation with a Soul of a Church* (San Francisco: Harper & Row, 1975), p. 79. The famous expression concerning "a wall of separation" is part of a single long sentence that provides the rationale for Jefferson's view:

> Believing with you that religion is a matter which lies solely between man and his God, that he owes account to none other for his faith or his worship, that the legislative powers of government reach actions only, and not opinions, I contemplate with sovereign reverence that act of the whole American people which declared that their legislature should "make no law respecting an establishment of religion, or prohibiting the free exercise thereof," thus building a wall of separation between Church and State.

CHAPTER THREE

1. Cited in Winthrop Hudson, *Religion in America* (New York: Charles Scribner's Sons, 1973), p. 138. One of the best studies of frontier revivalism is Charles A. Johnson, *The Frontier Camp Meeting* (Dallas: Southern Methodist University Press, 1955). Other reliable surveys of the Second Great Awakening include William McLoughlin, *Revivals, Awakenings, and Reform* (Chicago: University of Chicago Press, 1978) and Roger Finke and Rodney Stark, *The Churching of America, 1776-1990* (New Brunswick, NJ: Rutgers University Press, 1997).

2. See Sydney Ahlstrom's excellent summary of the historical significance of the Cane Ridge revival meeting in *A Religious History of the American People* (New Haven, CT: Yale University Press, 1972), pp. 433-434.

3. From "A Short History of the Life of Barton W. Stone Written By Himself," cited in Ahlstrom, p. 433.

4. Charles G. Finney, *Memoirs*, cited in Stuart C. Henry, "Revivalism" in Charles Lippy and Peter Williams, eds., *Encyclopedia of the American Religious Experience* (New York: Charles Scribner's Sons, 1988), p. 803.

5. Whitney Cross, *The Burned-over District: The Social and Intellectual History of Enthusiastic Religion in Western New York, 1800-1850* (Ithaca, NY: Cornell University Press, 1950), p. 155.

6. Charles G. Finney, cited in William McLoughlin's *Modern Revivalism* (New York: Ronald Press, 1959), p. 84.

7. Charles G. Finney, cited in William McLoughlin, *Revivals, Awakenings, and Reform*, p. 126.

8. A concise overview of Finney's "new measures" can be found in Stuart Henry's "Revivalism," p. 803.

9. A comprehensive and insightful discussion of how the "upstart sects" won America can be found in Finke and Stark, pp. 54-108.

10. Ibid., p. 76.

11. Among the early Presbyterian colleges were Transylvania (1783), University of Tennessee (1784), Washington and Jefferson (1802), Centre (1823), Lafayette (1826), Hanover (1833), Wabash (1834), and Davidson (1837). Congregationalists founded a number of colleges including Williams (1793), Middlebury (1800), Amherst (1821), and Oberlin (1833). A few colleges such as Hamilton (1812), Western Reserve (1826), Illinois College (1829), and Knox (1837) were founded jointly by Presbyterians and Congregationalists. Baptists launched Colgate (1817), Colby (1818), George Washington (1821), Furman (1826), Denison (1832), Richmond (1832), Kalamazoo (1833), Wake Forest (1834), and Franklin (1834). The Episcopalians founded fewer colleges, including Hobart (1822), Trinity (1823), and Kenyon (1824). Methodists established Wesleyan (1831), McKendree (1834), Albion (1835), Emory (1836), DePauw (1837), Willamette (1842), and College of the Pacific (1851). See Hudson, p. 155.

12. See Ahlstrom's helpful discussion of the term "sect" and its application to the specifically American historical context, pp. 473-477.

13. See Hudson's discussion of this issue, pp. 181-182.

14. A somewhat dated, but reliable study of the Shakers is Edward Andrews, *The People Called Shakers* (New York: Oxford University Press, 1953). A discussion of the sectarian religious—and sexual—attitudes of the Shakers, Mormons, and Oneida Community can be found in Lawrence Foster, *Religion and Sexuality: The Shakers, the Mormons, and the Oneida Community* (New York: Oxford University Press, 1981).

15. A helpful study of the life and thought of John Humphrey Noyes is Robert David Thomas, *The Man Who Would Be Perfect: John Humphrey Noyes and the Utopian Impulse* (Philadelphia: University of Pennsylvania Press, 1977).

16. Excellent sources with which to begin a study of American communal groups include Arthur E. Bestor, *Backwoods Utopias: The Sectarian and Owenite Phases of Communitarian Socialism in America, 1663-1829* (Philadelphia: University of Pennsylvania Press, 1950); Laurence Veysey, *The Communal Experience* (New York: Harper and Row, 1973); Mark Holloway, *Heavens on Earth: Utopian Communities in America, 1660-1880* (New York: Dover Publications, 1966); and Robert Forgarty, "Communitarians and Counterculturalists" in Mary Kupiec Cayton, Elliott J. Gorn, and Peter W. Williams, eds., *Encyclopedia of American Social History* (New York: Charles Scribner's Sons, 1993), III: 2241-50.

17. One of the earliest accounts of Millerism was Clara Endicott Sears' *Days of Delusion: A Strange Bit of History* (Boston: Houghton Mifflin, 1924). As her title suggests, Sears unapologetically treated the Millerites as irrational fanatics and may well have perpetuated unfounded rumors concerning the movement's "deluded" expectation of the Second Coming. Francis D. Nichol, a Seventh-Day Adventist minister,

responded to Sears' volume with his own partisan *The Midnight Cry: A Defense of the Character and Conduct of William Miller and the Millerites, Who Mistakenly Believed That the Second Coming of Christ Would Take Place in the Year 1844* (Washington, D.C.: Review and Herald, 1944). Among the most helpful of the subsequent histories are those by Ruth Alden Doan, *The Miller Heresy, Millennialism, and American Culture* (Philadelphia: Temple University Press, 1987); David L. Rowe, *Thunder and Trumpets: Millerites and Dissenting Religion in Upstate New York, 1800-1850* (Chico, CA: Scholars Press, 1985); Edwin S. Gaustad, ed., *The Rise of Adventism* (New York: Harper & Row, 1974); and Ronald L. Numbers and Jonathan M. Butler, eds., *The Disappointed: Millerism and Millenarianism in the Nineteenth Century* (Bloomington: Indiana University Press, 1987).

18. The Greek work *apokalypsis* means an unveiling, an uncovering, a revealing of what is normally hidden. As applied to biblical texts treating God's plan for the "final days," it means the disclosure of the true meaning of events that seem to be bringing the world to a cataclysmic end. The Book of Revelation states that in the end times an angel will seize Satan (the dragon) and throw him into a bottomless pit for a thousand years (millennium). During this millennium Christ will rule over a rejuvenated earth before destroying Satan forever.

19. William Miller used a King James version of the Bible that contained Archbishop Ussher's chronology of biblical dates and events in the margins. Ussher concluded that Daniel's visions occurred in 457 B.C.E. Using the standard evangelical assumption that a biblical day equals a human year, Miller concluded that the obscure reference to seventy weeks (490 days) in the Book of Daniel would have projected to the year 33 C.E.—precisely the year of Christ's resurrection. Miller then proceeded to interpret Daniel's reference that the sanctuary would be restored to its rightful state in "two thousand and three hundred days." Subtracting 457 from 2,300 gave Miller the precise year of 1843. A more extensive discussion of the system that Miller used for Bible interpretation can be found in Wayne R. Judd, "William Miller: Disappointed Prophet," in Numbers and Butler, eds., *The Disappointed*, pp. 20-21.

20. Some of Miller's followers were so taken up by his end-times predictions that friends and family considered them lunatics or deluded fanatics. Many were, in fact, admitted to insane asylums on the grounds of "Millerite-induced insanity." See Ronald L. Numbers and Janet Numbers, "Millerism and Madness: A Study of 'Religious Insanity' in Nineteenth-Century America," in Numbers and Butler, eds., *The Disappointed*, pp. 92-118.

21. Although it focuses on her health philosophy, Ron Numbers' *Prophetess of Health: A Study of Ellen G. White* (New York: Harper & Row, 1976) remains one of the best overall treatments of White's visions and outlook. A scathing critique of White's visions, alleging gross plagiarism, is Walter T. Rea's *The White Lie* (Turlock, CA: M & R Publications, 1982).

22. The best book-length study of Joseph Smith and the rise of Mormonism is probably Jan Shipps' *Mormonism: The Story of a New Religious Tradition* (Urbana: University of Illinois Press, 1985). A condensed version of her study titled "The Latter-day Saints" can be found in Charles H. Lippy and Peter W. Williams, eds., *Encyclopedia of the American Religious Experience* (New York: Charles Scribner's Sons, 1988), pp. 649-665.

Two other excellent overviews of Mormonism are Thomas O'Dea's *The Mormons* (Chicago: University of Chicago Press, 1957) and *The Mormon Experience: A History of the Latter-day Saints* (New York: Alfred A. Knopf, 1979) written by the two Mormon scholars, Leonard J. Arrington and Davis Bitton. The best-known, but decidedly iconoclastic, biography of Joseph Smith is Fawn Brodie's *No Man Knows My History: The Life of Joseph Smith, the Mormon Prophet* (New York: Alfred A. Knopf, 1945).

23. Brief accounts of the charges of fraud and deceit against Joseph Smith can be found in O'Dea, pp. 5-6; Arrington and Bitton, pp. 9-12; and Brodie, pp. 16-33.

24. Joseph Smith was familiar with a popular book professing to explain the Hebrew origin of the American Indians written by a Vermont pastor, Ethan Smith. This book, *View of the Hebrews; or the Ten Tribes of Israel in America* described Indian inscriptions as "hieroglyphical records and paintings." Fawn Brodie points out that at this time the Egyptian language was popularly believed to be indecipherable, suggesting that no one would ever be able to hold Joseph accountable for the accuracy of his Egyptian characters. See Brodie, pp. 46-50.

25. Accusations of plagiarism and outright fraud plagued Joseph Smith from the very beginning. As early as 1834, Philastus Hurlbut published *Mormonism Unvailed* (sic), a work destined to be but the first in a steady stream of anti-Mormon tracts that have developed alternative theories concerning the origin of the Book of Mormon. Some argue that the book was actually authored by Sidney Rigdon, an early convert to the cause. One version of this accusation is that Rigdon came across the missing manuscript that a Rev. Solomon Spaulding had written as a novel purporting to describe the early Indian inhabitants of the region. Others have accused Smith with deliberately concocting the entire Book of Mormon, including the story of its alleged discovery. Detractors have often pointed out that the manuscript is too full of references to issues germane to 1830 New York State to be authentic. Alexander Campbell made this point in his *Delusions: An Analysis of the Book of Mormon* (1832). Ironic, he noted, that this ancient text anticipated "every error and almost every truth discussed in New York for the last ten years . . . (including) infant baptism, ordination, the trinity, regeneration, repentance, justification, the fall of man, the atonement, transubstantiation, fasting, penance, church government, religious experience, the call to the ministry, the general resurrection, eternal punishment, who may baptize, and even the question of freemasonry, republican government, and the rights of man." Historian Sydney Ahlstrom observed that assuming there was a human author to the Book of Mormon, that "author apparently possessed absorptive powers far beyond the ordinary, a roving curiosity, boundless imagination, a facile, easygoing, uncommitted set of mind, and a keen sense of the religious needs of those who had been seared but not consumed, both by revivalism and by the various forms of dark and irrational eccentricity which swept over the land" (p. 503).

26. Arrington and Bitton offer a helpful explanation of the First Vision as well as a defense of its authenticity, pp. 5-10. My narrative of this vision in the preceding paragraph depends heavily on their account.

27. No scholar has more clearly demonstrated the importance of the "First Vision" for determining later Mormonism's understanding of their early origins than Jan Shipps. See her *Mormonism*, pp. 30-31.

28. Jan Shipps offers an insightful discussion of how Joseph's "surfeit of titles" allowed the Saints to utilize imagery from earlier epochs in Judeo-Christian history for their own community-building purposes. See *Mormonism*, pp. 37-38.

29. See R. Laurence Moore's chapter on "How To Become a People: The Mormon Scenario," in *Religious Outsiders and the Making of Americans* (New York: Oxford University Press, 1986).

30. The issue of Joseph Smith's sexuality continues to divide Mormon and non-Mormon scholars. There is no shortage of scandalous claims that have been made about Smith's sexual overtures to women over the course of his life. He is said, for example, to have had a relationship with a seventeen-year-old girl, Fannie Alger, whom Smith's wife, Emma, brought into their home. Perhaps even more scandalous are the charges that he attempted to seduce Sidney Rigdon's daughter, Nancy. It seems fairly certain that Joseph was eventually married to more than fifty women. Just how many of those he had sexual relations with is a matter of heated dispute. See Brodie, pp. 181, 310-311, 320-321, 345, 369, 376, and 434-465.

31. One of the most careful analyses of Mormon plural marriage can be found in Lawrence Foster's *Religion and Sexuality: The Shakers, the Mormons, and the Oneida Community* (Urbana: University of Illinois Press, 1984). It should also be noted that Arrington and Bitton estimate that between 1850 and 1890, no more than 5 percent of all Mormon men and 12 percent of all Mormon women entered into plural marriages.

32. Joseph Smith, *Doctrine and Covenants*, 135: 4, cited in O'Dea, p. 68.

33. Cross, *The Burned-Over District*, p. 183.

34. Charles G. Finney, cited in McLoughlin's *Revivals, Awakenings, and Reform*, p. 125.

35. See Cross, p. 183.

CHAPTER FOUR

1. See Sydney Ahlstrom's excellent discussion of harmonial piety in *A Religious History of the American People* (New Haven, CT: Yale University Press, 1972), pp. 1019-1036. Other studies of American metaphysical religion include Robert C. Fuller, *Spiritual, But Not Religious: Understanding Unchurched America* (New York: Oxford University Press, 2001); J. Stillson Judah's *The History and Philosophy of the Metaphysical Movements in America* (Philadelphia: Westminster Press, 1967); and Robert Ellwood's *Religious and Spiritual Groups in Modern America* (Englewood Cliffs, NJ: Prentice-Hall, 1973).

2. An excellent article describing the history of metaphysical piety in American life is Catherine Albanese's "Narrating An Almost Nation: Contact, Combination, and Metaphysics In American Religious History," *Criterion* 38 (Winter, 1999): 2-15. See also Jon Butler, *Awash in a Sea of Faith* (Cambridge, MA: Harvard University Press, 1990) and the essays covering the various strands of Western occultism in Antoine

Faivre and Jacob Needleman, eds., *Modern Esoteric Spirituality* (New York: Crossroad Publishing Company, 1992).

3. Ralph Waldo Emerson, included in Catherine Albanese, ed., *The Spiritual Writings of the American Transcendentalists* (Macon, GA: Mercer University Press, 1988), p. 48.

4. George Ripley, cited in the overview of Transcendentalism found in Winthrop Hudson, *Religion in America* (New York: Charles Scribner's Sons, 1973), p. 174. A helpful introduction to the Transcendentalist movement is Catherine Albanese's article in Charles Lippy and Peter Williams, eds., *Encyclopedia of the American Religious Experience* (New York: Charles Scribner's Sons, 1988), pp. 1117-1128. Readers also might wish to consult Catherine Albanese's *Corresponding Motion: Transcendental Religion and the New America* (Philadelphia: Temple University Press, 1977); Octavius Brooks Frothingham, *Transcendentalism in New England* (1876; reprinted in Philadelphia: University of Pennsylvania Press, 1972); and Perry Miller, ed., *The American Transcendentalists* (Garden City, NY: Doubleday Anchor Books, 1957).

5. Ralph Waldo Emerson, included in Albanese, *Spiritual Writings*, pp. 78-79.

6. Ibid., p. 81.

7. Ibid., p. 98.

8. Ralph Waldo Emerson, *The Complete Works of Ralph Waldo Emerson*, 12 vols. (New York: AMS Press, 1968), 1: 27.

9. Ibid., 2: 82.

10. Ralph Waldo Emerson, cited in Albanese, *Spiritual Writings*, p. 116.

11. Ralph Waldo Emerson, *Works*, 173.

12. Ahlstrom, p. 605.

13. Ralph Waldo Emerson, *Works*, 4: 35.

14. Ibid., 3: 26. Emphasis mine.

15. Ibid., 1: 76. Emphasis mine.

16. Ibid., 1: 63.

17. George Ripley, review of James Martineau's *The Rationale of Religious Enquiry*, *The Christian Examiner* 21 (1836): 254.

18. For a more complete account of Poyen's tour through New England and an explanation of mesmerism's role in nineteenth-century American religious thought, see Robert C. Fuller, *Mesmerism and the American Cure of Souls* (Philadelphia: University of Pennsylvania Press, 1982). Other accounts of mesmerism include Henri Ellenberger, *The Discovery of the Unconscious* (New York: Basic Books, 1970); Vincent Buranelli, *Franz Anton Mesmer: The Wizard from Vienna* (New York: McCann, Cowan, and Geoghegan, 1975); and Frank Podmore, *From Mesmer to Christian Science* (New York: University Books, 1963).

19. Charles Braden's chapter on Quimby in his *Spirits in Rebellion: The Rise and Development of New Thought* (Dallas: Southern Methodist University Press, 1977) is perhaps the best-known account of Quimby's life and thought. Readers should also consult Horatio Dresser's edited volume, *The Quimby Manuscripts* (New York: Thomas Crowell, 1921). Dresser's account (and also Braden's account, which relies heavily on Dresser's text) emphasizes a specific reading of Quimby's work influenced by three of Quimby's patient-disciples: Warren Felt Evans, Annetta Dresser, and Julius Dresser (Horatio's parents). Readers might also wish to consult Ervin Seale, ed.,

Phineas Parkhurst Quimby: The Complete Writings. 3 vols. (Marina Del Rey, CA: DeVorss, 1988). Finally, there is a helpful account of Quimby's role in American religious thought in Craig James Hazen, *The Village Enlightenment in America: Popular Religion and Science in the Nineteenth Century* (Urbana: University of Illinois Press, 2000).

20. George Quimby, cited in Hazen, p. 116.

21. Phineas P. Quimby, *The Quimby Manuscripts*, p. 30.

22. Ibid.

23. Ibid., p. 180.

24. Ibid., p. 319.

25. Ibid., p. 62.

26. Ibid., p. 243.

27. Stewart Holmes, "Phineas Parkhurst Quimby: Scientist of Transcendentalism," *New England Quarterly* 17 (September 1944): 357. Hazen expands upon this observation in *The Village Enlightenment in America*, pp. 124-125.

28. Quimby, *The Quimby Manuscripts*, p. 277.

29. Ibid.

30. Ibid., p. 287.

31. Ibid., p. 327.

32. Ibid., p. 396.

33. Ibid., p. 303.

34. Ibid., p. 319.

35. Mary Baker Eddy's indebtedness to Quimby has been the subject of heated debate. Julius Dresser's *The True History of Mental Science* (Boston: Alfred Budge and Sons, 1887) and his son Horatio's *The History of New Thought* (New York: Crowell Company, 1919) marshaled considerable evidence to show that Eddy's writings were little more than poor attempts to reconstruct Quimby's unpublished manuscripts. Other detractors of Christian Science's foundress include Richard Dakin in his *Mrs. Eddy: The Biography of a Virginal Mind* (New York: C. Scribner's Sons, 1929) and Stefan Zweig in his *Mental Healers: Anton Mesmer, Mary Baker Eddy, and Sigmund Freud* (New York: F. Ungar Publishing Co., 1962). Mary Baker Eddy's most able apologists are Stephan Gottschalk in his *The Emergence of Christian Science in American Life* (Berkeley: University of California Press, 1973) and Robert Peel in his three-volume biography *Mary Baker Eddy: The Years of Discovery* (New York: Holt Rinehart and Winston, 1966), *Mary Baker Eddy: The Years of Trial* (New York: Holt, Rinehart and Winston, 1971), and *Mary Baker Eddy: The Years of Authority* (New York: Holt, Rinehart and Winston, 1977).

36. In addition to Charles Braden's *Spirits in Rebellion*, which remains the most complete history of the Mind Cure or New Thought movement, demographic information can be obtained from David Moberg's *The Church as a Social Institution* (Englewood Cliffs, NJ: Prentice Hall, 1960), Bryan Wilson's *Sects and Society* (Berkeley: University of California Press, 1961), and an unpublished doctoral dissertation at Washington University written by Joseph C. Johnson, "Christian Science: A Case Study of Religion as a Form of Adjustment Behavior."

37. See Beryl Satter, *Each Mind a Kingdom: American Women, Sexual Purity and the New Thought Movement, 1875-1920* (Berkeley: University of California Press, 1999). Extended

discussions of the feminist underpinnings of mind cure can also be found in Donald Meyer, *The Positive Thinkers* (New York: Doubleday and Co., 1965) and Gail Thain Parker, *The History of Mind Cure in New England* (Hanover: University Press of New England, 1973).

38. Henry Goddard, "The Effect of Mind on Body as Evidenced by Faith Cures," *American Journal of Psychology* (1896): 431-502.

39. Ibid., pp. 450, 453.

40. Ralph Waldo Trine, *In Tune with the Infinite* (New York: Crowell Co., 1897), p. 172.

41. Ibid., p. 16.

42. Ibid., from the preface.

43. Ibid.

44. Biographical information on Andrew Jackson Davis can be found in William Fishbough's introduction to *The Principles of Nature, Her Divine Revelations, and a Voice to Mankind, by and through Andrew Jackson Davis, the "Poughkeepsie Seer" and "Clairvoyant"* (New York: S. S. Lyon and W. Fishbough, 1847); Andrew Jackson Davis, *The Magic Staff: An Autobiography* (New York: J. S. Brown, 1857); Robert Ellwood's account of Davis in *American National Biography* (New York: Oxford University Press, 1999), pp. 164-165; Robert W. Delp, "Andrew Jackson Davis: Prophet of American Spiritualism," *Journal of American History*, 54 (1967): 43-56; and Slater Brown, *The Heyday of Spiritualism* (New York: Hawthorn Books, 1970), pp. 73-97.

45. Andrew Jackson Davis, *The Great Harmonia* (Boston: Mussesy and Co., 1852), p. 26

46. Ibid., p. 31.

47. Ibid., p. 45. In his *The Discovery of the Unconscious*, historian Henri Ellenberger advanced a hypothesis concerning the instrumental role of what he termed "creative illness" in the discovery of psychological insights. It is interesting in this light to note that throughout his youth Davis was both physically and psychologically abused, causing him to retreat inwardly. Just prior to his "breakthrough," Davis underwent a severe emotional breakdown. Although the details are unclear, he is believed to have been unconscious for well over a day. He later claimed to have been "living wholly in the interior world." It was from this point onward that his journeys into the mesmeric state would be imbued with great spiritual significance.

48. Andrew Jackson Davis, *The Philosophy of Spiritual Intercourse: Being an Explanation of Modern Mysteries* (New York: Fowler and Wells, 1851), p. 38.

49. Excellent discussions of the cosmology found in the writings of Davis and other nineteenth-century spiritualists can be found in Bret Carroll, *Spiritualism in Antebellum America* (Bloomington: Indiana University Press, 1997), pp. 60-84; Catherine Albanese, "On the Matter of Spirit: Andrew Jackson Davis and the Marriage of God and Nature," *Journal of the American Academy of Religion* 60 (1999): 1-14; and Ann Braude, *Radical Spirits: Spiritualism and Women's Rights in Nineteenth-Century America* (Boston: Beacon Press, 1989), p. 40.

50. Andrew Jackson Davis, cited in Carroll, p. 77.

51. Ibid., p. 68.

52. Andrew Jackson Davis, cited in Delp, p. 48.

53. Ibid.

54. Mary Fenn Davis, cited in Carroll, p. 39.

55. Andrew Jackson Davis, cited in Robert W. Delp, "Andrew Jackson Davis and Spiritualism" in Arthur Wrobel, ed., *Pseudo-Science and Society in Nineteenth-Century America*, p. 116.

56. Ibid.

57. See the excellent discussion of the ideological differences between Davis and other spiritualists in Carroll, p. 125.

58. See the discussion of spiritualism's uncanny anticipation of what were to become the major themes of liberal religious and intellectual thought in America in R. Laurence Moore's *In Search of White Crows: Spiritualism, Parapsychology, and American Culture* (New York: Oxford University Press, 1977).

59. Ann Braude expands upon this point by commenting that, "While direct communication with individual spirits struck Emerson as a vulgar distortion of Transcendentalism, it struck many Americans as concrete proof of the immanence of God and as a literal interpretation of Emerson's advice to seek truth within their own souls. Spiritualism's concreteness liberated many of Emerson's ideas from their class-bound character by making them accessible to those without the intellectual bent to grasp their subtler implications." *Radical Spirits*, p. 46.

CHAPTER FIVE

1. Arthur Schlesinger, "A Critical Period in American Religion, 1875-1900," *Proceedings of the Massachusetts Historical Society* 64 (1930-1932): 523.

2. James King, "The Present Condition of New York City Above Fourteenth Street, 1888," in Robert D. Cross, ed., *The Church and the City* (Indianapolis: Bobbs-Merrill, 1967), p. 30.

3. See Robert Wiebe's excellent study of the period's social and cultural turmoil, *The Search for Order* (New York: Hill and Wang, 1967). Wiebe remarks that

> The health of the nineteenth-century community depended upon two closely related conditions: its ability to manage the lives of its members, and the belief among its members that the community had such powers. Already by the 1870's the autonomy of the community was badly eroded. . . . America in the late nineteenth century was a society without a core. It lacked those national centers of authority and information which might have given order to such swift changes (pp. xii, 12).

4. Washington Gladden, "The Fratricide of the Churches," in Cross, *Church and the City*, p. 44.

5. An excellent discussion of how psychological theories emerged to (1) "explain away" competing religious models and (2) advance new, more liberal religious models can be found in Ann Taves, *Fits, Trances, & Visions* (Princeton, NJ: Princeton University Press, 1999). Other helpful studies of religious factors in the rise of modern psychology are Peter Homans, "A Personal Struggle with Religion: Signif-

icant Fact in the Lives and Work of the First Psychologists," *Journal of Religion* 62 (1982); 128-44, Dorothy Ross, *G. Stanley Hall: The Psychologist as Prophet* (Chicago: University of Chicago Press, 1972); and Robert C. Fuller, *Americans and the Unconscious* (New York: Oxford University Press, 1986).

6. See Edwin Starbuck, *The Psychology of Religion* (New York: Charles Scribner's Sons, 1901) or James Leuba, *A Psychological Study of Religion* (New York: Macmillan, 1912).

7. The best study of the rise of America's liberal theological tradition is William R. Hutchison's *The Modernist Impulse in American Protestantism* (Cambridge, MA: Harvard University Press, 1976).

8. Henry Ward Beecher, cited in Winthrop Hudon's overview of the rise of Protestant liberalism in *Religion in America* (New York: Charles Scribner's Sons, 1973), p. 266.

9. Lyman Abbott, *The Theology of an Evolutionist* (New York: Outlook Company, 1925), p. 8.

10. John Fiske, *Through Nature to God* (New York: Houghton Mifflin, 1899), p. 191.

11. Ibid.

12. Lyman Abbott, *Reminiscences* (Boston: Houghton Mifflin, 1915), p. 462.

13. Although now quite dated and having some methodological shortcomings, an extremely helpful analysis of the theological spectrum in American religion is to be found in Rodney Stark and Charles Clock, *American Piety* (Berkeley: University of California Press, 1968).

14. William Hutchison, p. 3.

15. See E. Brooks Holifield, *A History of Pastoral Care in America* (Nashville: Abingdon Press, 1983) and William Clebsch and Charles Jaekle, *Pastoral Care in Historical Perspective* (New York: Jason Aronson, 1964).

16. See Carol George, *God's Salesman: Norman Vincent Peale and the Power of Positive Thinking* (New York: Oxford University Press, 1993). A helpful overview of Peale's efforts to use psychological insights to inform his theological positions—and the criticisms that these efforts drew—can be found in Roy M. Anker, *Self-Help and Popular Religion in Modern American Culture: An Interpretive Guide* (Westport, CT: Greenwood Press, 1999).

17. Discussions of American Judaism can be found in Joseph Blau, *Judaism in America: From Curiosity to Third Faith* (Chicago: University of Chicago Press, 1976); Nathan Glazer, *American Judaism* (Chicago: University of Chicago Press, 1972); Michael A. Meyer, *Response to Modernity: A History of the Reform Movement in Judaism* (New York: Oxford University Press, 1988); Jacob Neusner, *American Judaism* (Englewood Cliffs, NJ: Prentice-Hall, 1972); and Jacob Neusner, ed., *Understanding American Judaism* (New York: KTAV Publishing House, 1975).

18. See Julia Mitchell Corbett, *Religion in America* (Upper Saddle River, NJ: Prentice-Hall, 2000), p. 108.

19. See Edwin Scott Gaustad and Philip Barlow, *New Historical Atlas of Religion in America* (New York: Oxford University Press, 2001), p. 218.

20. The two most authoritative accounts of the history and doctrinal heritage of American fundamentalism are George M. Marsden, *Fundamentalism and American Culture: The Shaping of Twentieth-Century Evangelicalism, 1870-1925* (New York: Oxford University Press, 1980) and Ernest R. Sandeen, *The Roots of Fundamentalism: British and*

American Millenarianism, 1800-1930 (Chicago: University of Chicago Press, 1970). Also helpful is Nancy T. Ammerman's essay "North American Protestant Fundamentalism" in Martin E. Marty and Scott Appleby, eds., *Fundamentalism Observed* (Chicago: University of Chicago Press, 1991).

21. Curtis Lee Law, "Convention Side Lights," *Watchman-Examiner*, July 1, 1920, p. 3.

22. For extended discussion of twentieth-century fascination with premillennial or "end-times" theology, see Robert C. Fuller, *Naming the Antichrist: The History of an American Obsession* (New York: Oxford University Press, 1995); Paul Boyer, *When Time Shall Be No More: Prophecy Belief in Modern American Culture* (Cambridge, MA: Belknap Press, 1992); and Timothy Weber, *Living in the Shadow of the Second Coming* (New York: Oxford University Press, 1979).

23. See James F. Findlay, *Dwight L. Moody: American Evangelist 1837-1899* (Chicago: University of Chicago Press, 1969); William McLoughlin, *Modern Revivalism: Charles Grandison Finney to Billy Graham* (New York: Ronald Press, 1959); and William McLoughlin, *Billy Sunday Was His Real Name* (Chicago: University of Chicago Press, 1955).

24. Helpful studies of the decline of mainline denominations and the corresponding growth of conservative groups include Roger Finke and Rodney Stark, *The Churching of America, 1776-1990: Winners and Losers in Our Religious Economy* (New Brunswick, NJ: Rutgers University Press, 1997); Dean R. Hoge, Beton Johnson, and Donald Luidens, *Vanishing Boundaries: The Religion of Mainline Protestant Baby Boomers* (Louisville: Westminster/John Knox, 1994); and Dean M. Kelley, *Why the Conservative Churches Are Growing: A Study in the Sociology of Religion* (New York: Harper & Row, 1972; 2d ed., 1977).

25. The Book of Joel records the prophecy that, "And it shall come to pass afterward, that I will pour out my spirit on all flesh; your sons and your daughters shall prophesy, your old men shall dream dreams, and your young men shall see visions. . . . in those days, I will pour out my spirit" (2: 28-29). The Book of Matthew notes that John the Baptist predicted that "he who is coming after me . . . will baptize you with the Holy Spirit and with fire" (3:11). Acts 2: 1-18 describes how these prophecies were said to have been fulfilled on the day of Pentecost.

26. Among the biographies of William James are Ralph Barton Perry's *The Life and Character of William James*, 2 vols. (Boston: Little, Brown, 1935); Gerald Myers, *William James: His Life and Thought* (New Haven, CT: Yale University Press, 1986); Gay Wilson Allen, *William James* (New York: Viking Press, 1967); Howard Feinstein, *Becoming William James* (Ithaca, NY: Cornell University Press, 1984); Cushing Stout's "The Pluralistic Identity of William James," *American Quarterly* 23 (1971): 135-152; and Linda Simon, *Genuine Reality: A Life of William James* (New York: Harcourt, Brace & Co., 1998).

27. Erik Erikson, *Young Man Luther* (New York: W. W. Norton, 1962), p. 67.

28. William James in Henry James, Jr., ed., *Letters of William James* (Boston: Kraus Reprint Co., 1969), 1: 130.

29. See Joseph Adelson, "Still Vital After All These Years," *Psychology Today* 16 (April 1982): 52-58.

30. William James, "What Pragmatism Means" in *Pragmatism* (Indianapolis: Hackett Publishing Company, 1981), p. 38.

31. An excellent introduction to James' interest in psychical research is Robert McDermott's preface to William James' *Essays in Psychical Research* (Cambridge, MA: Harvard University Press, 1986). Readers might also wish to consult Gardner Murphy and Robert O. Ballou, eds., *William James on Psychical Research* (New York: Viking University Press, 1960), and Eugene Taylor, *William James on Consciousness Beyond the Margin* (Princeton, NJ: Princeton University Press, 1996).

32. William James, *Essays in Psychical Research*, p. 131.

33. William James, *The Varieties of Religious Experience* (Cambridge, MA: Harvard University Press, 1985), p. 403.

34. Ibid., p. 307.

35. Ibid., p. 15.

36. Ibid.

37. Ibid., p. 341. James' view of mystical experience (and the views of others like him who seem to maintain that a mystic first has an "ineffable" experience and then adds culturally defined definitions to this experience) has come under considerable attack in recent years by a cadre of scholars including Steven Katz, Robert Gimello, Wayne Proudfoot, and Hans Penner. Coming out of a philosophical tradition influenced by Heidegger, Wittgenstein, Foucault, and Derrida, they maintain that all experience—including mystical experience—is produced in a specific cultural context. Their position, generally referred to as constructivism, agues that our beliefs and concepts construct all experience; there is no such thing as unmediated experience. Their point is that the language, doctrines, and beliefs with which mystics describe their experience do not come *after* the mystical experience, they *produce* it. Readers may wish to consult Steven Katz, ed., *Mysticism and Philosophical Analysis* (New York: Oxford University Press, 1978); Steven Katz, ed., *Mysticism and Religious Traditions* (New York: Oxford University Press, 1982); and Wayne Proudfoot, *Religious Experience* (Berkeley: University of California Press, 1986). Robert Forman argues against the constructivist position in his *The Innate Capacity: Mysticism, Psychology, and Philosophy* (New York: Oxford University Press, 1997).

38. Ibid., p. 406.

39. William James, *A Pluralistic Universe* (New York: E. P. Dutton, 1971), p. 264.

40. Ibid., p. 266.

41. William James, "The Will To Believe," in *The Will to Believe* (New York: Dover Publications, 1956), p. 25.

42. William James, "Pragmatism and Religion," in *Pragmatism*, p. 126.

43. Ibid., p. 127.

44. James, *Varieties*, p. 399.

45. Ibid., p. 400.

46. See Ernest Kurtz, *Not-God: A History of Alcoholics Anonymous* (Center City, MN: Hazelden Press, 1979) and Ernest Kurtz, "Twelve Step Programs" in Peter H. Van Ness, ed., *Spirituality and the Secular Quest* (New York: Crossroad, 1996), pp. 277-304.

47. Kurtz, p. 177.

48. See Robert C. Fuller, *Spiritual, But Not Religious: Understanding Unchurched America* (New York: Oxford University Press, 2001).

Chapter Six

1. Will Herberg, *Protestant-Catholic Jew: An Essay in American Religious Sociology* (Garden City, NY: Doubleday and Company, 1955).

2. One of the first discussions of this trend was Dean M Kelley's *Why Conservative Churches Are Growing: A Study in the Sociology of Religion* (New York: Harper & Row, 1972, 2nd ed., 1977). Two other studies that investigate the decline of many mainline churches are Roger Finke and Rodney Stark, *The Churching of America, 1776-1990: Winners and Losers in Our Religious Economy* (New Brunswick, NJ: Rutgers University Press, 1977) and Dean R. Hoge, Benton Johnson, and Donald A. Luidens, *Vanishing Boundaries: The Religion of Mainline Protestant Baby Boomers* (Louisville: Westminster/John Knox, 1994).

3. William McLoughlin provides a succinct summary of Graham's career and its place in recent American religious history in *Revivals, Awakenings, and Reform* (Chicago: University of Chicago Press, 1978), pp.186-190.

4. The most complete biography of Paul Tillich is Wilhelm Pauck and Marion Pauck, *Paul Tillich: His Life and Thought* (New York: Harper and Row, 1974). Tillich's own *On the Boundary* (New York: Charles Scriber's Sons, 1966) links important themes in his life and work. Useful assessments of his thought include David Kelsey, *The Fabric of Paul Tillich's Theology* (New Haven, CT: Yale University Press, 1967) and Charles Kegley, ed., *The Theology of Paul Tillich*, 2d ed. (New York: Pilgrim Press, 1982).

5. Paul Tillich, *The Protestant Era* (Chicago: The University of Chicago Press, 1963), p. 202.

6. See the excellent discussion of the structural similarities between Tillich's thought and Transcendentalism in Amanda Porterfield's *The Transformation of American Religion: The Story of a Late Twentieth-Century Awakening* (New York: Oxford University Press, 2001), pp. 216-218.

7. Paul Tillich, *The Shaking of the Foundations* (New York: Charles Scribner's Sons, 1948), p. 181.

8. Paul Tillich, *Systematic Theology* (Chicago: University of Chicago Press, 1967), 2: 81.

9. Paul Tillich, *The Dynamics of Faith* (New York: Harper & Row, 1957), p. 16.

10. Ibid.

11. Tillich, *Systematic Theology*, 2: 7.

12. Tillich, *Shaking of the Foundations*, p. 57.

13. Tillich, *Systematic Theology*, 1: 133.

14. Paul Tillich, *Theology of Culture* (New York: Oxford University Press, 1959), p. 5.

15. Tillich, *Systematic Theology*, 3:398. See the introduction to the third volume of his *Systematic Theology* for his identification of Chardin as a leading influence on his later thought.

16. Porterfield, pp. 213-214.

17. Helpful overviews of the status of feminist theology during this time period can be found in Deane William Ferm's chapter on feminist theology in *Contemporary American Theologies: A Critical Survey* (New York: Seabury Press, 1981) and Carol Christ's and Judith Plaskow's *Womanspirit Rising* (New York: Harper and Row, 1979).

18. Examples of feminist theology from the early 1970s include Rosemary Reuther, *New Women, New Earth: Sexist Ideologies and Human Liberation* (New York: Seabury Press, 1975); Letty Russell, *Human Liberation in a Feminist Perspective—A Theology* (Philadelphia: Westminster Press, 1974); and Sheila Collins, *A Different Heaven and Earth* (Valley Forge, PA: Judson Press, 1974). An excellent short article that outlines the principal themes of a feminist approach to Christian theology is Sheila Collins, "Toward a Feminist Theology," *The Christian Century* (August 2, 1972).

19. Brief autobiographical information about Mary Daly's life appear in "Sin Big," *The New Yorker* 72 (February 26, 1996): 76-85 and in the preface to the 1975 edition of *The Church and the Second Sex* (New York: Harper & Row, 1975).

20. Daly, *Church and the Second Sex*, p. 74.

21. Ibid., p. 180.

22. Ibid., p. 66.

23. Ibid., p. 223.

24. Daly, "Sin Big," p. 82.

25. See the introduction to the 1975 edition of *The Church and the Second Sex*. This "feminist postchristian" introduction provides an excellent overview of the gradual evolution of Daly's thought.

26. Mary Daly, *Beyond God the Father: Toward a Philosophy of Women's Liberation* (Boston: Beacon Press, 1973), p. 4.

27. Ibid., p. 65.

28. The hostility that Daly expressed toward Paul Tillich's thought in her later writings is somewhat difficult to interpret. For example, in *Pure Lust: Elemental Feminist Philosophy* (Boston: Beacon Press, 1984), Daly notes that the "vast scope and rigor of his thought" inspires profound ontological reflection. Yet she then subjects immediately his thought to hypercriticism, calling him a "philosopher of phallicism" despite the fact that the very passages of Tillich's she cites could easily be argued to be consistent with her own views. See pages 29-30. Daly also adds an "ad hominem" criticism of Tillich's work by drawing attention to his wife's, Hanna Tillich's, autobiography, which claims that Paul Tillich showed a porn film for his own private entertainment—an event prompting Daly to pronounce that "sado-masochistic fantasies were the juice/sap of his impressive theologizing." See *Gyn/Ecology: The Metaethics of Radical Feminism* (Boston: Beacon Press, 1978), p. 94.

29. Daly, *Beyond God the Father*, p. 21.

30. Ibid., p. 37.

31. Ibid., p. 23.

32. Daly, *Gyn/Ecology*, p. 10.

33. Helpful starting points for a study of African American religious history are George Eaton Simpson, *Black Religions in the New World* (New York: Columbia University Press, 1978) and Albert Raboteau, *Slave Religion: The "Invisible Institution" in the Antebellum South* (New York: Oxford University Press, 1978).

34. See Sydney Ahlstrom's chapter on "Black Religion in the Twentieth Century," in *A Religious History of the American People* (New Haven, CT: Yale University Press, 1972), pp. 1055-1078. Although Ahsltrom's chronicle of American religious life is perhaps the single most comprehensive ever published and includes helpful information on African American religion, this chapter strangely focuses on several aberrant manifestations (e.g., Father Divine, Sweet Daddy Grace) of modern black spirituality and omits most of the important themes that appear in my overview.

35. One of the best overviews of black theology is the chapter on this topic in Deane William Ferm's *Contemporary American Theologies: A Critical Survey*, pp. 41-58.

36. My account of the life and works of both Martin Luther King, Jr. and Malcolm X rely heavily upon James Cone's acclaimed *Martin and Malcolm and America: A Dream or a Nightmare* (New York: Orbis Books, 1991).

37. Ibid., p. 66.

38. Ibid., p. 69.

39. Ibid., p. 54.

40. Ibid., p. 176.

41. Ibid., p. 151.

42. Ibid., pp. 165, 130.

43. Perhaps the best overall introduction to James Cone's life and thought is the address he delivered at the University of Chicago on the thirtieth anniversary of his *Black Theology, Black Power*. See "Looking Back, Going Forward: Black Theology as Public Theology" in *Criterion* 38 (Winter, 1999): 18-27. Cone further discusses the development of his thought in *My Soul Looks Back* (Nashville: Abingdon, 1982) and *For My People: Black Theology and the Black Church* (New York: Orbis Books, 1984).

44. Ibid., p. 22.

45. James Cone, *Black Theology, Black Power* (New York: Seabury Press, 1969), pp. 1, 6, and 8.

46. Ibid., pp. 42, 38, and 2.

47. Ibid., p. 17.

48. Ibid., p. 56.

49. Ibid., p. 68.

50. Ibid., p. 152.

51. Cone, *Martin and Malcolm*, p. 160.

52. James Cone, *A Black Theology of Liberation* (New York: J. B. Lippincott, 1970), pp. 49, 136.

53. Joseph Washington, *Black and White Power Subreption* (Boston: Beacon Press, 1969).

54. Major Jones, *Black Awareness: A Theology of Hope* (Nashville: Abingdon Press, 1971); J. Deotis Roberts, *Liberation and Reconciliation: A Black Theology* (Philadelphia: The Westminster Press, 1971); and Cecil Cone, *The Identity Crisis in Black Theology* (Nashville: African Methodist Episcopal Church, 1975). Readers might wish to consult the epilogue to Gayraud S. Wilmore and James H. Cone, eds., *Black Theology: A Documentary History, 1966-1979* (New York: Orbis Books, 1979), in which Cone offers interpretation of the debate this his work sparked among black theologians. Also, Cone offers a lengthy response to Roberts' charge that his

thought insufficiently addresses the issue of reconciliation in the last two chapters of *God of the Oppressed* (New York: Seabury Press, 1975).

55. Cone, *God of the Oppressed*, p. 245.

56. James Cone, *A Black Theology of Liberation* (New York: Orbis Books, rev. ed., 1986), from the "preface to the 1986 edition," pp. xv-xix.

57. Ibid., p. 64.

58. Cone, *God of the Oppressed*, p. 137.

59. Cone, "Looking Back," p. 27.

CHAPTER SEVEN

1. A more complete account of unchurched American spirituality can be found in my *Spiritual, But Not Religious: Understanding Unchurched America* (New York: Oxford University Press, 2001).

2. Cited in Wade Clark Roof, *Spiritual Marketplace: Baby Boomers and the Remaking of American Religion* (Princeton, NJ: Princeton University Press, 1999), p. 85.

3. See Wade Clark Roof, *A Generation of Seekers: The Spiritual Journeys of the Baby Boom Generation* (San Francisco: HarperSanFrancisco, 1993), p. 79.

4. The most complete account of the origins and teachings of Theosophy is Bruce F. Campbell's *Ancient Wisdom Revived: A History of the Theosophical Movement* (Berkeley: University of California Press, 1980).

5. A helpful discussion of Watts' involvement with the 1960s counterculture can be found in Robert S. Ellwood, *The Sixties Spiritual Awakening* (New Brunswick, NJ: Rutgers University Press, 1994), pp. 41-44. I also include a discussion of Watts in *Spiritual, But Not Religious*, pp. 83-84.

6. Alan Watts, *This is It: and Other Essays on Zen and Spiritual Experience* (New York: Vintage Books, 1973), p. 90.

7. Ibid., p. 79.

8. Starhawk, *Dreaming the Dark: Magic, Sex and Politics* (Boston: Beacon Press, 1982), p. 25. Readers might also wish to consult the helpful introductions to modern American witchcraft and the larger neo-pagan movement of which it is a part in J. Gordon Melton's chapter on the "Magick Family" in *Encyclopedia of American Religions*, 5th ed. (Detroit: Gale Research, 1996), pp. 163-170; Margo Adler's *Drawing Down the Moon: Witches, Druids, Goddess-worshippers and other Pagans in America Today* (New York: Penguin, 1986); and James R. Lewis, *Magical Religion and Modern Witchcraft* (Albany: State University of New York Press, 1996).

9. Starhawk, *Dreaming the Dark*, p. 4.

10. Catherine Albanese, *Nature Religion in America: From the Algonkian Indians to the New Age* (Chicago: University of Chicago Press, 1990).

11. Charlene Spretnak, *Spiritual Dimensions of Green Politics*, cited in Albanese, p. 175.

12. See Robert Wuthnow, *After Heaven: Spirituality in America Since the 1950s* (Berkeley: University of California Press, 1998), p. 137.

13. Wade Clark Roof, *Spiritual Marketplace: Baby Boomers and the Remaking of American Religion* (Princeton, NJ: Princeton University Press, 1999), p. 7.

14. Ibid., p. 121.

15. William James, *The Varieties of Religious Experience* (Cambridge, MA: Harvard University Press, 1985), p. 399.

16. Ibid., p. 408. Emphasis added.

Index